The Age of the Bachelor

★

THE AGE OF
THE BACHELOR

CREATING AN AMERICAN
SUBCULTURE

✳

Howard P. Chudacoff

PRINCETON UNIVERSITY PRESS

PRINCETON, NEW JERSEY

Copyright © 1999 by Princeton University Press
Published by Princeton University Press, 41 William Street, Princeton,
New Jersey 08540
In the United Kingdom: Princeton University Press, Chichester, West Sussex
All Rights Reserved

Library of Congress Cataloging-in-Publication Data
Chudacoff, Howard P.
The age of the bachelor : creating an
American subculture / Howard P. Chudacoff.
p.   cm.
Includes bibliographical references and index.
ISBN 0-691-02796-X (cloth : alk. paper)
1. Bachelors — United States.   I. Title.
HQ800.3.C58   1999
305.38′9652 — dc21   98-35154   CIP

This book has been composed in Sabon typeface

The paper used in this publication meets the minimum requirements of
ANSI/NISO Z39.48-1992 (R1997) (*Permanence of Paper*)

http://pup.princeton.edu

Printed in the United States of America

1   3   5   7   9   10   8   6   4   2

DEDICATED TO

IRVING CHUDACOFF AND BERNARD FISHER

I AM THANKFUL THAT THEY

DID NOT REMAIN

BACHELORS

✳ *Contents* ✳

✳ *Acknowledgments* ✳

A NUMBER OF individuals have provided vital assistance and stimulation for this book. I thank first Brigitta van Rheinberg, who showed interest from the very beginning and provided welcome support at every step in its preparation. I owe a deep debt of gratitude for research assistance to Todd Nelson, Michael Oates Palmer, Leah Gordon, Rebekah Scheinfeld, and Jeremy Derfner. Several colleagues have given direct and helpful input to the manuscript, particularly Tony Rotundo, Elaine May, Gail Bederman, Judy Smith, and Fran Goldscheider. Some of the concepts and perspectives developed in this book began to take shape many years ago, when I studied family history in collaboration with John Modell, Maris Vinovskis, Tamara K. Hareven, and Glen Elder. I never have met Jon Kingsdale or Leonard Ellis, but Kingsdale's passing reference to the demographic and institutional contexts of bachelor society in his article on nineteenth-century saloons provided the embryo for my own study, and Ellis's insights in his dissertation on nineteenth-century male interrelationships propelled my research. I also wish to acknowledge the intellectual stimulation and support I have received from colleagues in the Brown University Department of History, especially Jim Patterson and Jack Thomas. The creative research and sensitive eye of Pembroke Herbert have given this book its visual content, and the Brown University Interlibrary Loan staff, especially Elizabeth Coogan and Beth Beretta, aided immeasurably in obtaining many of the materials used in my research. Staff members at the Boston Public Library, the Chicago Historical Society, and the Bancroft Library of the University of California, Berkeley, also gave valuable assistance. I, of course, assume all responsibility for errors of fact, interpretation, and judgment.

As always, Nancy Fisher Chudacoff has provided invaluable

ix

contribution with her editorial assistance, support, and love. I am ever grateful that she lured me away from the subculture of bachelorhood.

The Age of the Bachelor

★

Introduction

THE AGE OF THE BACHELOR

O<small>N</small> J<small>ANUARY</small> 31, 1977, *U.S. News and World Report* announced authoritatively that "an emerging life style centered around the activities of unmarried men and women is adding a new dimension to American cities and towns." According to this article, single people made up one of every three households in the United States and represented a new historical phenomenon with far-reaching consequences. The magazine quoted Joseph Peritz, a New York City pollster and market analyst, as proclaiming, "This is a trend with enormous implications for business, Government, and everyone else in our society."[1] A bachelor lifestyle, in other words, was becoming common across the country.

The phenomenon of a bachelor lifestyle, however, was not new, even in the so-called modern era. Nearly a century before Peritz offered his breathless prediction, unmarried men and women constituted a considerable proportion of the population in many American communities, raising consternation among their families, instigating disorder on city streets, provoking admonitions from clergy and educators, but mostly minding their own business. The male component of this group, the bachelors, especially attracted attention. Satirized but rarely appreciated or respected, these men became associated with a variety of images, almost all of them negative. In the minds of some observers, bachelors exhibited arrogance and selfishness, because they stubbornly refused to marry. To others, bachelors were simply misfits, misanthropes who purposely rebuffed all civilizing influences, especially those virtues presumably instilled by the sacred institution of marriage. Still others considered bachelors as degenerates, social outcasts who were socially or sexually repugnant and who had no choice but to remain single because they were physically or psychologically unacceptable to women. Useless to both family and society, bachelors seemed to be individuals who had slipped their social moorings and were drifting in an open sea. Or, as an old American proverb decried, "Bachelors are but half a pair of scissors."[2]

By the late nineteenth century, when their numbers and proportions had seemed to grow almost out of control, bachelors had become a serious social problem. Social analysts expressed heightened distress not only over the crime and disorder attributed to unmarried men but also over the possibility of "race suicide" linked to the falling birth rates that were attributed to declining marriage rates. So despised had bachelors become that by the 1930s, historian Mary Beard could assert that dangerous leaders and power-hungry political groups such as Adolph Hitler and the German Nazi Party had arisen from a society that harbored excesses of unmarried men.[3] Throughout the twentieth century, psychologists often have referred to bachelors as men who fail to marry or as those who do not make positive choices, viewing such individuals as hostile toward marriage and/or toward women. At the same time, "bachelor" became an even more loaded term, signifying to some that the labeled individual was unmarried because he was homosexual. The possibility that some men actually chose to be single, for however short a period beyond the age at which they were expected to marry, seldom was believed possible or acceptable.[4]

Americans have always revered and depended on the family as the chief institution for promoting citizenship and social order. They have celebrated family life as a basic stabilizing influence in society. Those who valued the family in this way considered individuals and groups living outside the family setting as outcasts, people handicapped by an inability to participate in wholesome social life. These individuals were said to be destabilizing influences and they thus inhabited what could be called "the 'edges' of family life."

4

As a result of this attitude, unmarried people, and bachelors in particular, have been excluded from family and social history; when given any attention at all, they have usually been classified as deviants. Some scholars have examined certain portions of the class of unmarried men, particularly those groups that ran afoul of the law or otherwise transgressed social norms by being homeless, unemployed, or unwed parents. Recently, a few historians have focused attention on such related topics as homosexuals in the male population (most, though certainly not all, of whom were unmarried) and the socially constructed meanings of manhood—meanings that, as a later chapter will contend, had deep roots in bachelor life. No one, however, has fully examined bachelor lifestyles and institutions in a comprehensive, objective way. Such an examination is the task I have set before me.

With the exceptions of the first and last chapters, this book concentrates on the period between 1880 and 1930, the peak years of bachelor subculture in America. The book follows a two-pronged approach: a general overview, surveying broad, overarching trends of bachelor culture nationally and in various cities (chapters 1–2 and 4–8); and a focused inquiry, intensively examining discrete bachelor populations in three selected cities (chapter 3). The text presents descriptive analysis, including the demography of single males (numbers, family statuses, and ages), as well as their lifestyles and livelihoods (occupations, housing, leisure activities, and social organizations, such as gangs and clubs). The book also examines interactions between single males and the larger urban community in which they lived, addressing such cultural and institutional issues as legal status, moral concerns, and commercial establishments that arose to service the bachelor subculture (cafés, pool halls, sports, leisure-time amusements). Because until quite recently, the numbers and proportions of divorced men and confirmed bachelors (men who remained unmarried for their entire lives) were relatively insignificant, almost all of the following analysis focuses on the lives that unmarried men led when they were in their late teens, twenties, and thirties, a time that for most preceded eventual marriage.

The study's significance lies in three basic assumptions that pervade the analysis, sometimes explicitly, sometimes implicitly. One assumption posits that a bachelor subculture and accompanying identity as a social group emerged as young men increasingly acquired control over their own adult careers. When not only marriage but also social and economic life remained under the supervision of parents, church, and community, the state of singlehood was seldom considered acceptable and the unmarried were deemed pariahs. When these forms of control broke down as a result of urbanization, migration, and new economic opportunities, bachelors, though still partial outcasts, were able to achieve some forms of recognition and perhaps even power in the urban community through their numbers if in no other way. Bachelors, in others words, became an active and identifiable social group, and the status and treatment of that group reflect American attitudes toward marriage and the family.

Every male is a bachelor for at least some portion of his life. Thus a second assumption defines bachelorhood as a subculture of unattached (unmarried) male individuals within the larger culture of masculinity. In this regard, the history of single men is inextricably tied to the history of all men. During the closing decades of the nineteenth century and opening decades of the twentieth, when the modern bachelor subculture first flourished, American commentators engaged in a reexamination of the meaning of masculinity, and images of bachelors played a major role in the new definitions of masculinity and manhood that circulated in the general culture. In addition the subculture of bachelorhood sometimes intersected with another male subculture: that of gay men. This book draws upon recent scholarship regarding urban gay culture and attempts to extend it by integrating perspectives on homosexual men into the analysis of unmarried men in general.

Finally, the city, with its special spatial, demographic, eco-

nomic, technological, and social characteristics, was vital to
the context of bachelorhood, and, conversely, bachelorhood
was vital to the context of the city. By considering the city as
both the site of bachelor subculture and also as an organic
environment whose changing elements shaped and were shaped
by bachelor subculture, I believe it is possible to reach a better
understanding of the dynamic processes which changed the
character of urban family life and, by extension, nonfamily life.
There has long been a tendency to consider high numbers of
bachelors as evidence of the disorganization and anonymity
that seemed to characterize city life in the late nineteenth century and early twentieth — and that attitude to a considerable
extent remains true today. This book, however, attempts to sit-
uate bachelor subculture within an environment of *re*organization, not *dis*organization. Rather than identifying a negative
breakdown, it views the transformation of urban society in the
modern age as a reordering and often positive process. The
diversity of cities and the multiple social possibilities that resulted from the massing of diverse peoples — including unmarried men — allowed new forms of social order to emerge, and
these forms were not necessarily disorganized. Thus, rather
than conceiving the city as purely a place of disorder and loneliness, this study adopts historian George Chauncey's view that
the city was, and remains, a place of multiple, overlapping subcultures involved in a process of reorganization that made possible the creation and flourishing of a variety of institutions
and behaviors.[5]

THE ANOMALIES OF SINGLEHOOD

Throughout history, boys who have reached a level of physical
maturity at which they are presumed ready to enter the emotional and economic independence of adulthood have undergone the experience of becoming "immigrants" to adult society. Moreover, social norms have made the phenomena of

adulthood and maturity synonymous with marriage and parenthood, and such norms thus have equated the proper and responsible life with married life. Most cultures have prescribed that marriage and family should serve as the natural pathways to what is productive and moral in human existence, and they have measured individual identity as well as maturity in terms of adult roles. That is, a girl becomes a woman through marriage and motherhood; a boy becomes a man through his role as father and provider.[6] Though the emphasis on marriage may have varied in intensity according to time and place, even so-called primitive societies have made the link between adulthood and marriage explicit and strong. In such native societies, anthropologists have observed, every person was expected to marry, and the class of acceptable unmarried persons was limited to the widowed, the deformed, the diseased, and the mentally incompetent. According to Margaret Mead, such native communities differ from modern society "not because children are married at puberty but because marriage for all individuals must take place when they arrive at a certain age, and after this there are no unmarried adults."[7] Marriage thus has a universal quality.

In modern Western society, any choice of lifestyle that diverts or prevents a presumably marriageable person from the social obligation to settle down and to start a family has been considered inappropriate. Yet, these same societies also have given some recognition to a single state among people presumed to be adults, and they have tolerated that state as at least a temporary transitional period before marriage. The unmarried person has acquired an independent status in modern times that did not exist previously. Thus, for example, census tabulations consistently list "single" as a legitimate category of a country's or region's population characteristics. Moreover, in connection with their existence within a separate class, single people have developed their own social lives and institutions, as well as their own living arrangements. In that respect, the unmarried can be seen as constituting a recognizable minority group.[8]

Though modern societies may have accorded unmarried people more recognition as occupying a civil status than in the past, the social standing of singleness remains an ambiguous one. Nothing represents this ambiguity more directly than the lack of precise, objective terminology with which to refer to individuals who are not married. Designations such as "the un-married" and "singlehood"—terms that because of a dearth of more vivid and graceful labels are used in the following chapters—are invariably awkward. Technically, the term "celibacy" applies to this group, because its dictionary meaning is "the state of being unmarried." Yet in most Western societies, including the United States, the concept of celibacy has come to refer more explicitly to its secondary definition, describing a person who has taken a religious vow to remain unmarried and to renounce sexual behavior. Such a term certainly would not apply to most bachelors of the past 150 years. In addition, the Anglo-Saxon etymology of the word "celibacy" denotes wholeness and health, rather than the deviance and defiance often ascribed to the unmarried. The labels "bachelor," "spinster," and "old maid," which most often are used to refer to individuals who are not married, carry a variety of connotations, most of which are pejorative. People who exist in an unmarried state usually are conceptualized within a residual category related to marriage. That is, government surveys and other statistical collections aggregate the subcategory of single people under the general category of "marital status." There is an anomaly, however, to the consideration of singleness as a marital status, because to define it as such creates a contradiction in terms.[9] The most common characteristic of single people is that literally they do not have marital status.

Thus modern Americans manifest confusion over how to consider the single people in their midst. The United States is and has always been a couples-oriented society, and the general culture has usually had difficulty integrating those adults who are single. Sociologist Erving Goffman has highlighted this problem by drawing contrasts between "singles" and "withs" — that is, between individuals whose personal lives involve activities that mostly are carried out alone (singles) and those who live their daily lives as part of a primary group (withs), such as a married couple. As Alan Davis and Philip Strong, two sociologists who have adopted Goffman's concept, have pointed out, singles encounter unique challenges in public places, even when they engage in ordinary activities such as finding a place to sit, asking others for information, or going to a bar or restaurant. "Those who drink alone," write Davis and Strong, "may be suspected of alcoholism or else of using drinking as a cover for some other and more disreputable activity. . . . Public activities are consequently curtailed or else singles learn to be properly circumspect on such occasions. . . ."[10]

Couples, or "withs," according to Davis and Strong, experience few such problems. In public settings their demeanor usually conveys the appearance of comfort, stability, and safety. Couples normally are allowed (or are expected) to have interest in each other as well as in the object of their activity, whether it be drinking in a bar, eating in a restaurant, or sitting on a park bench. Moreover, Davis and Strong assert, unlike singles, couples can depend on each other in social situations, because each partner bears an obligation toward the other partner. "To be part of a couple," they note, "is to have someone on whom you have first call, and in whom you have guaranteed rights. The extent and nature of such rights is [sic] obviously a matter of negotiation, but more can theoretically be asked of and expected from such a partner." Single persons, of course, often lack someone in whom they have guaranteed rights and consistent expectations of partnership. Their approaches to friends must of necessity be more circumspect than those of couples.[11]

In the instance of men, the concepts of bachelorhood and individualism glide together almost naturally. The autonomous status of the unmarried man, which prompts him to engage alone in a quest for self-realization, contrasts with the communal obligations of the husband, who has responsibilities to a group (wife and children) that derive from his status in his family of procreation. These differences between the married and the unmarried state affect how a man spends his time away from work. A husband presumably experiences structured time, as well as mutual obligations and responsibilities that focus him back toward his family; such obligations and responsibilities create predictable, negotiable schedules that govern his daily life. A bachelor, however, can construct more of his own time schedules unencumbered by the needs of family members; he does not have to coordinate with others. But because the bachelor receives no rewards from others for attending to scheduled responsibilities and tasks, such as cleaning and shopping, he is conceivably susceptible to "drift," to losing track of time. At the same time, because he has less opportunity to share mundane tasks with someone else, he may actually have less freedom for leisure time than a husband has, because there is no compulsion for a bachelor to budget his time. Moreover, he does not have a readily available companion for leisure activity; he must do things alone or actively recruit a companion.[12]

The bachelor's individualism can be seen as an anomaly in another way as well. A set of fundamental values of American culture has entangled bachelors in a web of contradiction. On the one hand, individualism and the independence that inheres in it form the cornerstone of Americans' belief in their exceptionalism. The media and the educational system have always lauded self-reliance and independent action. Who, then, could be more individualistic and self-reliant than the unattached, unencumbered bachelor? On the other hand, the norms of mutuality and conformity pervade American culture. Since the late nineteenth century, the corporate organization of industrial and postindustrial capitalism has put a premium on cooperation and unity. Though the society ostensibly appreciates individual initiative, it constructs moderate limits to individuality and imposes penalties on persons who exceed those limits. As sociologists Leonard Cargan and Matthew Melko have pointed out, this contradiction is felt most strongly by minority populations, not only racial and ethnic minorities but also such groups as the poor and physically handicapped, all of whom stand out as exceeding the bounds of socially acceptable difference. And in this sense, bachelors themselves constitute a nonconforming minority group because, by crossing the lines of acceptable individuality, they too do not accede to what is believed to be the natural order of things.[13]

Subculture and Counterculture

In a society, such as that of the modern United States, in which marriage exists as one of the strongest cultural norms, bachelors, as persons who deviate from the norm, stand in a peculiar relationship to the rest of society. As the succeeding chapters will attempt to suggest, unmarried men have developed their own way of life, and the surrounding society has recognized that way of life and dealt with it in a number of ways. If such a bachelor way of life did form, the question then arises: Did the values, behaviors, and institutions of bachelors comprise a subculture — in other words, a subset of the general culture — or were they part of a counterculture that openly conflicted with the general culture?

The term "subculture" has been defined as "an ethnic, regional, economic, or social group exhibiting characteristic patterns of behavior sufficient to distinguish it from others within an embracing culture or society." In this sense, a subculture exists as a reasonably benign component of a more general culture. The defining characteristics of a subculture may include such qualities as age, ethnicity, region, or occupation. The elderly, the Irish, southerners, and carpenters are all subcultures. As well, a subculture may consist of people tied to each other by mutual special interests, such as birdwatching, gun ownership, or vegetarianism. According to one authority, the most important element in distinguishing a subculture is the degree to which values, artifacts, and identities are shared among members. Such sharing is normally enhanced by the extent of conscious social separation between members of the smaller behavioral group and members of the larger society.[14] Thus hair color can characterize a group but in itself is not a strong enough criterion for social separation — though certain cohorts of redheads or blonds might disagree. Youth or an interest in birdwatching, by contrast, more likely would be sufficient qualities to create a subculture.

In an article published in 1960, J. Milton Yinger, a sociologist and leading authority on subcultures, separated the distinguishing characteristics of subcultures into four types: (1) aspects of life, such as religion, language, diet, or moral values; (2) duration over a period of time; (3) a common origin; and (4) a mode of relationship — indifferent, positive, or conflictual — with the surrounding larger culture.[15] Yinger also distinguished between two types of subcultures: (1) those groups characterized by ascriptive qualities that differentiate the group from the larger society, qualities such as language and religion; and (2) those groups with norms that arise specifically from tension or conflict between that group and the larger society, separate norms common to groups such as youth gangs or homosexuals. He dubbed the second type "contracultures," which he notes could develop a series of inverse or counter values that stand in opposition to those of the larger society.[16]

The term "contraculture" evolved into "counterculture" in the 1960s. "Counterculture" is defined as "the culture and lifestyle of those people, especially among the young, who reject or oppose the dominant values and behavior of society." Rejection and opposition are key qualities here. Yinger elaborated on the concept, writing in 1982:

The term counterculture is appropriately used whenever the normative system of a group contains, as a primary element, a

13

theme of conflict with the dominant values of society, where the tendencies, needs, and perceptions of the members of that group are directly involved in the development and maintenance of its values, and wherever its norms can be understood only by reference to the relationship of the group to the surrounding dominant society and its culture.[17]

According to Yinger, practically every person is born into a culture and is automatically a member of several subcultures, but an individual must actively and voluntarily join a counterculture. Moreover, conflict constitutes an essential element in the concept of counterculture, and such conflict differentiates a counterculture from a subculture. As sociologist William Zellner has written, "A *subculture* is part of the dominant culture, but some aspects of the subculture's value system and life-style set its members apart from the larger culture. . . ." That is, a subculture normally does not pose a threat to the dominant culture. A *counterculture*, on the other hand, "is deliberately opposed to certain aspects of the larger culture."[18] Yinger has added that to understand a subculture, it is not necessary to understand its interaction with the larger society. But a counterculture's identity is a product of such interaction and can be understood only through that relationship.[19] Thus, the Amish are a subculture who may be understood as existing outside the surrounding general culture, but, unlike countercultures such as the Ku Klux Klan or the Church of Scientology, the Amish are not at war with the larger culture.

I contend in the following pages that bachelors in America created, and to some extent are continuing to create, essentially a subculture, though at times they acted as, or were considered to be, a counterculture. There were distinct ways that bachelors lived alternative lives, sometimes harmlessly different from the lives of married people, at other times at odds and even at war with a conjugal, domestic existence. The subculture of bachelorhood was not monolithic; it contained several variations that differed by such factors as age and social class.

14

Nevertheless, I contend also that beginning in the final decades of the nineteenth century and accelerating in the early decades of the twentieth, a singular array of lifestyles, associations, and institutions formed among, and characterized the everyday existence of, a large number of unmarried men in urban America. These lifestyles, associations, and institutions reinforced the identity of bachelors as a subcultural group and differentiated bachelors from the larger society in more ways than just the bachelors' civil (i.e., marital) status.

Bachelors and Manhood

A historical study of bachelorhood in the United States reveals two kinds of social contests, two forms of tension. One contest, alluded to above, involves bachelors as individuals and groups who are contending with the larger society in which they live over the status of unmarried life and its subculture. The other contest, however, has engaged bachelors in contention with themselves and with married men over the significance of their maleness. As a number of historians recently have pointed out, until the early twentieth century, gender cultures in the United States operated primarily within separate spheres that cultivated same-sex relationships. From the colonial period onward, men, regardless of their marital, or civil, status, dominated the so-called public sphere, which consisted of the marketplace and the political arena, while women were mostly confined to the so-called private sphere of the domestic hearth and home. Except for rare formal and/or family gatherings and activities, the two sexes rarely interacted intensively with each other, even within marriage. Men socialized in separate, homosocial (same sex) institutions of taverns, street corners, and clubs, while women cultivated their own homosocial associations that included church and voluntary organizations as well as the household. Thus, in many respects the history of unmarried men does not diverge appreciably from the history

15

of all men, and in that history sex often counted for more than marital, or civil, status did in determining a person's social identity.[20]

As studies by gender historians have concluded, masculinity does not consist simply of some biological "essence of manhood." Rather, masculine identity is socially constructed, and it develops as the result of complex cultural interactions. The nature of a man's masculinity also can vary across historical time and cultures.[21] Until recently, however, historians had seldom considered men as gendered beings; the cultural construction of womanhood has undergone much scrutiny, but males have been what gender historian Nancy Cott has labeled as the "unmarked sex." Men usually received scholarly attention not as males alone but in terms of their relationship to historical categories of politics, warfare, religion, and work, to name a few; analysts of men's lives rarely focused on gender itself as a frame of reference. To be sure, as Cott has pointed out, all men as male beings did not and do not share the same consciousness, and thus a universal definition — or even a definition in the context of American culture — of masculinity is fraught with drawbacks.[22] Yet I contend that there are plausible ways, which will appear in the following chapters, to refer to "men's culture" without being too reductive. Moreover, viewing bachelors as gendered men may indeed expand the boundaries established by those few scholars who have investigated men's general history. Investigating bachelorhood within the gendered context of masculinity provides insights into the adaptations that a "different" social group of men embraced within their own particular settings of the male sphere.[23]

The social status of bachelors as akin to that of immigrants or a minority group made unmarried men "others" in a male-oriented society dominated by married men. But unlike foreign immigrants or racial minorities, whom their society deemed emasculated and inferior because of their economic dependency and their physical and cultural deviations from the host culture, bachelors possessed the presumably manly characteristics of autonomy and male-oriented sociability that accounted for the paramount symbols of manhood. For most of American history, differing attitudes toward marriage have distinguished male culture from female culture, and a large number of males, regardless of ethnic, racial, regional, or religious identities, have often perceived women as either nuisances or saints. From colonial times to the peak of approbation of marriage in the 1950s, misogyny and joshing references to marriage have been staples of male-to-male interaction. Because bachelors represented the ultimate escape from the domesticated female culture and society, they have always exerted a strong influence on general male attitudes.[24] The images of escape and freedom that have characterized bachelor existence have served as both an asset and a liability.

Near the end of the nineteenth century, especially within the American middle class, a certain softening of the meaning of masculinity did commence, and that moderation has reappeared in various guises and at various times down to the present. During the Progressive period of the early 1900s, social arbiters revived and increased the emphasis on a man's contributive role within the family. They tried to create new norms for men's behavior and image through the rhetoric and goals of such campaigns as temperance and moral purity (especially antiprostitution crusades), through the integration of men and women in white-collar and bureaucratic occupations, through the family-centered activities and "domestic masculinity" thought to exist in suburban homes, and through heterosocial (mixed-sex) family-oriented recreations such as vaudeville and museums.[25] This enhanced emphasis on familial and heterosocial relationships and responsibilities privileged husbands and fathers and accordingly undermined the homosocial bachelor/married-male culture of previous eras. The result was a more distinct separation between the lives of married men and their unmarried brothers that became increasingly evident by the 1920s. Nevertheless, I will contend in the following pages that the bachelor subculture developed certain institutions, attitudes, and practices that remained influential on all of male culture even after these fissures between married and single men began to widen.

STIGMA, DEVIANCE, AND SOCIAL IDENTITY

On the surface, the concepts of individualism and group association appear as mutually exclusive. But upon reflection, one can see that a person often gains individual identity by belonging to a social group and by contrasting his or her membership in a particular group with nonmembership in other groups. If a group helps to define individual identity, then it must have some common qualities that bind its members together. Identity depends on a specific set of attributes shared by those within a group. And a shared set of social identities can enable individuals not only to be identified as a group but also to unite into a *conscious social group*.[26]

To the extent that those attributes reduce a group's social power and access to resources and institutions, they can be understood to be a *stigma*. Thus, for example, a diseased group, such as lepers, is assumed to be stigmatized because the larger society — the non-lepers — believe that group's shared attribute of their disease to be stigmatizing. But nature — that is, the disease — does not create the stigma; people, or society, create it and the disadvantages that accompany it. At the same time, however, a stigma can prompt those who share it to experience what sociologist Barry Adam has called the "coming to consciousness" and the "translation of commonality to community." A common attribute can enable people to unite into a conscious social group and to utilize their deviance for their own advantage.[27] I suggest that this model can apply to bachelors in American society. Unmarried men, because of their presumed contrary relationship toward marriage, suffered from a socially-constructed stigma, yet through their actions, their affiliations, and occasionally their words, they constituted

18

a legitimate social group. Though they rarely organized in a conscious way to advance their own ends, the sum of their individual and communal actions often worked to their own advantage.

In another sense, however, the bachelor subculture need not necessarily be considered as a stigmatized one. It can be more reasonably defined as a variant social group, one that constructed a functional existence for itself in society. The relationships that bachelors nurtured in their gangs and on the street corners, in the saloons and pool halls, and in their clubs and other associations created systems of norms, ideals, and standards of evaluation that bridged the distance between the isolated individual and that individual's social identity as a bachelor. By reconstructing these relationships, I hope to illuminate ways in which bachelors actually negotiated their everyday existence. As well, I contend that the components of the bachelor subculture, when combined with the numbers of bachelors and the larger society's attempts to deal with them, helped to reorient the blossoming American consumer culture of the late nineteenth century and early twentieth in the direction of youth and the individual, rather than toward the family.

The following analysis is intended as a beginning step toward the understanding of a complicated topic. I cannot and do not claim to provide full and intensive coverage of every aspect of bachelor life. The perspective is one of overview; though I occasionally attempt to recognize distinctions among bachelors by race, ethnicity, religion, and region, I do not include detailed differentiations. I have, however, tried to pay some attention to issues regarding sexual orientation, a theme thus far overlooked in most historical examinations of men in general. Most of the analysis in the following chapters concentrates on the period between 1880 and 1930 when, I believe, the modern bachelor subculture took shape and bachelors began to influence the direction of consumer culture. For comparative purposes, I have included brief examinations of bachelor life in America before the late nineteenth century (chapter 1) and between 1930 and the present (chapter 8), but these chapters cannot claim comprehensive analysis of all aspects of bachelor life in early America or in the contemporary period.

Bachelorhood in Early American History

ROGUE ELEPHANTS. That is how one contemporary commentator on colonial American society referred to bachelors. Another observer, Anne Macvicar Grant, a Scottish poet who wrote a memoir of her years living in Albany, New York, in the late eighteenth century, described unmarried men as "passing in and out [of society] like silent ghosts and seeming to feel themselves superior to the world." Referring to eighteenth-century New York, Arthur Wallace Calhoun, in his *Social History of the American Family*, labeled bachelors in that colony as "misfits," "misguided," and "pariahs." Perhaps, however, Mrs. Grant best described the status of unmarried men in early American society when she disdainfully remarked, "Their association was almost exclusively with one another though sometimes one took part in the affairs of the family with which he lived."[1]

As Anne Grant's and Arthur Calhoun's observations suggest, bachelors in colonial and early nineteenth-century American society straddled two worlds. Like other people with kinfolk, unmarried adult males held membership in the family into which they were born, their family of orientation, whether that family was distant or nearby. And, as Mrs. Grant intimated, obligation and/or convenience brought bachelors into the family circle at certain times. They attended family gatherings, visited and corresponded with siblings and parents, and sometimes exchanged money or services with their close relatives. But like rogue elephants, bachelors also roamed freely, moving about their environment unshackled from responsibility to anyone except themselves, and, as rogues are wont to do, they occasionally stirred up trouble for the rest of the population. On the social continuum that ranged from the isolated individual at one end to the integrated community member on the other, bachelors stood close to the former edge, existing as socially detached persons whose choices and behavior presumably did not induce them to conform to group restraints. Yet, in contrast to what their status would become in the late nineteenth century, bachelors in colonial and antebellum America still were tethered to their family and community in ways that prevented them from constituting a fully countercultural group. The norms and institutions of the larger society exerted more force on bachelors' lives than they would in the industrial age and beyond.

Though intensities of community and interpersonal involvement varied by region, the social life of any individual white American in the seventeenth, eighteenth, and early nineteenth centuries can be described generally as a matrix of overlapping experiences.[2] Not only was each person's status defined and regulated by the multiple institutions of family, community, and church, but also the boundaries between and among those institutions were fluid and indistinct. Though — or perhaps because — early American society was hierarchical in its social structure, the interrelationships between social groupings were reciprocal and interdependent. As a result, distinctions between private and public life blurred, and the family and community circumscribed practically every individual's, including every bachelor's, activities.[3]

The nature of early American communities, especially urban communities, affected unmarried men in two particular ways. First, as individuals who functioned outside the basic unit of social organization, namely the family, bachelors were generally considered social outcasts, if not outright threats. In fact, in some instances they ranked in the same category as suspected criminals. On the other hand, as part of a milieu in which social relationships were interdependent and overlapping, bachelors as a social group were not as separate or as isolated as they might have been and would become in an industrial and postindustrial society in which public and private roles were more distinct. Premodern Anglo-American societies could not and would not tolerate the kind of unrestrained individualism that bachelorhood represented.

Bachelors in the Seventeenth and Eighteenth Centuries

The scarcity of pertinent and extant records makes it very difficult to determine precisely how many and what proportions of adult men in colonial America were unmarried. Those demographic records that do exist offer only hints. For example, between about 1620 and 1770, an estimated 900,000 to 1.2 million people migrated to the colonies that would later become the United States, and it seems quite certain that a large majority of these immigrants were adult males, especially young adult males and more especially unmarried young adult males. Records from the earliest communities in British North America reveal that men, especially men under the age of forty, consistently outnumbered women, ranging from six to one in Virginia to three to two in New England. Records for a later period reveal the same pattern. For example, ships' lists of arrivals at the Philadelphia port between 1728 and 1748 show ratios of seven men for every five women. A study of six thousand English emigrants who moved to the American colonies just before the Revolution indicates that 80 percent were adult males, 12 percent adult females, and 8 percent children. In Middlesex County, Virginia, in 1688, the number of males between the ages of twenty and twenty-four alone outnumbered the total of *all* females in the county. And, there were heavy preponderancies of men among the 17,000 convicts who were sent out from England, mostly to Georgia, and among the 350,000 unwilling migrants from Africa who arrived in North America after 1700.[4]

Most of these sources do not specify the marital status of the individuals listed, but with sex ratios so unbalanced and so many migrants being young, large numbers of men must have been unmarried, especially in colonies of the Chesapeake and South Atlantic regions, where white males outnumbered white females by substantial ratios.[5] In these regions as well, the population consisted of thousands of indentured servants, most of whom were unmarried young males. According to one estimate, 85 percent of immigrants to the Chesapeake colonies in the seventeenth century were indentured servants.[6] The requirement that these males had to work out their terms of indenture usually postponed their marriages until they were in their late twenties.

Moreover, free white males in American communities during the seventeenth and eighteenth centuries duplicated the European pattern of late marriage, normally delaying matrimony until they were in their late twenties and thus prolonging the period of bachelorhood even among those who could afford to marry and who desired to do so.[7] Even though a male's average marriage age declined in some American communities over the course of the eighteenth century, it still remained relatively high — in the mid-twenties — by the time of the Revolution.[8] To be sure, most of these men — over 90 percent — ultimately married, but custom and the unavailability of marriageable women prevented or postponed marriage for at least some segments of the colonial American male population.

Demographic historians have been able to determine more precisely the proportions of unmarried people in selected populations in the late colonial period, but even the data for that period are limited. Using town records, demographer Thomas Monahan estimated the proportion of women who were unmarried in a number of New Hampshire towns in the 1760s and 1770s. He calculated that almost exactly one-third of all adult women in these communities were single, widowed, or divorced between 1767 and 1773, and just under one-fourth had never or not yet married. Monahan did not estimate similar rates for men, but because men outnumbered women in most age groups, it seems safe to assume that large numbers of men were unmarried as well.[9] More directly, Arthur W. Calhoun examined tax records for several Maryland parishes between 1755 and 1763, where, to raise revenue for fighting the French and Indian War, parish governments levied a special tax on unmarried men over the age of twenty-five. (Light wines, which some people might have considered a possible cause for the evasion of military service, were subject to a similar tax.) Calhoun found that there were "many [bachelors] to pay this tax" in St. Thomas and St. Anne's parishes. A European traveler touring Pennsylvania colony commented, "As for bachelors, who should be rarer here than in Europe, . . . they are more numerous in Philadelphia than in any other city. . . ."[10] Other observers identified what they believed to be a rising number of single men by the mid-eighteenth century.[11] More important than the numbers and proportions of unmarried men, however, were the ways in which their society attempted to deal with them.

Benjamin Franklin, perhaps the most incisive commentator on life in eighteenth-century America, voiced a prevailing value judgment in 1745 when he wrote, "A single man has not nearly the value he would have in a state of union. He is an incomplete animal."[12] It was this attitude that prompted colonial governments to keep bachelors under rein and make them subject to a wide variety of legal restrictions, many of which represented clear discrimination. The Maryland tax mentioned above provides just one example. As early as 1619, the Virginia House of Burgesses enacted a law decreeing that all men in the colony were to dress according to their social rank and marital status. In eighteenth-century Pennsylvania, the colonial legislature passed a "Batchelor's [sic] tax," which ordered, "Every male person twenty-one years old and still improvided with a wife pays from that time on 12s 6d . . . a year." According to the German visitor Johann Schoepf, who published his travel account just before the American Revolution, such a tax was necessary "because young men will not long expose themselves to mockery of this sort in a country where working hands can so easily find support for a family."[13]

The New England Puritans, as might be expected, made conditions hard for "unyoked individuals" who might seek to live their lives independent of domestic and community restraints. In order to ensure obedience to the town and the church, Puritans in seventeenth-century Massachusetts and Connecticut tried to encourage all individuals to live in "well-ordered" households—meaning legally-constituted families—by taxing adult men and women who failed to marry and requiring unmarried persons to reside in established households as boarders or servants. In Hartford, Connecticut, for example, an ordinance required a weekly levy of twenty shillings from those who indulged in "the selfish luxury of solitary living," and in New Haven the town meeting of 1656 resolved

> that no single person of either sex do hence forward board, diet, sojourn, or be permitted to do so, or to have lodging; or house room within any of the plantations of this jurisdiction but either in some allowed relation, or in some approved family licensed thereunto, by the court, or by a magistrate . . . ; the governor of such family, so licensed, shall as he may conveniently duly observe the course, carriage and behavior of every such person, whether he, or she walk diligently in a constant lawful imployment, attending both family duties, and publick worship of God, and keeping good order day and night, or otherwise.[14]

Similar statutes were passed in Massachusetts and Plymouth colonies. In Plymouth, "henceforth no single person be suffered to live by himself or in any family but such as the selectmen of the Towne shall approve of. . . ." Such laws were no idle threats, for as late as 1762 in Plymouth, "Thomas Henshaw and Thomas Hall, single men, being convicted of living from under family government, . . . are ordered forthwith to submit themselves [to the government] and to appear at the next court and bring with them certificates thereof."[15]

All of these penalties and restrictions suggest that to a considerable extent a single adult male in the American colonies actually gained his freedom, rather than lost it, when he married. In New England towns, a married man was allocated a much larger home lot than was an unmarried man, and elsewhere wedlock released a man from special bachelor taxes and residential regulations. Moreover, marriage allowed a man to escape the community-imposed social stigma that branded him in much more restrictive ways than it would later in the nineteenth century.

BACHELORS IN THE EARLY NATIONAL PERIOD

After the Revolution — indeed, some historians would say because of the Revolution — the patriarchal glue that had held together traditional family systems in the colonies began to dissolve. As gender historian E. Anthony Rotundo and other scholars have observed, notions of Lockean individualism, which gave precedence to the autonomous being in relation to external institutions such as the state, laws, and the economy, replaced the corporate communalism that characterized colonial society. Such individualism had informed the ideology of American independence, and it persisted into the early nineteenth century.[16] The urge for personal independence particularly motivated young, unmarried men, who after the Revolution found new labor markets open to them in an expanding country. "[B]oys are men at 16," complained Thomas D'Arcy McGee. "They all work for themselves."[17] Such young men were not necessarily separating themselves completely from parental control and family obligations, but their desires and opportunities to support themselves in waged labor created tensions within households that sometimes resulted in adolescent and young adult sons moving out when their parents became too demanding.[18] Combined with ever-increasing migration, these strivings for independence created an enhanced population of nondomestic bachelors, "elephants" who were even more "roguish" than their counterparts of the colonial era.

As was the case in the previous two centuries, statistical evidence relating to unmarried men in the early nineteenth century is sparse, but most demographers and social historians agree that both the numbers and the proportions of single men were increasing, mostly as a result of the migration of some males to the frontier where they postponed their marriage until they were settled.[19] The proportions of bachelors might have been even higher had not the average age at which men married declined somewhat by the early 1800s, dropping from the late twenties to about twenty-five. Nevertheless, even though some studies have shown that adult sons were remaining in their parents' homes longer than had been the case among their immediate ancestors, earlier marriage still left a number of years in a young man's life for a relatively unfettered bachelor existence.[20] More importantly, however, regional and class differences created a variety of patterns in both the numbers and experiences of these unmarried males.

This book focuses chiefly on the experiences of bachelorhood in the urban environment, but an example of rural patterns can provide useful insights for comparison and contrast. Historian Merle Curti, in his classic study of Trempeleau County, Wisconsin, on the rural frontier, found very high percentages of single men there in the early and mid-nineteenth century. According to records from the Wisconsin town of Black River, for example, 67 percent of all gainfully employed males were unmarried in 1850. In Trempeleau County as a whole, 31 percent of employed men were single in 1860 and 34 percent were bachelors in 1870. According to Curti, a large percentage of these men were likely to pick up and go elsewhere after staying only a few years in Trempeleau County. Some 84 percent of unmarried adult men living in the county in 1860 had left by 1870; 80 percent who lived there in 1870 were gone by 1880.[21] Bachelors, so it seemed, were becoming ever more footloose.

Similarly numerous and mobile bachelor populations could be found in mining towns and agricultural centers throughout the West in the nineteenth century.[22] As a result of the California gold rush, for example, men comprised over 90 percent of that state's total population in the late 1840s and early 1850s, and over 70 percent were in the age range of twenty to forty. In all probability most of these men were unmarried. In heavily male and mostly bachelor communities such as mining towns, a kind of rude freedom developed, in which drinking, gambling, and fighting replaced family life and church services, and this lifestyle prompted residents to affix the term "California prayer book" to a simple deck of cards.[23]

More complex than the rural bachelor subculture in the antebellum era, however, was the cluster of experiences that characterized the lives of unmarried men in the nation's booming cities. From Boston to San Francisco, it was common for 40 to 50 percent of men in the age range of twenty-five to thirty-five to be single and for close to one-third of adult men of all ages to be unmarried.[24] In the urban environment, distinctive class-defined bachelor subcommunities began to form in the early nineteenth century as a result of the influx of young men and of expanding economic opportunities. Though these subcommunities were not as well defined and visible as they would become later in the century, they nevertheless provided crucibles in which both bachelor subculture and general male culture fused and flourished.

Much of the variety in the ways that bachelors experienced their lives depended on social class, particularly differences between working-class men on the one hand and middle- and upper-class men on the other. In the antebellum years, many large cities developed discernible districts in which sizable numbers of unmarried working-class men lived, labored, and enjoyed their leisure. Mostly these men were individuals who had recently arrived in the city and needed cheap housing relatively close to their employment. With their newly acquired disposable incomes, these individuals, mostly young and distant from family, were able to patronize commercial establish-

FIGURE 1.1. The sheet music cover for the popular song, "Home Sweet Home," portrays the domestic joys of a model middle-class family linked together physically as well as emotionally. Societal values in the early nineteenth century exalted family life and disparaged those who shirked familial responsibility by remaining unmarried. (Smithsonian Institution)

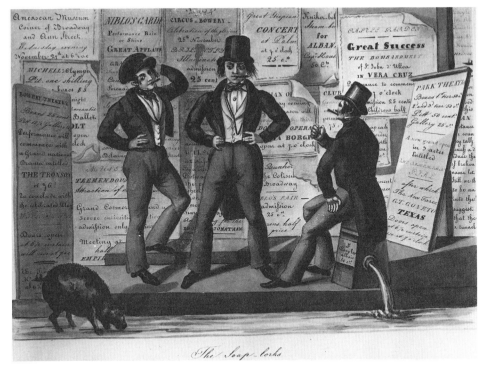

FIGURE 1.2. By contrast, Nicholino Calyo's 1847 watercolor of "Soap-Locks, or Bowery Boys" depicts unattached, brazen young men loitering on a city street in front of signs for disreputable entertainments and, symbolically, next to a gushing sewer. (The New York Historical Society)

ments that catered to their needs for inexpensive clothing, low-cost prepared food, and male-oriented entertainment.

New York City's Bowery section exemplified one of these working-class, male-dominated neighborhoods. According to historian Richard Stott, the unmarried male workers who inhabited the Bowery in the 1850s earned around twenty-five to thirty dollars a month, enough to board in relatively comfortable quarters—relative, that is, to what they had left behind in the small towns and farms when they moved to the city. Such incomes also enabled these men to dress in polished boots, shiny hats, and other forms of attire that were emblematic of a "man about town."[25] Detroit's Lower East Side developed into a similar core of working-class bachelor subculture in the mid-nineteenth century. This area became a center, according to historian John C. Schneider, for amusements such as billiard halls, taverns, and houses of prostitution as well as for bachelor residences such as hotels, boarding houses and rooming houses.[26]

As was the case with all members of the working class, married or not, the living standard of the men who inhabited these crowded and sometimes sordid neighborhoods was precarious. Wage cuts, unemployment and other afflictions of economic distress could strike at any time, leaving unattached men (and most independent working-class women as well) especially vulnerable because they often lacked some resource of the family support system that they could summon for help. As a result, they sometimes were forced to wander about, homeless, ill-clad, and hungry. Indeed, such possibilities prompted some commentators to equate bachelorhood with vagrancy. In his notations to *Blackstone's Commentaries*, for example, St. George Tucker wrote in 1803 that "any able bodied man, without a wife and child, who not having wherewithal to maintain himself, shall wander abroad, or be found loitering without betaking himself to some honest employment, or shall go about begging, shall be deemed and treated as a vagrant."[27] Undoubtedly, the majority of men arrested for loitering and homelessness in these cities were unmarried.

The early nineteenth century marked the emergence of the boarding house as an important social as well as residential institution for single men. A sample of forty-five boarding houses in New York City's working-class districts of 1850 revealed that 533 of the 698 residents (76.4 percent) were unmarried men. As Stott has shown, these establishments provided attractions and amenities besides just a room and a bed. The sleeping spaces may have been cramped, to say the least, but the common rooms and group dining offered sociability, a feeling of camaraderie for young workingmen separated from their families. Living and eating with peers whose conditions and aspirations were similar to their own, working-class bachelors created communities that, according to Stott, resembled a twentieth-century fraternity house. In these residences, men shared social activities such as gathering to smoke and converse in the parlor or on the rooftop, going out to a tavern, attending the theater, or patronizing other places of amusement. Disparate evidence exists to verify that intense friendships developed among these men, complete with horseplay, generosity, gossip, and intimate conversation.

Stott claimed to have found almost no indication, direct or indirect, that homosexuality existed among these friendships.[28] More recently, however, other historians have discovered hints and even direct evidence that same-sex emotional and sexual relationships actually did develop among some working-class males in antebellum cities. Independence from family supervision in the anonymous urban environment offered young men opportunities to explore their sexuality in a variety of liaisons and romantic partnerships, and boardinghouse life provided unique opportunities for men to develop intimacies with each other in their rooms away from public surveillance. The abundance of transients, which included seamen, soldiers, day laborers, and others, also provided possibilities for the development, temporary or more long-lasting, of same-sex unions. Historians John D'Emilio and Estelle Freedman note, for example, that in the antebellum era poet Walt Whitman "frequently brought home young working-class men whom he met while visiting or living in New York, Brooklyn, and Washington, D.C."[29] Arrests for sodomy and other "crimes against nature" attest to the existence of homosexual behavior within the antebellum bachelor subculture. In 1846, for example, New York City police prosecuted two young wage earners who allegedly had engaged in carnal intercourse while living together in the same boardinghouse room.[30]

Middle-class bachelors differed from working-class counterparts in some respects, because they tended less to cut themselves loose from family ties. Large numbers of them remained with their family of origin—that is, in their parents' households—longer than their counterparts of earlier generations had. Historian Mary Ryan found, for example, that among middle-class families in Utica, New York, in 1860, 60 percent of native-born and presumably unmarried middle-class males aged fifteen to thirty were living with one or both parents, and the practice of boarding seemed to be decreasing. Such prolonged dependence, or semi-independence, of young men occurred in other northern cities as well.[31] A strategy of protracted family support supposedly provided a means by which young men could cushion themselves from the unpredictable economic future in the expanding capitalist marketplace of the city.

Middle-class male migrants to the cities also populated boardinghouse districts, and they indulged in many of the same activities and diversions as did their working-class counterparts, including same-sex unions. But perhaps more than working-class bachelors, single men of the middle class seemed to retain or recreate quasi-family relationships within their urban subculture. Numerous young clerks and other aspiring middle-class bachelors ventured away from their parents' homes, temporarily or permanently, to associate with others of their ilk in voluntary organizations that served as surrogate families. They joined literary organizations, music societies, evangelical church groups, the Young Men's Christian Association (YMCA), and fraternal clubs where they could socialize with those who, like themselves, were seeking self-reliance and self-identity in the socially and morally challenging urban environment. The diary of Henry Peters, a young unmarried clerk living in a Boston boardinghouse in the 1840s, reveals an active after-work social life of meetings, concerts, and other activities. Peters belonged to two music societies and was a member in the aptly named Bachelors Club and an Odd Fellows lodge. However, as historian Stuart Blumin has pointed out, once Peters married and became the proprietor of a hat store, he dropped all of this bachelor associational life to devote his spare time to family activities and responsibilities.[32] Peters's abandonment of his bachelor pastimes, however, may have been the exception rather than the rule, as we shall see in later pages of this book.

The Sporting Culture

The most notable social phenomenon involving urban bachelors in the early and mid-nineteenth century was the emergence of what historians have called the sporting-male culture. Sporting males received their identity from their patronage of various illicit pastimes involving gambling (card games, horse racing, pugilism, and animal blood sports such as cock-fighting and dog-fighting); their commerce in saloons, gambling houses, billiard parlors, and brothels; and their aggressive street behavior as members of gangs, volunteer fire brigades, and political clubs. Though sporting males in Europe usually belonged to the upper class, in American cities they established themselves simply in contrast to "respectable men" and included among their fraternity members from all social classes. And though some married men participated in the typical sporting-male activities, the sporting subculture primarily was coincident with bachelor subculture.[33]

According to historian Timothy Gilfoyle, the sporting-male culture, especially its patronage of gambling and prostitution, derived from several factors new to American cities after 1820. First, the increased transiency caused by heightened numbers of immigrants, visitors, seamen, and other temporary inhabitants fractured old forms of social surveillance, further loosening the moral restraints of a family-centered society. Second, economic changes that included the replacement of the precapitalist artisanal production system by waged labor and the accompanying uncertainty of employment made it increasingly difficult for young males to accumulate enough resources to marry and start a family. (This factor may be exaggerated, as the next chapter will show.) Third, courtship and sexual mores became liberalized as peer socialization, rather than tradition and parental guidance, began to define the boundaries of accepted behavior among young adults. Fourth, the enhanced status of women and agitated discussions of women's proper place raised apprehensions among some men about their prerogatives to control the women of their family, causing those men to become misogynist and to seek company with other males of similar disposition.[34] These developments served to reinforce what historian David Courtwright has identified as the natural tendencies of young men toward aggressive and criminal behavior.[35]

Most of all, sporting bachelors cultivated adamantly antimarriage sentiments. Gilfoyle cites as an expression of this mind-set a popular diatribe against marriage and panegyric to bachelorhood titled *Reveries of a Bachelor*, published in 1850 by the British essayist Donald Mitchell. Mitchell, whose works frequently appeared in American journals, attacked the institution of marriage for turning men into captives of women. No intelligent man, he asserted, "free to chase his fancies over the wide world" would exchange his independence and comfort for a "relentless marriage," even when others might define for him "a nice match." And no self-respecting bachelor would ever consider relinquishing his cherished freedom of male sexuality. To Mitchell, whose words foreshadowed a philosophy promulgated by Hugh Hefner over a century later (see chapter 8), a variety of female companions provided a man with the ultimate inspiration. "Surely," he wrote, "imagination would be stronger and purer, if it could have the playful fancies of dawning womanhood to delight in."[36]

The era's popular music also expressed these themes. In the years just before and during the Civil War, Tony Pastor, later to become one of the nation's leading vaudeville impresarios, composed and performed numerous comic and sentimental songs during his early career as a music hall singer. The lyrics to some of these tunes celebrated the unmarried state. One ditty, titled "I'm Not a Single Man," for example, bemoaned that the singer no longer could attract attention from, or lavish attention on, women, now that he had married. One verse described what would happen if the unfortunate singer dared to compliment another woman in front of his own new wife:

> Others may hint a lady's tint
>   Is purest red and white—
> May say her eyes are like the skies,
>   So very blue and bright;
> I must not say that she has eyes,
>   And if I so began,
> I have my fears about my ears—
>   I'm not a single man.

The chorus to each verse repeated the same lament:

> With my whack row do dow
>   Why did I ever think of marriage
> Whack row do dow
>   I'm not a single man.[37]

Another Pastor song, "The Single Young Man Lodger," related a particularly humorous tale of a man who convinced his wife to take in an unmarried lodger so the couple could have more income. But the husband soon found that the lodger, named Roger, let his rent lapse and became insolent when pressed for his bill. In the end, the husband learned a hard lesson from his lustful visitor:

> I've been married seven years,
>   And during all that time,
> We were without those dears
>   That make marriages so fine.
> All at once she had
>   Two thumping little codgers;
> They said one was mine, egad,
>   But the other was the lodger's![38]

As Gilfoyle and others have pointed out, the bachelor creed pronounced by Donald Mitchell's book and these song lyrics reflected new social mores that tolerated promiscuity and supported commercialized sex. Before about 1820, prostitution, though common throughout almost all of American society, seems to have existed as a relatively marginal form of male indulgence. By mid-century, however, sexual activity outside of marriage increased as growing numbers of transient young men strayed from traditional forms of courtship that once had placed interaction between potential marriage partners under community and parental control. In burgeoning, fast-paced cities, a new form of behavior, which Gilfoyle has called the "promiscuous paradigm," elevated the value of sensual pleasure and nurtured an ethic through which unattached — and, occasionally, married — men could create common bonds with each other. This promiscuous paradigm furnished the ideological foundation for the lifestyles of "sporting men," and it crossed class, ethnic, religious, racial, and even age boundaries. It also provided patrons for the brothels, model-artist shows, concert saloons, and other commercial sex establishments that sprang up in cities from one coast to the other.[39]

The case of Richard Robinson encapsulated the temptations and tragedies that could engulf a bachelor sporting male who had been set loose in the city. In 1836, Robinson, a nineteen-year-old clerk, was arrested and charged with murdering a prostitute named Helen Jewett in a New York City brothel. The grisly event became one of the era's most sensational crime stories, attracting emotional coverage from the press and igniting fervent debates over the dangers of youthful independence. Helen Jewett, aged twenty-three and famous for her glamour and refinement, was found in her room bludgeoned to death and her body set afire on an early April morning. Richard Robinson, known as a "nabob" who bragged that "like the Grand Turk I had a harem," was Jewett's last known customer. Other circumstantial evidence implicated Robinson — police found his cloak and ax discarded in a nearby yard — and he was brought to trial less than two months later. Robinson's speedy acquittal sparked rumors that his sporting friends had bribed jurors and procured false testimony from witnesses, but the trial itself paled in comparison to the public debate that surrounded its aftermath.[40]

Newspaper writers continued to rage for weeks after Robinson's acquittal. Some commentators vindicated Helen Jewett as a goddess who "gave grace to licentiousness — elegance to its debauchery."[41] Others, however, complained that prostitution and murder were the expected consequences when once innocent but unsupervised young people were lured into the city's corrupt depths. Though these observers rebuked Robinson for his "intense selfishness," they also branded him as a symbol of "the whole frame of society which debauch [sic] young women and young men, and root out virtue and morality."[42] In a brash attempt to construct an argument of victimization, Robinson adopted these attitudes in his defense, reputedly confessing in a public letter that his nighttime meanderings had received no supervision from his employer. "I was an unprotected boy," he abjured, "without female friends to introduce me to respectable society, sent into a boarding house, where I could enter at what hour I pleased — subservient to no control after the business of the day was over."[43] Helen Jewett, Robinson and his apologists would have the public believe, was an insouciant corrupter of unsuspecting men, and, according to one defender, "no man ought to forfeit his life for the murder of a whore."[44]

Though Richard Robinson's acquittal may have been a quirk and a miscarriage of justice, the intense emotions that the case sparked signaled that rising expectations of individual gratification now contested with the emotional haven of the family. No less an intellect than John Stuart Mill had praised human progress in the nineteenth century as evidenced by what he believed to be the considerable extent to which men had committed themselves to home and family life at the expense of their former amusements.[45] Mill, however, was probably indulging in wishful thinking because an extraordinary expansion of male-oriented public amusements and commercial sex was proving him wrong, even with regard to the loyalties of presumably domesticated middle-class men. Moreover, Mill's conclusions and the contradictory evidence that undermine their credibility starkly reveal how attitudinal distinctions between married and unmarried men were pervading antebellum American culture. There were strongly implied cultural assumptions separating husbands, who presumably returned to the haven of the domestic hearth after the workday was done, from bachelors, who lacked families to which they could commit their nonwork attention and who therefore could indulge in unprecedented personal choice and sexual freedom. The fact that various commentators lamented family breakdown certifies the extent that such indulgence was reaching. Thus an editorial writer in the Santa Clara (California) *Argus* of September 8, 1866, complained, "The idea of looking beyond the sphere of home for enjoyment is at the root of many of our modern ills. Home should be the very center and sanctuary of happiness; and when it is not there is some screw loose in the domestic machinery."[46] To individuals like the *Argus* writer, the "loose screw" could result in acts like the murder of Helen Jewett.

MALE RETREATS

In spite of cases like the indictment of Richard Robinson in the murder of Helen Jewett, the emerging homosocial, male-centered world of the cities, though frequently misogynist, was not always amoral and disorganized. The flourishing of formal clubs and fraternal orders as male retreats also accompanied and encouraged the growth of bachelor society. Most middle-class service organizations such as the Eagles and the Sons of the American Revolution were formed later in the nineteenth century, but by mid-century a few associations such as the Elks Club, founded in 1868, were already beginning to offer native-born white males an opportunity for combined masculine sociability and community service. Even earlier, middle-class single men in large cities had begun to form *"clubs en famille,"* cooperative group residences in which members shared the expenses of rent, meals, and a cook-housekeeper. Such arrangements proved a practical solution to the economic stringencies that clerks and other white collar workers encountered as they tried to reconcile the expenses of urban living with their slender resources.[47]

Many of these middle-class associations began with, and/or developed, special themes and/or functions. One such club was San Francisco's Olympic Club. Founded in 1855 by two German immigrant brothers, Charles and Arthur Nahl, the Olympic Club attracted young men who were primarily interested in gymnastic exercises. In just a few years, these enthusiasts constituted themselves into a formal organization by electing officers and renting a meeting hall. By 1860, the club could count twenty-three members, and their building housed an elaborate gymnasium and a ballroom. Initial Olympic Club activities included gymnastic exercises, track and field events, boxing, baseball, wrestling, cycling and dances. By the end of the nineteenth century, the club had built a swimming pool and was utilizing its facilities to sponsor the training of Olympic athletes and other competitors in amateur athletic contests. By this time, however, it had also evolved into an exclusive men's social club and eventually added a golf course and club house, located outside of the city.[48]

More common than middle-class organizations in the mid-nineteenth century, however, were the exclusive patrician male enclaves, such as Boston's Somerset Club, New York's Knickerbocker Club, Philadelphia's Rittenhouse Club, and San Francisco's Bohemian Club. These were places where, according to one member, a gentleman found "his peculiar asylum from the pandemonium of commerce and the bumptiousness of democracy."[49] Though several of these clubs housed members as residents, the wealthy nature of the membership was such that even those who lived at the club did so voluntarily rather than out of financial necessity.

Elite men's clubs provided a homey alternative to domestic life for wealthy bachelors. The buildings and their facilities were open at all hours, and they included well-appointed parlors and sitting rooms, wood-paneled reading rooms, billiard tables, card rooms, fine wines and cuisine, and good books and cigars—every mark of manly ease. But because they so conveniently offered the comforts of home, they often provoked challenges from critics. Thus New York journalist Junius Henri Browne charged in 1867, "Every club is a blow against marriage, . . . offering, as it does, the surroundings of a home without women or the ties of a family."[50] The next year, a writer for *The Nation* railed that in England (and, by implication, in the United States as well), "the root of all evil is 'those hateful clubs. . . .'"[51] Accusations such as these reflected an assumption that elite clubs encouraged men to avoid marital and domestic commitments, and they elicited avid disavowals from the clubmen themselves. For example, Francis Gerry Fairfield, in his apologetic survey *The Clubs of New York* (1873), wrote, "It has been alleged in some quarters that the rolls of these associations are mostly recruited from the ranks of unmarried men. It would be natural to suppose so, but . . . the facts are at variance with the terms of fiction. At least three-fourths of the clubmen of New York are married men. . . ."[52]

Elite clubs certainly held attractions to unmarried men who, for whatever reason, lived apart from their families, and the clubs served especially as preferred alternatives to solitary living in a rooming house. According to Fairfield, not only was the number of unmarried men who lived *en club* large but also forming a club was easy for bachelors to accomplish. He described, "A half dozen or a dozen—friends and cronies—all club together and rent a house in an eligible quarter, paying rent by apportion, or according to the quality of rooms occupied. A caterer and two or three servants complete the organization, which is a true club in the old, exclusive sense of the word."[53] Living and eating in such an arrangement proved to be less expensive than living at a hotel and taking meals in a restaurant. By paying twenty dollars apiece per month, twelve men could, according to Fairfield, "take a Fifth Avenue mansion at the rent of $5,000 and still have $7,480 left for table expenses, which is more than equal to the necessities of the case. . . ."[54] Widowers also could find some replacement for their broken domesticity in the clubs.[55]

According to sociologist Leonard Ellis, who has researched early club life, the topics of conversation in which club members engaged reinforced male social relationships and buttressed the emerging bachelor subculture. Such conversation usually included four types: ribaldry, competitive ribbing, gossip, and serious discussion. Ribaldry was not completely misogynous; rather, it reflected the general sexism of society and often focused on the foibles of men in their dealings with women. Good-natured teasing provided a way for men to interrelate and often involved use of first names and nicknames, a practice generally uncommon in polite society. Gossip offered members a chance for mutual exchange of confidences, which normally could not be possible when women were present. Serious discussions of politics and intellectual topics provided an alternative to the blandness of the home and the formality of mixed-sex, drawing-room society.[56] All brands of conversation acted, says Ellis, to create sympathetic social relationships within a "bounded and emotionally-grounded all-male peer group."[57] The group pressured each member to act "as a gentleman" — or "as a clubman" — and reprimanded, often in prescribed ways according to club bylaws, those who behaved in an objectionable manner and to the annoyance of their fellow members.[58]

Did elite male clubs actually encourage bachelorhood? That is, did the supposed easy life and congenial sociability of clubhouses deter men from committing themselves to marital unions? Probably not. Contemporary accounts indicate that virtually all single club members eventually married, usually within a few years of joining; clubs were home for very few confirmed bachelors. Perhaps these associations provided the kinds of alternative attractions and diversions that helped postpone marriage for a short time, but there is no real evidence that distraction turned into absolute avoidance.

The French traveler Mme. Olympe Audovard, who journeyed through North America in 1869–70, thought that she had recognized an important social and demographic trend. "The bachelor," she wrote, "is an exception and [has] very much disappeared. At eighteen, or twenty, or later, the Yankee marries."[59] Mme. Audovard does not seem to have been a very keen observer, however, because throughout Yankee society, and Southern and Western society as well, unmarried men were far from exceptional and their numbers certainly were not lessening. Indeed, bachelors were beginning to make their presence felt in a variety of ways. Until the mid-nineteenth century, although bachelors had endured special burdens of an inferior status, they had remained integral parts of society. But as the nineteenth century entered its final decades, unattached individuals, epitomized by the growing numbers of single men, were increasingly being viewed as being in contention with society, particularly with its domestic component. Indeed, the flourishing of boardinghouse districts, young men's clubs and organizations, and the sporting culture in which single men enlisted signified that bachelors were becoming an important social group in American cities and beginning to take on the characteristics of a distinct subculture. How these bachelors would adjust to their independent urban life and how urban institutions would in turn adjust to the bachelors' major presence framed some of American society's important challenges at the turn of the century.

Why So Many Bachelors?

Iₙ ₐ ₓₐₘₒᵤₛ ₛcₑₙₑ from George Bernard Shaw's *Man and Superman*, Jack Tanner, the hard-headed marriage object of Ann Whitefield, proclaimed that it is "a woman's business to get married as soon as possible and a man's to keep unmarried as long as he can." For Tanner, whose resolute bachelorhood ironically turned out to be only temporary, marriage was "apostasy, profanation of the sanctuary of my soul, a violation of my manhood, sale of my birthright, shameful surrender, ignominious capitulation, acceptance of defeat."

Tanner aimed his stinging diatribe against one of society's most sacred affiliations: the union of man and woman in holy matrimony. And his outburst of contrariness exalted one of society's most reviled characters: the bachelor. Though as Jack Tanner vituperatively implied, marriage and bachelorhood stand at the opposite ends of the family pole, the two statuses form a unitary package. The status of being single can be considered only in relation to marriage; without marriage, the concept of bachelorhood has no meaning.

With its unique qualities of emotional, sexual, and social intimacy, the institution of marriage distinguishes human relationships from those found among all other organisms. According to Ernest Groves, whose sociological discourses on marriage in the early twentieth century have withstood many revisions, three basic sets of motives have always drawn people into matrimony: first, those interests that cluster around an emotional need for love and sexual expression; second, the personal desire and cultural obligation to produce offspring; and third, the mutual helpfulness that mates can provide to each other.[1] But as a public institution, marriage also serves as a building block of public policy; it is a legal as well as a social

45

and religious act, created and regulated by public authority. Through marriage, the state creates and enforces civic statuses and expectations for both men and women — as evidenced by the current debates over the legality of marriages between homosexuals. As historian Nancy Cott has observed, "One might go so far as to say that the institution of marriage and the modern state have been mutually constitutive. . . . One of the principal means that the state can use to prove its existence — to announce its sovereignty and hold on the populace — is its authority over marriage."[2]

If the establishment and enforcement of social norms are essential to the public institution of marriage, then those who do not conform to common expectations usually are made to feel the coercive power of whatever corporate body defines those norms. In some societies, especially in premodern times, a person had no more freedom to evade marriage than to decide whether or not to be born. But one of the distinguishing qualities of modern society has been the opportunity for individuals voluntarily to remain single. In spite of intense pressures from the tradition of family continuity, from the ridicule of public opinion, and even from the penalties of legal restrictions, there always have existed some individuals who have chosen to disdain marriage or at least to postpone it beyond the age at which their society has determined that they should be married.[3] Obviously, the status of being single can be, and usually is, only a temporary transitional period between childhood, a time when an individual is considered unqualified for marriage, and the actual entry of a responsible adult into married life. But the acknowledged independent social status of an unmarried mature person has existed as, according to sociologist Ernest W. Burgess, "peculiarly a phenomenon of modern times."[4] Those who occupy this "peculiar" status have been labeled by society as "spinsters" (or "old maids") and "bachelors."[5] These terms carry both neutral and negative connotations; rarely, however, have their images been complimentary.

Psychologists and popular commentators often describe those

who are single as people who have failed to marry, as if the unmarried state represents some major personal and social shortcoming, and they occasionally refer to someone who has left the single condition as being saved by marriage. Moreover, most people commonly assume that anyone can marry if she or he really wants to do so. Thus it is because of the supposed failure that the labels "bachelor," "spinster," and "old maid" have acquired derogatory connotations. Persons who are not wedded at an age when society expects them to be married often are accused of being hostile toward the sacred institution of matrimony or toward persons of the opposite sex (hostile, sometimes, because they are homosexual). Or else they are described as being repugnant physically or psychologically to potential mates, as being afraid of responsibility and involvement, or as being single-mindedly obsessed with themselves and/or their career.[6] The possibility that they willingly choose to be single is seldom considered plausible. Rather, they exhibit a differentness that social arbiters somehow need to explain and overcome.

Numbers of Bachelors

As their numbers and proportions increased in American urban communities in the last third of the nineteenth century, bachelors became, in the minds of some people, an ever visible social problem. At the same time, however, in the minds of others, unmarried men occupied an enviable position in society, one reflecting Jack Tanner's disdain for marriage and his implied revelry in the sanctuary and birthright of male freedom and self-indulgence. When they referred to marriage and family, the authors of almost every prescriptive publication of the era viewed the unmarried state as unnatural, and they strained to define means that would encourage "the singular to become plural." Meanwhile, other pundits voiced thinly veiled admiration for the ways in which bachelors could freely roam the city and enjoy the new commercial and consumer culture. Either way, as objects of scorn or envy, bachelors were identified as a genuine social group.

The numbers and proportions of bachelors inhabiting American cities were impressive. The following few pages present a detailed descriptive analysis of how many, how old, and where the bachelors were. The major point of this exercise is to show that in the decades ending the nineteenth century and beginning the twentieth, American cities contained consistently large numbers and proportions of unmarried men in their populations. Those readers who are interested in the details of these numbers and proportions should read on. On the other hand, those who are willing to accept my word may wish to skip to the next section of the chapter (page 55), where I analyze and offer an explanation of why there were so many unattached men at this particular time.

In 1890 the U.S. Census Bureau counted 41.7 percent of all American males over the age of fifteen as single, the highest national proportion recorded by the Bureau until the most recent past (see chapter 8).[7] That year an estimated 67 percent of men aged fifteen to thirty-four were unmarried.[8] Median marriage age for men in 1890 was 26.1, also a historic high, and it remained at just below that peak into the first two decades of the twentieth century before dropping to 24.3 in 1930 and bottoming out at 22.8 in 1960.[9] Demographer Paul Jacobson has estimated that of those men born in the decade between 1865 and 1874, 37.3 percent were still single in the early 1900s, when they were aged twenty-five to thirty-four—ages at which, according to the averages and to the norms of virtually every ethnic, religious, and racial group, they should have been married.[10] Advanced marriage ages meant fewer matrimonial ceremonies. The country's marriage rate—that is, the number of marriages per 100,000 population—dropped from 98 in 1870 to 91 in both 1880 and 1890, and the number of marriages per 100,000 *un*married people aged fifteen and above reached an all-time low of 316 also in 1890.[11] Although between 1886 and 1915 the American marriage rate remained quite high compared to that of other nations of the Western world (the rates in the Scandinavian countries and especially in Ireland were considerably lower—60 marriages per 100,000 people in Sweden, for example, and just 51 per 100,000 in Ireland), bachelors nevertheless comprised an important and conspicuous segment of individual communities in every region of the United States.[12]

It is ironic—and significant—that at a time of extensive urbanization, when migration and population growth in the nation's cities enlarged the range of potential marriage partners, the extent of bachelorhood in major cities surpassed that of the nation as a whole. As table 2.1 reveals, only in Detroit and Baltimore did the proportions of unmarried adult males in the population fall below the national figure of 41.7 percent in 1890. In the western boomtowns of Denver and San Francisco, considerably more than half of all adult males were single, figures significantly higher than the national average. The relatively advanced age at marriage is reflected in the fact that in almost all cities (again Detroit and Baltimore, plus New Orleans, are exceptions) more than half of all males between the ages of twenty-five and twenty-nine in 1890 were unmarried. Even among men in their late thirties and early forties, one in five or one in six had not married.

By 1920 the proportions of adult men in major cities who were single had fallen somewhat but in most places still remained above the national average of 35.1 percent. Table 2.1 shows that with the exceptions of San Francisco, Boston, and Louisville, between 36 and 40 percent of men over the age of fifteen in the selected cities were unmarried in 1920, proportions that ranged about five percentage points lower than they had been thirty years previously. Though the marriage age had fallen by 1920, reflected in the lower proportions of single men in the twenty-to-twenty-four age bracket, the percentages of single men in the thirty-five to forty-four age group remained about the same as they had been in 1890 or even rose in most

49

TABLE 2.1

Percentage of Men Aged Fifteen and Older Who Were Single
Selected Cities, 1890 and 1920

| | 1890 | | | | | | | |
	Total 15+	15–19	20–24	25–29	30–34	35–44	45–64	65+
Baltimore	41.2	99.8	82.4	45.4	27.6	16.6	9.8	5.2
Boston	46.3	99.8	87.5	59.1	37.9	22.5	11.1	6.6
Chicago	44.0	99.9	85.1	51.0	29.3	17.5	8.2	4.7
Cincinnati	44.0	99.9	85.6	49.7	29.4	18.4	8.9	5.2
Denver	56.4	99.7	89.7	70.2	49.7	31.3	14.5	7.7
Detroit	38.8	99.7	83.8	43.4	20.8	11.1	4.8	4.9
Louisville	45.4	99.6	83.7	50.2	30.8	17.9	8.1	7.7
Minneapolis	49.5	99.8	90.1	62.7	36.8	22.1	19.0	16.9
New Orleans	43.8	99.7	81.7	47.8	30.3	19.4	10.8	9.7
New York	44.9	99.7	84.2	51.8	32.5	20.6	11.0	6.9
St. Louis	46.5	99.6	86.6	52.6	31.8	18.8	11.7	7.8
San Francisco	56.8	99.4	90.1	70.8	56.0	42.0	25.3	18.1

| | 1920 | | | | | | |
	Total 15+	15–19	20–24	25–34	35–44	45–64	65+
Baltimore	35.6	98.2	68.9	32.0	18.3	11.1	10.8
Boston	41.3	99.3	83.2	44.1	24.3	16.8	11.0
Chicago	36.5	98.9	78.2	36.3	18.8	12.4	6.8
Cincinnati	36.1	98.4	74.6	38.1	20.8	15.6	10.6
Denver	35.8	98.4	75.4	39.9	22.8	16.3	12.7
Detroit	39.1	98.4	75.2	38.7	19.1	10.5	5.1
Louisville	34.3	97.1	67.1	32.7	19.0	13.0	8.4
Minneapolis	37.7	98.9	78.7	39.1	20.6	14.0	10.9
New Orleans	40.1	97.3	72.2	37.1	20.7	13.8	11.3
New York	38.1	99.1	80.8	36.9	17.5	12.1	9.0
St. Louis	36.5	97.9	71.9	35.3	20.4	15.9	11.6
San Francisco	43.8	97.5	79.1	47.4	31.2	25.3	21.2

Source: U.S. Bureau of the Census, *Eleventh Census of the United States, 1890, Volume 1: Population* (Washington, D.C.: Government Printing Office, 1892), pp. 883–908; U. S. Bureau of the Census, *Fourteenth Census of the United States, 1920, Volume 2 Population* (Washington, D.C.: Government Printing Office, 1922), pp. 288–304 and 993–1008.

cities. (It is important to note, however, that even in 1920, average age at marriage was still quite high relative to what it would become between 1930 and 1960.) The consistency of singlehood among older age groups over the thirty-year period represented by the table suggests that confirmed bachelor-hood—that is, men who never married as opposed to those who only postponed marriage—was an established cultural pattern in the years surrounding the turn of the century. In fact, findings by demographer Kingsley Davis support such an observation. Davis compiled figures showing that among men reaching marriageable age between 1870 and 1920, consistently about 10 percent never married. Only after 1920 did these percentages fall, reaching 5.9 percent for men who were in the most marriageable age range in the decade between 1950 and 1960.[13]

The sheer numbers of unmarried men make the various percentages even more remarkable. In 1890, the city of Chicago counted 170,571 single males, and 151,362 of them were between ages fifteen and thirty-four. That year the number of bachelors in Chicago outnumbered the total population of the entire city of Louisville, Kentucky. In 1890, Boston contained 74,112 unmarried men; 63,031 were between fifteen and thirty-four. San Francisco had 75,091 bachelors, 55,147 of them between fifteen and thirty-four. The young (fifteen to thirty-four year old) bachelor populations of Boston and San Francisco in 1890 were approximately the same numerical size as the total (male and female, young and old) populations of Memphis, Tennessee, and Trenton, New Jersey.[14] With tens or even hundreds of thousands of their cohorts in one place, bachelors certainly contained the numbers for a powerful social force.

By 1920 the numbers of bachelors had grown impressively. Chicago contained 362,178 single men that year, 287,796 of them between the ages of fifteen and thirty-four — just slightly less than the total population of Rochester, New York, which was 295,750. In 1920 as well, Boston counted 111,245 unmarried males, 97,845 of whom were between fifteen and thirty-four while San Francisco was home to 97,940 bachelors, 62,931 of whom were between fifteen and thirty-four. Boston's young bachelor population equaled the total population of Lynn, Massachusetts, while San Francisco's young bachelor contingent was approximately equal to the total number of people living in Sacramento, California.[15]

Within the individual cities, considerable variation in the extent of singlehood occurred depending on race and nativity, making generalizations more difficult and complicated. Detailed figures are presented in the appendix, but a few notable patterns can be mentioned here. The country's population of African American males, for example, tended to marry earlier than white males and therefore tended to have lower percentages of unmarried men, especially in younger age groups. In places with substantial communities of African Americans, such as Baltimore, New Orleans, and St. Louis in 1890, the proportions of all African American men over the age of fifteen who were unmarried were three to five percentage points lower than those of white men, and they were five to thirteen percentage points lower than those of whites among all men aged twenty-five to twenty-nine. By 1920 in these cities, the disparities between blacks and whites in the twenty-five to thirty-four age cohort had evened out, but among men aged twenty to twenty-four, blacks were considerably more likely to be married than whites.

Even more significant differences showed up when white males were divided into nativity groups. Generally, the percentages of bachelors among a particular city's men who were native whites born of native parents quite closely matched the city's total percentages of bachelors. Thus in Chicago in 1890, 44 percent of all men over fifteen were unmarried and 46 percent of native white men born of native parents were unmarried. In Boston in 1920, 41.3 percent of all males over fifteen were unmarried and 43.0 percent of native white males born of native parents were unmarried. In each of these cases, the differences between all males and native white men born of native parents were statistically insignificant. Throughout most cities, the similarities in rates of bachelorhood between native white men of native parents and all white men in the city persisted through the various age groups. In other words, in Chicago in 1890, 83.0 percent of native white men who were between the ages of twenty and twenty-four and who had native-born parents were single, compared to 85.1 percent of all men in that age category. And in Boston in 1920, 44.3 percent of native white men who were between the ages of twenty-five and thirty-four and who had native-born parents were unmarried, compared with 44.1 percent of all Boston men in that age category.

Significant differences did exist, however, between native-born men of foreign parents[16] on one hand and foreign-born men on the other as well as between both of these groups and the general rates for all white men. Intuitively one would expect that the disruptions of immigration would have induced foreign-born men to postpone marriage and therefore that high rates of bachelorhood would have resulted among them. Also, one would expect that native-born men of foreign parents, presumably having acclimated themselves to the American environment, would have had less trouble finding mates than would those who had directly experienced the disruptions of immigration. Yet just the opposite occurred with remarkable consistency over the entire turn-of-the-century period. That is, the proportions of foreign-born men who were single were considerably lower than those for other nativity groups (and lower than those for African Americans as well), and proportions of native-born men of foreign parents who were unmarried were considerably higher than those for other nativity groups.

Just why these contrasts existed has remained somewhat of a mystery to demographers, but the patterns occurred with remarkable consistency. For example, in 1890 in cities such as Boston, Cincinnati, Detroit, New York City, and St. Louis, all of which had high aggregations of immigrant males but very different economies, the percentages of all men over fifteen who were unmarried ranged between 39 and 46 percent while the percentages of foreign-born men who were unmarried ranged between only 26 and 35 percent, almost a third lower. In Cincinnati, just 21.2 percent of foreign-born men aged fifteen and over were unmarried in 1890. The same pattern of smaller proportions of single men among the foreign-born persisted in 1920 as well. For example, while 38.1 percent of all adult New York men were unmarried in 1920, only 25.3 percent of immigrant men were single. The 1920 figure for Cincinnati's foreign-born bachelors was 19.6 percent. This low extent of bachelorhood among immigrant men relative to native white men extended throughout all age categories. Indeed, the fact that immigrant groups in general contained fewer never-married men than did native-born groups even among those aged forty-five and older suggests that confirmed bachelorhood was not an acceptable alternative among most immigrant cultures.[17] It may also be true that more immigrant men entered the United States already married than historians previously have assumed, but this possibility must await future research.

In direct contrast to foreign-born men, those males born in the United States to one or two foreign-born parents showed an extraordinary propensity to stay unmarried through their early and mid-twenties. In all the selected cities, the proportions of single men among those who were native-born of foreign or mixed (one foreign-born, one native-born) parents greatly exceeded the proportions of all other nativity and racial groups. (See appendix for details.) For example, in Boston in 1890, while 46.3 percent of all males aged fifteen and over were unmarried, 70.0 percent of native-born men of foreign parents were single. In Chicago in 1890, while 44.0 percent of all men aged fifteen and over were unmarried, 76.7 percent of native-born men of foreign parents were single. Similar contrasts occurred in other cities: Cincinnati, 44.0 percent versus 61.6 percent; Louisville, 45.4 percent versus 62.6 percent; New York City, 44.9 percent versus 68.6 percent; San Francisco, 56.8 percent versus 74.8 percent.

The same patterns persisted by 1920, though the differences were not quite so wide. In Boston in 1920, 41.3 percent of all males fifteen and over were single while 58.6 percent of native-born men of foreign-born parents were unmarried. In Chicago, the difference was 36.5 percent versus 51.0 percent; in New York, 38.1 percent versus 54.7 percent; in San Francisco, 43.8 percent versus 48.6 percent. Only in Cincinnati and

Louisville were differences between the two groups relatively small: 36.1 percent versus 36.9 percent in Cincinnati and 34.3 percent versus 34.5 percent in Louisville.

Though native-born men of foreign-parents contained higher percentages of single men in every age cohort, the differences were especially notable among the oldest age categories. Among men aged 35 and older, the proportions of bachelors among native-born men of foreign parents doubled those of foreign-born men and were 50 percent higher than those of native-born men of native-parents in both 1890 and 1920. Thus for example, in Boston in 1890, 16.4 percent (one in six) of native-born men aged forty-five to sixty-four who were born to foreign parents were single, while 8.8 percent of foreign-born men in the same age category were single and 11.1 of all Boston men in that category were unmarried. In Chicago in 1920, 12.1 percent (almost one in eight) of native-born men aged sixty-five and older who had foreign parents had never married, compared to 5.4 percent of foreign-born men and 6.8 percent of all Chicago men in that age category. These patterns show that not only did second-generation immigrants delay marriage more extensively than did both first-generation immigrants and men of third generation and above, but also a significant proportion of them permanently avoided wedlock.

WHY WERE THERE SO MANY BACHELORS?

A bachelor who is asked why he is not married may have myriad explanations, each of which may be unique to that particular man. Some males may have wanted to get married but found, or imagined, specific obstacles in their way. As would be the case currently, examples of such explanations in the late nineteenth century and early twentieth could be amusing. In 1906, a twenty-seven-year-old bachelor wrote to the "Bintel Brief," the folksy advice column published in the widely-read Yiddish-language newspaper the *Daily Forward*, that he desired to marry a seventeen-year-old girl but was reluctant to do so because she was very short and he was very tall. The column's editor gently assured him that all sizes can be happy in marriage and that he should be grateful that he was taller and she was shorter, not the opposite. Other bachelors seeking advice met with less patience. When a twenty-five-year-old wrote to the "Bintel Brief" in 1908 that he was afraid to marry because his beloved had a dimple on her chin and he had heard that people with dimpled chins were fated to lose their first spouse, the columnist responded with characteristic Jewish sarcasm. "The tragedy," the "Brief" answered, "is not that the girl has a dimple in her chin but that some people have a screw loose in their heads!"[18]

In spite of all the idiosyncratic rationales, fears, and excuses for not marrying, some systematic and historical examination of the explanations for bachelorhood still is possible. The foregoing pages have outlined the extraordinary extent of bachelorhood—especially among certain groups such as native-born men of foreign or mixed parents—in the United States in the late nineteenth century and early twentieth. What possible overarching reasons might exist to explain why so many men were postponing or avoiding marriage? Demographer Ruth Dixon has cited three factors that have affected the timing and prevalence of voluntary[19] nuptiality in western society: (1) the availability of mates (demographic explanation); (2) the availability of resources (economic explanation); and (3) the desirability of marriage versus the alternative (cultural explanation).[20] The following pages offer a critical examination of each of these factors.

Demographic Theory

The simplest explanation for the extent of bachelorhood in American cities around the turn of the century would be the demographic one. That is, there was an imbalance in sex ratios, an excess of males and shortage of females that limited the "market" of marriageable women, thereby constraining men's choices. Such disparity could result from differential birth rates: more males being born than females; or it could result from differential mortality rates: men dying earlier (especially in infancy, childhood, and early adulthood) and more frequently than women.

However, neither of these demographic trends, both of which normally occur in most human populations, fully explain why there were large surpluses of single men in the United States during the years under discussion. Though human biology causes more males than females to be born, this fact alone is not sufficient to cause very large excesses of males. Since male infant mortality is higher than female infant mortality, gender disparities at birth tend to level off, even resulting in a surpluses of females. To be sure, females have had, and continue to have, higher survival rates and longer life expectancies than males, a fact that accounts for the almost universally high ratio of widows to widowers. But advantageous survival and longer life expectancy rates would increase, rather than decrease, the pool of potential female mates, thereby acting as an incentive for men to marry rather than a disincentive to remain single. As well, the brief but significant mismatches in sex ratios that occurred after the Civil War, which killed hundreds of thousands of men of prime marrying age, and to a lesser extent after World War I, which also killed large numbers of young men, created a shortage of men that should have resulted in higher rather than lower rates of marriage among men.

Instead, those imbalanced sex ratios that did exist resulted from differential migration patterns rather than from contrasts in birth and death rates. Census data show heavy excesses of men over women in many of those urban communities that were growing rapidly from migration in the late nineteenth century and early twentieth.[21] In San Francisco, for example, there were more than 130 males for every 100 females in the city's population during every census year but one between 1870 and 1920.[22] The gender imbalance was even more severe among people of marriageable age. In San Francisco in 1890, single men between the ages of twenty-five and thirty-four outnumbered single women in that age range by almost four to one, and the ratio was still high at two to one in 1920. Not surprisingly, nearly 57 percent of all adult men in San Francisco in 1890 were single, and, as noted in the previous section of this chapter, 75 percent of San Francisco's adult men with at least one foreign-born parent were unmarried. In Chicago in 1890, where 44 percent of all males over the age of fifteen were unmarried, single men between twenty-five and thirty-four outnumbered single women in that age group by almost two and one-half to one, and in 1920 the sex ratio of unmarried men to women was still over three to two. Such figures suggest a logical conclusion: many men had to stay unmarried because there simply were not enough women to go around.[23]

The overrepresentation of men in the sex ratios of cities such as San Francisco and Chicago, however, comprised only one variant of a more complicated pattern. One might speculate, for example, that since women married at younger ages — usually three to five years younger — than did men, a more useful investigation of the marriage market would be to compare numbers of single men aged twenty-five to thirty-four to numbers of single women aged twenty to twenty-nine. This comparison reveals somewhat smaller imbalances in San Francisco in 1890, with men outnumbering women by five to three, and in Chicago the ratio is almost exactly one to one. But in other cities, including — significantly — those with quite high proportions of bachelors in the male population, there were heavy *surpluses* of women of marrying age. For example, in Baltimore in 1890, single women aged twenty to twenty-nine outnumbered single men aged twenty-five to thirty-four by almost two to one, yet 37.0 percent of all Baltimore men aged twenty-five to thirty-four were unmarried and 53.4 percent of all Baltimore men aged twenty to thirty-four were bachelors. In Boston in 1890, single women aged twenty to twenty-nine outnumbered single men aged twenty-five to thirty-four by three to two even though 49.6 percent of all Boston men aged twenty-five to thirty-four were unmarried and 62.7 percent of all Boston men aged twenty to thirty-four were bachelors.

Moreover, ratios such as these did not follow a strictly regional pattern. For example, there were close similarities in the 1890 sex ratios among unmarried persons living in Cincinnati (a midwestern city), Louisville and New Orleans (southern and border cities), and Boston and Baltimore (eastern cities). At the same time, the ratios for Chicago (a midwestern city), Denver (a mountain city), and San Francisco (a West Coast city) resembled each other while differing from those of the other five places.[24]

The manner in which the U.S. Census Bureau aggregated age categories changed in the federal censuses from 1900 onward, making comparison with 1890 somewhat difficult,[25] but the pattern looks the same. Even though practically every major city had surpluses of single men to single women among people aged twenty-five to thirty-four,[26] most places also had relatively high proportions of unmarried *women* in these same age groups. Thus in 1910, the proportions of women aged twenty-five to thirty-four who were single were: Baltimore, 30.0 percent; Boston, 38.9 percent; Chicago, 24.8 percent; Cincinnati, 31.8 percent; Denver, 24.3 percent; Louisville, 29.4 percent; New Orleans, 26.3 percent; and San Francisco, 28.2 percent. Nationally, the percentage of women aged fifteen and above who were unmarried was 29.7 percent in 1910 and 27.3 percent in 1920,[27] but in almost every large city it was several percentage points higher.

Adna Weber, whose statistical analysis of American urban society at the turn of the century remains one of the most thorough of its kind, remarked that higher numbers of men than women were the norm in virtually all cities of the Western world. Weber attributed these imbalances to differential migration and concluded that high rates of out-migration among males, rather than high rates of in-migration among females, was more likely to cause excesses of women in cities.[28] Such a

conclusion makes intuitive sense; the rapid growth of the agricultural, ranching, and mining regions of the American West in
the late nineteenth century tended to attract more men than
women, and this migration tended to leave women behind in
the eastern cities.[29] In fact, there certainly were far more men
than women in western cities such as San Francisco, Denver,
Seattle, and Portland in the years between 1890 and 1920. But,
as the above analysis suggests, age breakdowns seriously undermine Weber's conclusion because census figures for young
adult age groups — those most likely to be shopping in the marriage market — reveal excesses of men in virtually *every* city
and also high proportions of unmarried women even in those
cities with surpluses of single men.

Furthermore, if, as Weber and others have hypothesized, migration had a deterrent effect on marriage, one would expect
those who traveled the farthest distances to have exhibited the
highest rates of bachelorhood. In fact, as the previous section
pointed out, the opposite occurred: foreign-born immigrants
manifested the *lowest* rates of bachelorhood, relative to native-
born groups, in every city examined. To be sure, the highest
proportions of unmarried men consistently occurred among
native-born men with at least one foreign-born parent, but
these men apparently were trying to reconcile their immigrant
backgrounds with their new American environment and seem
to have postponed marriage for reasons other than migration.

Most importantly, however, it is problematic to use sex ratios, including those resulting from differential migration patterns, as an explanation for the extent of unmarried people
because sex ratios can affect marriage patterns in a given community only if that community is endogamous. That is, excesses of one sex compared to another can influence the propensity to marry or remain single only if people select or accept
their mates from the same community in which they live. In an
endogamous society, a preponderance of one sex over another
would certainly influence the proportion marrying because the
marriage market would not be able to match up men and

women in a one-to-one fashion. But in virtually all of modern Europe and the United States, no community, especially no large city, has ever been endogamous; countless people seek, select, and accept marriage partners from outside their own community. Thus, it is not necessarily logical to conclude that non-marriage is correlated with unbalanced sex ratios.[30] Furthermore, as anthropologist Stanley Brandes has noted, *late* marriage is not necessarily correlated with *non*-marriage. In a society such as the United States was at the end of the nineteenth century, where a somewhat advanced marriage age relative to the mid-twentieth century was the norm, an individual remained eligible to marry for a longer number of years than did someone living in a low-marriage-age society that might deem a person increasingly ineligible for marriage after the person passed that normative age.[31]

Economic Theory

Age breakdowns of census figures suggest that, contrary to Weber and other analysts in the late nineteenth century and early twentieth, the high proportions of unmarried people in American urban populations may not have been that closely related to unbalanced sex ratios. In other words, what some have called the law of numbers did not act as strongly as contemporary demographers had assumed.[32] Rather, other explanations need to be found, especially for the low rates of marriage among people of both sexes normally considered to be of marriageable age.[33] The next most accessible rationale is the economic one: that is, the argument that people, mainly men, avoided committing to marriage because they could not afford it. This theory has a lengthy history. As long as the United States was expanding and land remained relatively plentiful from the Revolution through the first half of the nineteenth century, according to the theory, a man could, with relative ease, acquire a farm, marry his sweetheart, and start a family at a relatively early age. But then, the economic uncertainties attendant to the urban-industrial transformation of the late nineteenth century presumably prompted the temporary or permanent postponement of marriage. As well, the transiency of men in search of work, also attendant to urbanization and industrialization, supposedly created difficult obstacles to marriage.[34] A variation of this theory posits that rising standards and expectations of comfort resulting from technological and scientific advance increased the incidences of marriage, but a worsening of material conditions as a result of economic downturn postponed marital plans and increased the number of yet-to-be-married and never-married persons. Only after the Great Depression and well into the mid-twentieth century, when economic opportunity and expectations became more stable and the institution of marriage became less of an economic and social commitment—shifting more to an emotional relationship—did marriage age and rates of nonmarriage fall.[35]

Economist Richard Easterlin has presented a more sophisticated version of the economic explanation with a theory based on a rational-actor model of behavior. Easterlin asserts that individuals considering marriage (mostly males) normally assess the ratio between their earnings potential and the level of their material aspirations. Expectations for living standards, he says, are influenced by childhood experiences. Thus, according to the Easterlin theory, if a young adult's relative income rises above that of the parental family, then that person will feel lessening economic pressure and would be ready to marry and have children. When many people experience this readiness, the results are lower marriage age and higher birth rates. If, however, the person's relative income falls compared to that of the parental family, the individual will experience economic stress, and, as a consequence of the decisions by multiple persons encountering this situation, marriage rates and fertility will decline. More generally, relative income can be equated with economic outlook. If times are good and potential earning power appears to be high, then a person's economic outlook can be said to be optimistic. Conversely, uncertain times obviously would induce pessimism.

According to Easterlin, when the national economy was relatively strong, as in the 1920s and again in the 1950s, rates of marriage and childbearing accelerated. When times were hard or uneven, as in the late nineteenth century and during the depression of the 1930s, many people deferred marriage.[36] Thus, according to the Easterlin theory, it was such an economic perspective, influenced by the severe nationwide economic depression that had occurred in the early and mid-1890s, that prompted Adna Weber to assert in 1899 that postponement of marriage, especially by native-born Americans, reflected prudence and foresight.[37]

There is a basic drawbacks to the economic explanation for why people would avoid or postpone marriage. The theory is just that—a theory. Even though it makes intuitive sense, there is little direct evidence to substantiate the assumption that scarce resources or relative decline in economic outlook would necessarily induce people to delay marrying. It is true that in colonial times, sons often postponed marriage until they inherited or received by gift or purchase some land from their fathers.[38] And even into the mid-nineteenth century, the necessity for having enough income to establish an independent household and farm often forced men to postpone marriage until they were in their late twenties and early thirties.[39] But as the nineteenth century advanced and the agrarian economy gave way to one oriented toward commerce and manufacturing, access to land-based resources became less important in determining the timing of marriage. Personal decision making seems to have become more complicated, especially in urban communities, and without survey information that would have asked individuals why they married when they did, applying a general economic theory of marital timing to a large population is very difficult. For example, immigrants' lack of full information about and access to resources in American cities should have induced them to delay marrying. Yet, according to the figures presented earlier in this chapter, the marriage rates and ages at marriage of foreign-born men suggest that they delayed wedlock less often than native-born men did. On the other hand, for some, if not many, immigrant men, the United States might have offered better resources and opportunities relative to what they had available in their countries of origin, so that once they encountered American society, they were encouraged to marry.

In the late nineteenth century, presumably a time when the uncertain dynamics of the urban-industrial transformation clouded many people's economic outlook, the highest rates of marriage and earliest marriage ages were occurring among the immigrant and native working classes, the least economically advantaged groups of the population.[40] Conversely, those on the highest end of the socioeconomic scale, supposedly those with the rosiest economic outlooks, were marrying later and less often. Though the data are not definitive, marriage records from Providence, Rhode Island, in 1879 showed that men in the three lowest occupational categories — skilled, semi-skilled, and unskilled — were marrying earlier than those in the three highest occupational categories — professionals, managers, and proprietors. The differences were somewhat small but suggestive. Almost 42 percent of men in the lowest occupational groups who married did so before they were twenty-five, while just 37 percent of men in higher occupational groups did so. Also, 54 percent of those relatively well-off men who married did so between the ages of twenty-five and thirty-four, compared to 49 percent of blue-collar men who married.[41] Nationally, by the late nineteenth century, the high marriage and birth rates of the working classes, especially those of racial and ethnic minorities, relative to those among native-white upper classes created fears of race suicide. This was being carried out by the supposedly superior middle and upper classes who appeared to be avoiding marriage and limiting their family size.

The end result, in some people's minds, would be the collapse of American civilization.[42]

It is possible that Richard Easterlin's theory may indeed be partly applicable in explaining high rates of marriage among the working classes. That is, some young working-class men, believing that their prospects were better than those of their fathers, might have married at relatively young ages. As well, some young middle-class men, believing that they might fall below their fathers' socioeconomic status, might have remained unmarried for a few years after the age that previously had been the norm for their social rank. The point here is that many subtle factors were and are involved in the decision to marry, and general economic theories can explain them in only overly general and sometimes contradictory ways. Data and logic lead toward an explanation other than either the demographic or the economic theory.

Cultural Theory

What remains, then, is the sociocultural explanation, the assumption that a plethora of social and personal motivations unrelated to sex ratios and/or economic market forces induced large numbers of men to remain unmarried, even if temporarily. These motivations can be subsumed under a rubric of desirability. That is, we can hypothesize that the availability of alternatives to marriage, such as opportunities for economic, social, and sexual independence, could have influenced individuals — in this case men — in a manner such that they would prefer to forego or delay marriage as a means of attaining personal satisfaction.[43] The possibility of such alternatives was suggested as early as 1868 by J. Bixby, a writer for *The Nation*, who penned an article titled "Why Is the Single Life Becoming More General?" Bixby, alluding to the "fact established by abundant statistical proof" that "marriage has become less frequent" than in previous decades, dismissed most

FIGURE 2.1. In the closing decades of the nineteenth century, a host of new commercial amusements presented young, unmarried people with diversions that altered their courting habits and temporarily curbed their willingness to marry. Here, the Midway of New York's Coney Island shows the variety of establishments — beer hall, burlesque house, cigar shop, and cafés, as well as the park itself — that attracted hordes of patrons. (Library of Congress)

explanations for this "fact"—such explanations as migration and female employment—as effects rather than causes. Instead, he asserted that modern civilization and its "social developments" produced the single life. In other words, modern American society's diversions, rather than its economic constraints and the numbers game of potential marriage mates, were the principal causes of bachelorhood.[44] Later in the century, a writer for *Forum* magazine echoed Bixby's comment, noting that in the city "men's matrimonial discouragements and bachelor compensations are many."[45]

The late nineteenth century certainly marked a time when American cities began to harbor myriad leisure-time diversions, many of which tempted and filled the everyday lives and leisure time of young, independent men and women. Historians have equated this period with the rise of commercial amusements, such as dance halls, spectator and participation sports, amusement parks, vaudeville, saloons, theaters, popular literature, sensational journalism, social clubs, pool halls, red-light vice districts, cafés and cabarets, and many more that occupied the time of young urban adults who had newfound spendable incomes.[46] Going somewhere by trolley or automobile became the common mode by which middle-class young people socialized and entertained themselves, but also all classes of urban youths shared in the new activity of "going out."[47] Historian David Nasaw has cited an 1899 *New York Times* description of the wide openness of public entertainment in the city. An amusement district, notes Nasaw, was "a world like no other, . . . where the city's people came together to have a good time in public. There were no restrictions as to gender, ethnicity, religion, residence, or occupation in the new amusement space."[48]

Such diversions helped create a new heterosocial culture, one that brought together young, unattached men and women in social and sometimes sexual relationships that minimized personal commitment. Literary critic Henry Canby recalled his youth in turn-of-the-century Chicago as a time when social life consisted of "free associations of boys and girls in their teens and early twenties."[49] These associations contrasted with the traditional courtship ritual that had prevailed in the early nineteenth century and that was supposed to lead to marriage. Rather, the new patterns of socializing with the opposite sex taking place in a city's amusement centers gave youths freedom to pursue fun and personal satisfaction to an extent previously unavailable. Remarking on the new instruments of transportation and communications that revolutionized social life for urban dwellers in the early twentieth century, sociologist Ernest W. Burgess asserted that "in towns and cities marriage tended to be delayed, the period of courtship and engagement extended. With the growing economic independence of youth, their social life became an end in itself."[50]

For men, these pursuits often exacerbated the double standard in moral behavior. While women were identified and glorified for their purity, men were seen as creatures of passions that sometimes could not be controlled. Thus men's occasional searches to satisfy their sexual appetites in illicit ways were tolerated as long as the men otherwise safeguarded and honored the moral virtue of their wives and other women of their family. Two different categories of women resulted from this double standard: those whose moral purity could nurture men and "cleanse" them from temptation, and those "morally loose" women, usually but not always prostitutes, who catered to men's "beastly needs." The expanded world of leisure and amusement in burgeoning cities in the late nineteenth century and the resulting dilution of the formalities of courtship provided new outlets for men's sexual energies, desires that in earlier decades marriage had confined. Thus one observer remarked in 1894 that men "raided the amusement parks or the evening streets in search of girls that could be frankly pursued for their physical charms."[51]

The availability of new leisure-time pursuits and outlets for male sexual energies, however, would not alone have diverted young urban dwellers from a commitment to marriage; the

FIGURE 2.2. Dance halls represented new places of commercial amusement where young people could exercise control over their courtship without parental supervision. The dance hall particularly brought together unmarried young men and women in an environment in which they could interact with each other yet avoid relationships that would lead directly to marriage. Small and informal, dance halls such as the one depicted here became venues for the social life of many an urban bachelor. (The New York Historical Society)

new entertainments were accompanied and reinforced by a new attitude. That is, young men (and to some extent young women also) avoided marriage because they, rather than their parents, the marriage market, or the economy, had seized control over the choices of what they did with their lives and their time, including when and whether they married. The proliferation of dance halls, amusement parks, motion picture theaters, cabarets, and countless other sites of commercial amusement provided young people with spaces in which they could attain a heightened degree of escape from the watchful eyes of older adults. First streetcars and then automobiles facilitated access to these places where youths of every class could explore all kinds of liberties: in the way they spent their money, in the people with whom they associated, and in the social and sexual intimacies they had with others.[52] In addition, the telephone diluted the formality that previously had reigned when unattached men and women met face to face, and it too provided another opportunity for unsupervised interaction.[53]

These unchaperoned activities enabled courtship between men and women to be transformed from the act of keeping company (often under watchful supervision of a parent or other chaperone) into unsupervised dating, with the result that the social lives of adolescents and young adults came to be peer controlled.[54] In the 1930s, Ernest W. Burgess articulated this cultural theory to explain bachelorhood when he suggested that heightened individual control over marriage combined with the growing independence of youths in cities to make social life an end in itself rather than a means to marriage.[55]

At the same time, the escape that young people made from the social supervision of adults meant that they also freed themselves from parental guidance in the timing and selection of their potential marriage mates. Historian Ellen K. Rothman has pointed out that parents surrendered control over their children's marriage choices early in the nineteenth century, but she asserts also that the more that commercial amusements, school life, and other independent activities drew young people

outside of the family circle, the more those young people selected marriage mates from among strangers — people, that is,
formerly unknown by the family. These choices positioned
youths even further from parental influence. Though parents
might express concern and anxiety over marital choices, they
would not and could not interfere. As Rothman has written,
"Young people belonged even more [than ever before] to a
peer society where parents had less opportunity, and less authority, to take an active part in the lives of their young-adult
offspring."[56]

Challenge to parental authority created special tensions within
immigrant families, as children used New World customs to
cut themselves adrift from ancient moorings. M. E. Ravage, a
New York City labor radical and aspiring medical student who
immigrated from Rumania as a young man in the late nineteenth century, noted the breach that opened when immigrant
children learned English, began patronizing new commercial
establishments, and adopted new forms of sexual interaction.
The younger generation, he wrote in his memoirs, became

> master of the situation and kept the older in wholesome terror
> of itself. Mere slips of boys and girls went around together and
> called it love after the American fashion. The dance-halls were
> thronged with them. The parks saw them on the benches in pairs
> until all hours of the morning, and they ran things in their par-
> ents' homes to suit themselves.[57]

Moreover, as the economic and procreational motivations
for marriage became less important than in previous eras, qualities such as emotional compatibility, companionship, and sexual attraction rose to prime importance and young adults asserted their own prerogative to determine those qualities in a
potential marriage mate.[58] That determination process often
took several years once the individual reached marrying age, a
period longer, for the most part, than it would have taken parents to identify the suitability of a potential spouse in a more
traditional manner. As Burgess remarked, "The introduction of

71

choice of partners by young people rather than by parents naturally increased the difficulty of concluding engagements and marriages."[59] Contemporary experts acknowledged the trend toward companionability and the resulting delay in marriage, and they often justified delaying marriage as necessary for potential partners to explore and be certain of their compatibility. In an article otherwise dedicated to making divorce easier, writer Elizabeth Lynn Linton declared in 1891 that "the good of society necessitates late marriages; for those youthful mores which make the charm of poetry and the staple of romance, in practice mean pauperism and misery."[60]

Diaries, correspondences, and other personal literature of the late nineteenth century and early twentieth are full of uncertainties about love, suitors, and potential marriage partners, and there are numerous accounts of refused marriage proposals that reflected heightened anxiety about selecting and accepting the perfect person for a spouse. A varied range of men agonized over how to define and find the ideal mate. Larue Brown, a New York lawyer, wrote of his ideal in a 1915 letter to his future wife (to whom he had postponed marriage for several years). "Since first I came to think as a man thinks there has been ever with me in my heart a picture of a kind of girl. I could love that kind of girl and be to her what I wished to be to the woman whose life was linked to mine."[61] Abe Hollandersky, who spent much of his adulthood as a prize-fighter and newsboy on a navy ship, disdained a romance with a beautiful, wealthy woman named Carlotta Puertos and shunned marriage until late in life because of his attitude about marriage. "When you marry," he declared in his autobiography, "you must marry someone of your own faith, your own mental equipment; some girl who, when she gets tired of your style, will have to be tired of her own style too, because you are both the same style."[62]

There is one final point that combines the sociocultural and demographic explanations for bachelorhood in the late nineteenth century and early twentieth. It seems plausible to hypothesize that at this particular time the profusion of bachelors may have become self-reinforcing and self-generating, that the existence of large numbers of unmarried men somehow encouraged other men, who might otherwise have been contemplating marriage, to "stay with the fraternity" and remain single, at least for a while. In other words, there may have been an "epidemic" of bachelorhood in American cities. Though, as chapter 1 pointed out, the statistics from the early eras of American history are not very abundant, nonetheless it seems that before 1870 or 1880 the size of the bachelor populations in various communities provoked some vaguely expressed concerns but only slowly moved in the direction of constituting a distinctly subcultural group. By the last quarter of the nineteenth century, however, the numbers and proportions of men who were single may well have reached a tipping point, a juncture at which those men who had postponed their own marriages served to "infect" other men with similar sentiments. This "contagion," when combined with the burgeoning alternatives that the urban commercial culture was providing, diverted a larger-than-might-be-expected cohort of marriageable men away from matrimony. Then, after 1920, as society became accustomed to the institutions and situations that previously had distracted men from marital commitments, the epidemic subsided and both marriage age and the proportions of men who were bachelors in the population declined. Not until the 1970s, when new sexual standards made cohabitation between unmarried people acceptable and new social and economic conditions discouraged marriage, did the proportions of people who were single once again rise. But that is a topic for discussion later in this book (see chapter 8).

J. Bixby, the writer for *The Nation* quoted earlier in this chapter, summed up the situation perceptively at the beginning of this new period of bachelor ascendancy when he observed that the single life was caused by modern civilization and its social developments. Bixby explained,

By the general diffusion of education and culture, by the new inventions and discoveries of the age, by the increase in commerce . . . and wealth, the tastes of men and women have become widened, their desires multiplied, new gratifications and pleasures have been supplied to them. By the increase of the gratifications of existence the relative share of them which married life affords has become just so much less. The domestic circle does not fill so large a place in life as formerly. . . . Married life has lost in some measure its advantage over single life.[63]

Moreover, as Bixby well knew, the city and its institutions strongly influenced the choices young people were making. "The city," he reflected, "is the habitat of the single. . . . The single must have public amusements and public resorts, and those only flourish in great cities. . . . The city bachelor and young miss of today . . . have a surfeit of independent resources," and thus did not need domestic life to sustain their needs.[64] Herein lay the major explanation for why there were so many bachelors and how the basis formed for the subculture that flourished as the nineteenth century melded into the twentieth.

The Domestic Lives of Bachelors

As THE NINETEENTH CENTURY reached its closing decades, the burgeoning numbers of single men occupying American cities were stirring up comment. Reports from state bureaus of labor statistics in the 1880s noted the impermanence of work-force participation among unmarried men, and employers be-moaned the inconstancy and irresponsibility that they believed these "wanderers" exhibited. Moral reform groups voiced fears that unrestrained single males were forming the van-guards of social breakdown, threatening the presumed stability of family and community.[1] Young and unmarried men had al-ways inhabited cities, but now their huge numbers and visi-bility provoked more anxiety than ever before. Jane Addams, settlement house founder and one of the country's leading so-cial reformers, articulated these fears when she wrote at the turn of the century,

> The social relationships in a modern city are so highly made and often so superficial, that the old human restraints of public opin-ion, long sustained in smaller communities, have also broken down. Freed from the benevolent restraints of the small town, thousands of young men and women in every great city have received none of the lessons in self-control which even savage tribes imparted to their appetites as well as their emotions.[2]

Of particular concern to reformers such as Jane Addams was the involvement of bachelors in the "boarder problem" that resulted when hordes of otherwise unattached men sought do-micile with families and in group residences. This social mal-ady had dual symptoms. In the first place, the nature of board-ing itself—inexpensive, anonymous, free from the wholesome social supervision of kin—allegedly attracted antisocial people:

ne'er-do-wells, thieves, prostitutes, and other deviants who, because they defied common conventions, could live nowhere
else. These individuals threatened sexual propriety, especially
that of the girls and young women living in households that
rented rooms to boarders or who themselves boarded in establishments that rented to men. Living among strangers, stated
one U.S. Bureau of Labor report, "cannot help but blunt a
girl's sense of proper relations with the other sex and foster
standards which are not acceptable in this country."[3] In the
minds and discourses of moralists, these "strangers" invariably
were unmarried men.

Second, according to observers, the social isolation and presumed depravity of the boarding population could corrupt not
only young women but also unsuspecting young men moving
to the city who lacked family and were in need of inexpensive
lodging. Writing in the early twentieth century, charity worker
Elizabeth Y. Rutan labeled the boardinghouse as the enemy of
home life. Referring to the residential experiences of what she
believed to be a typical unmarried male, Rutan observed, "Life
in a boarding house is at best an uninviting and monotonous
one; he is fortunate if it is not evil."[4] Several years later, Chicago sociologist Harvey W. Zorbaugh lamented the individualism that boardinghouse districts cultivated. "It is a world of
atomized individuals, of spiritual nomads," he wrote.[5] The
themes of "spiritual nomads" and the "lodger evil" continued
to pervade the meetings and writings of moralists and social
workers well into the twentieth century.[6]

Statistics substantiate that boarding and lodging were common practices in urban America at the turn of the century. In
cities growing rapidly from influxes of young, unmarried people, boarding and lodging offered a sensible solution to housing needs, and thousands of people took advantage of the opportunity. For example, the total number of boardinghouses,
lodging houses, and resident hotels in Boston grew from 927 in
1860 to 1,412 in 1880 and to 2,703 in 1900, tripling in just
four decades. Social reformer Alfred Benedict Wolfe counted

over 54,000 boarders and lodgers in Boston in 1895, two-thirds of whom were men. Wolfe estimated that in 1905, just a decade later, the number of boarders and lodgers had grown to between 70,000 and 80,000.[7] Wolfe also calculated that in 1900, Chicago had one boardinghouse or lodging-house proprietor for every 723 people in the total population. San Francisco may have contained a proportionately greater number of boarding establishments and proprietors than any other city; in 1900 there was one such proprietor for every 233 people, the highest ratio in the country.[8]

When the actual living situations of bachelors are examined more closely, however, the boardinghouse population greatly misrepresented reality. Certainly a very large proportion of the boardinghouse and lodging-house population consisted of unmarried men, but a very large proportion, usually the majority, of bachelors did *not* live as boarders. In fact, a surprising number of bachelors lived inside their own nuclear or extended family household, sometimes well into adulthood. How and with whom did unmarried men actually live? What consequences and conclusions can be drawn from their patterns of residence? This chapter provides some unexpected answers.

THE SAMPLE POPULATIONS

The data used as evidence for much of the analysis in this chapter were derived from nine separate populations of unmarried men, aged sixteen and over, sampled from the federal manuscript censuses of Boston, Chicago, and San Francisco for the years 1880, 1900, and 1920. The manuscript censuses are the actual schedules on which census enumerators recorded each individual's name, age, relationship to the head of household, race, marital status, place of birth, parents' place of birth, occupation, and other characteristics. A full discussion of the methodology used in selecting and recording the samples and in selecting cities and years for the samples is presented in the appendix. Suffice it to say at this point that the samples were drawn systematically, so as to ensure maximum representation of each city's total unmarried adult male populations. The three cities were chosen to reflect varying economic and ethnic environments of turn-of-the-century urban America.

Only two major points about the samples should be noted in this context. First, the composition of each of the samples generally matched the actual ethnic patterns in the particular city that each sample represented. Thus, about one-third of the Boston bachelors sampled were foreign-born, dominated by Irish in 1880 but consisting of more southern and eastern Europeans by 1920; the city's total unmarried male population was divided in the same way in those years. As well, slightly over 40 percent of the Chicago samples were immigrants, heavily German, Irish, and Scandinavian early in the sample period and also shifting toward higher proportions of Russian and Italian immigrants by 1920. These distributions of Chicago samples closely resembled those of the city's total unmarried male population for those years under consideration. In contrast to Boston and Chicago, San Francisco contained large numbers of Chinese immigrants in 1880, and, because of this component, its bachelor population was almost 60 percent foreign-born. By 1900 and 1920, however, immigrants accounted for 40 percent of the San Francisco samples, and Italians became the largest single nativity group. Again, the samples closely reproduced the ethnic distributions of single males in San Francisco's total population.

Second, although occupational distributions of unmarried men in the three cities' total populations were unavailable from the published census volumes (only occupational distributions for the combined married and unmarried male populations were published), and thus comparisons between the sampled and full populations were impossible to make, the occupational distributions of the samples followed expected and consistent patterns. In all three cities in all three sample years, foreign-born bachelors were more concentrated in blue-collar occupations than were native-born bachelors, with the Irish most heavily engaged in unskilled, as opposed to skilled and semiskilled, working-class pursuits. At the same time, in all three cities, German-born bachelors held more skilled jobs than did samples from other nativity groups. Among native-born bachelors, there were virtually no significant differences in occupational patterns between those samples born in the state in which they were residing (Massachusetts, Illinois, and California) and those who had been born in a state different from the one in which they were residing.

THE RESIDENTIAL EXPERIENCE

As table 3.1 reveals, only in San Francisco in 1880, a relatively young and highly transient port city, did the proportion of sampled bachelors who were not living as family members (that is, who were boarders, lodgers,[9] and servants) exceed half. Even the 1880 figure for San Francisco is somewhat of an anomaly because that city's boarding population was inflated by large numbers of single Chinese immigrants living as boarders and lodgers, who constituted 23 percent of the total bachelor sample for that year. After the Chinese Exclusion Acts of 1881 and 1882, the proportion of Chinese in the San Francisco bachelor population dropped precipitously as those who returned to China or left for other American destinations were not replaced by new immigrants. Equally remarkable in the table is the large proportion of unmarried adult men who, except in San Francisco, were living within a family as sons, grandsons, brothers (of the head), nephews, cousins, and ascendants (parents and uncles who were coresident with a head from the younger generation). In fact, in Boston and at times in Chicago, close to 60 percent of all bachelors lived with one or more of their kin.

Not surprisingly, the data revealed that in all three cities the residential experiences of the sampled bachelors differed ac-

TABLE 3.1
Relation to Head of Household (by percentage)

	Head	Ascendant	Son	Grandson	Brother	Nephew	Cousin	Boarder	Servant	Number
Boston 1880	2.4	0.2	50.1	0.4	4.2	1.4	0.3	32.1	1.8	993
Boston 1900	6.2	0.8	47.4	0.3	7.9	1.3	0.4	34.3	1.2	994
Boston 1920	10.5	1.7	38.7	0.2	9.4	0.8	1.4	36.3	0.7	877
Chicago 1880	3.3	1.0	42.2	—	4.2	0.7	0.1	43.8	4.0	780
Chicago 1900	5.4	1.0	46.2	0.3	7.8	0.9	0.4	37.6	0.5	1209
Chicago 1920	8.4	2.3	41.3	0.2	11.5	2.5	0.4	32.9	0.5	930
San Francisco 1880	2.8	0.4	26.5	0.1	2.6	0.4	0.1	64.3	2.8	1372
San Francisco 1900	6.6	0.8	36.4	0.2	6.7	1.3	0.8	44.6	2.7	960
San Francisco 1920	13.3	0.7	33.3	0.2	7.1	1.0	3.3	42.4	1.3	899

Source: Sample data.

cording to occupation—which is to some extent a surrogate for social class. Consistently in all three cities and in all three sample years, bachelors in higher-status, white-collar occupational groups (managers, proprietors, and clerk/salesmen) tended to live with kin (as household heads or as sons, brothers, or other relatives of the head) to a greater extent than did bachelors in lower-status, blue-collar occupations (skilled, semiskilled, and unskilled employees). Conversely, those single men who had blue-collar occupations tended to live as non-kin boarders more frequently than did those who worked at white-collar occupations. The differences, however, were not especially large. Usually about 25 to 30 percent of those bachelors who lived with family members held white-collar occupations, compared to 20 to 25 percent of those who lived as boarders or servants. About 50 to 60 percent of single men who lived with kin had blue-collar occupations, compared to 60 to 70 percent of those who did not live with kin. And, as would be expected, some 8 to 10 percent of those bachelors who lived with kin were dependents (that is, they had no listed occupation or were designated by the enumerator as living at home) while only 3 to 5 percent of single men who lived as boarders had no listed occupation. Most of the dependents who lived at home were attending school. These patterns confirm findings by other scholars that middle-class families tended to retain adult sons in their households longer than did working-class families, but, as noted above, the class differences within the samples—at least as roughly approximated by general occupational categories—were not significantly large.

A closer examination of those single males living with kin reveals two intriguing patterns. First, as shown in table 3.1, there was a consistent increase from 1880 to 1920 in all three cities in the proportion of sampled bachelors who lived as heads of their own household. The vast majority of these men had not previously been married, and thus the increase cannot be explained by a rise in the number of widowers or divorcees. Moreover, with but a few minor exceptions, the increase in

81

bachelors who headed a household occurred in all age groups. For example, in Boston, (from analysis not presented in table 3.1) the proportion of presumably confirmed bachelors (those never married and aged 50–59), who were heads of their own household rose from 11.4 percent in 1880 to 25.4 percent in 1920, but also the proportion of bachelors aged 30–39 who were heads of households rose from 3.3 percent in 1880 to 17.4 percent in 1920.

Since widowhood and divorce were negligible, it appears that shifts in attitudes and/or housing and economic opportunities were related to the rise in headship among bachelors. I tried to probe more deeply into this issue by comparing three groupings of bachelors who were heads of households: solitaries, who lived completely alone; semisolitaries, who lived with only one or two other people whether they were related or not; and those who lived with three or more people—the last group were usually proprietors of boardinghouses. In this regard, there was a difference between Boston on the one hand and Chicago and San Francisco on the other. In all three cities, there was only insignificant change over the forty-year period in the proportions of these bachelors who lived as solitaries. But in Chicago and San Francisco, there was a notable decrease in the proportions who headed a household containing many people (four or more) and a concomitant increase in the proportions of semisolitaries who headed a household containing just one or two others, usually a sibling or two. Boston's proportions in all categories remained relatively constant over time.

Just what these trends mean is difficult to discern, given the paucity of direct evidence. In all probability, housing in Chicago and San Francisco became available at a faster pace than it did in Boston because the economies of the two western cities were booming relative to that of Boston. As a consequence, increased housing availability provided those Chicago and San Francisco bachelors seeking to share a domicile with a sibling or some other person easier access to a small dwelling unit—whether it was a house or apartment—in which they could act as head. Such opportunities existed in Boston but only to a lesser extent. The data in table 3.1 also show an increase over time in the proportions of sampled unmarried men who were living in households headed by a sibling, often a brother but sometimes a sister. This pattern suggests an enhanced ability, willingness, or necessity of the family — or at least of adult siblings — to incorporate adult brothers into their midst. This trend mirrors and reinforces the increase noted above in small sibling groups in the higher (by 1920) frequency of Chicago and San Francisco bachelors who lived as heads of small (two- or three-person) households. In the context of active, dynamic cities, such as those from which these data are drawn, it is logical to assume that independent and unmarried adult siblings would create joint residential units, preserving some form of family familiarity to counter the city's anonymity and uncertainty. Moreover, a sibling who already had become established in a house or flat could have provided a haven for a brother migrating away from the family of orientation into both the physical and psychological uncertainty of adult independence. At the same time, the coresident siblings could help each other with rent, errands, and other domestic and financial needs.

Examples abound, but two from the census samples can illustrate the phenomenon. In 1880, Joseph Thayer (I substitute fictitious names for actual names), a twenty-four-year-old bachelor, lived in Boston's eleventh ward in a residence headed by his older brother Edward and also containing Edward's wife and their young son. Both Joseph and Edward Thayer had been born in New Hampshire, and both worked as salesmen in a furniture store. Quite probably Edward had moved to Boston and established his household before Joseph left New Hampshire, and then Edward helped Joseph obtain a job as well as housing once Joseph had moved to the city.[10] In Chicago in 1920, John Dembrowski, a thirty-three-year-old machinist who had been born in Poland, shared a flat with his thirty-eight-year old brother, Paul, who also had immigrated from Poland and who worked as a dipper in a candy factory.

Though John was listed in the census as household head, in this case it seems likely that both brothers immigrated at the same time and depended on each other for mutual assistance. Occasionally, there were cases of coresident siblings taking in boarders with whom they had no blood relationship, but usually the household group that contained a bachelor and one or more siblings consisted only of the siblings themselves, as in the case of the Dembrowskis, or of a bachelor sibling living with his brother's or sister's nuclear family, as in the case of the Thayers.

As would be expected, there was a relatively strong tendency for bachelors to live with heads who had the same occupational skill level — and therefore similar socioeconomic class — as their own. This trend was strongest among bachelor sons who lived in a household headed by their father, and it was especially common when the father was a salesman or agent. That is, in all three cities around half of those bachelor sons who had clerical occupations and who lived in homes headed by their father had fathers with white-collar or sales occupations similar to their own. Those bachelor boarders who resided with a family (not their own) rather than in a boardinghouse also tended to have an occupation similar to that of the head, a pattern reinforced by other historical studies. In his examination of Boston's boarders and lodgers, for example, historian Mark Peel found relatively high proportions of lodgers living with heads who had the same occupation as their own, though, unlike the case of my own samples from Boston, Chicago, and San Francisco, these proportions declined somewhat over the period between 1860 and 1900.[11]

THE BOARDING EXPERIENCE

Even though the majority of bachelors shared residential space with one or several of their kin, a substantial number of them did engage in the more impersonal experience of boarding or lodging.[12] Indeed, the experience of boarding and lodging was so common in the late nineteenth century and early twentieth that it is possible to assume that even some of those who lived with kin at the time of the three censuses from which I took samples had previously lived with non-kin as boarders or lodgers or else subsequently did so.[13] In cities across the country, well-known lodging-house districts or furnished-room districts arose, such as Boston's South End and West End, the areas contiguous to Chicago's Loop, New York's Bowery, and the region south of San Francisco's Market Street.[14] These neighborhoods usually were located on or near major transportation lines that fed the central business district, and the lodging houses themselves often were converted buildings where wealthier people had once lived because of the proximity to downtown.[15] In addition to these better areas, each city contained one or more flophouse districts of run-down, cheap rooming houses and hotels. Such residences usually were located above a saloon on a business street and housed transient and/or unemployed men whom contemporaries called tramps.[16]

The residential spaces occupied by boarders and lodgers varied greatly in size and amenities, ranging from elegant bachelor apartments for the middle and upper class to tiny cubicles for the poorest men and, in San Francisco, cells called cribs mostly inhabited by Chinese immigrant workers. The most luxurious quarters were the bachelor flats, which were multiple-room settings that combined the features of an apartment with those of a boardinghouse. Often located in what became known as apartment hotels, these types of residence first appeared in New York City in the 1870s. They spread to other cities over the next three decades and became particularly attractive to affluent bachelors. In New York, they included the aptly named Bachelor Apartments, built at 15 East 48th Street in 1900, and the Hermitage Hotel, built in 1907 on 7th Avenue near 42nd Street. The flats in these and similar buildings provided spaciousness and privacy while at the same time the management furnished amenities that a bachelor was presumably unwilling

FIGURE 3.1. Boardinghouse rooms came in various sizes and configurations. Simply and sparsely furnished, many probably resembled this one, occupied by a Lithuanian immigrant in Chicago—though probably not as ornately decorated. (Chicago Historical Society)

to maintain for himself, services such as maid and laundry facilities plus common meals in a downstairs restaurant. Some apartments even contained sufficiently spacious common rooms so that the occupants could sponsor dinners and receptions for the entertainment of their friends.[17]

Lodging facilities for the middle class were less commodious but still reasonably comfortable. In separate articles published in the early 1900s, social reformers and analysts Alfred B. Wolfe and Frederick Bushee described the floor plan and facilities of a typical four-story lodging house for white-collar and higher income blue-collar bachelors living in Boston's South End. The first floor of such a building usually contained front and rear rooms called parlors, which actually served as living quarters. With high ceilings and the best furniture in the house, these rooms commanded the highest rents, usually four or five dollars a week for a front view, though often two men shared such a room. The second floor housed the building's only bathroom, which included a sink, tub and toilet (hot water, however, was a rarity), plus four more bedrooms, each with a closet and sink. Rooms on this level rented for a dollar less than those on the first floor. The third and fourth floors contained even smaller bedrooms, and because the fourth-floor rooms usually lacked furnace heat they therefore were the least expensive, often renting for no more than $1.50 a week. The furniture in each bedroom typically included an iron bed, cheap carpet, small table, dresser (the only place to store clothes; closets were mostly nonexistent), one chair, and some inexpensive wall decorations. The basement housed the dining room and kitchen, possibly also the living quarters for the owner's family or the housekeeper. Sometimes, the dining room of a large boarding-house was operated under separate management.[18]

Those men who rented space in a household, rather than in a boardinghouse or lodging house, might have enjoyed a little more privacy but not necessarily better ambiance. Journalist Ray Stannard Baker recounted his experiences as a bachelor-lodger when in 1892, after graduating from the University of Michigan at the age of twenty-two, he journeyed to Chicago to find work. Baker discovered a house on North State Street with a sign "Room to Rent" where he leased quarters from "a heavy, dull, slatternly woman" who had "a suspicious look in her eye." For three dollars a week, Baker got "a hall bedroom, up one long flight of stairs, with a single narrow window opening on a dingy court. It was a close-pinched room hardly larger than one of the closets of my boyhood home, with a single gaslight set high above the bed, so high and so dim that when I read by it I had to stand up on my only chair. Even on that warm June morning, the atmosphere of the room seemed damp, and there was a sour, gassy odor."[19]

Quarters such as these could seem luxurious compared to those available for the poorest bachelors. Conditions were crowded, regardless of whether they were in a boardinghouse or a household. Artist and cartoonist John T. McCutcheon recalled that as a struggling young bachelor he often shared cramped living space with several others like himself on the Near North Side of Chicago. In one apartment on Chestnut Street, "there were as many as five of us living there at once. . . ."[20] Journalist Will Irwin told a similar story, reminiscing that in New York he and his bachelor roommates "lived five in a room with two double beds and a single one."[21] M. E. Ravage told of how he first lodged in the home of his Rumanian cousins, who opened their five-room flat to numerous others. "The sofa in the parlor," he reported, "alone held four sleepers of whom I was one. We were ranged broadside, with the rocking-chairs at the foot to insure the proper length. And the floor was by no means exempt. I counted no fewer than nine male inmates in that parlor alone one night."[22]

In San Francisco, an ordinance required that all lodging houses provide a minimum of five hundred cubic feet of air for each resident, but Chinatown and waterfront landlords frequently evaded the law. Journalist J. W. Buel described the most lurid of Chinese lodging houses after a police detective gave him a tour of the district in 1882. Inside the houses, he found tiny booths, where often two or three Chinese men slept on one bed. And located in the cellars underneath these floors of cubicles were the opium dens. Buel wrote,

> Along each side of this byway are shelves arranged one above the other to a height of ten feet or more. Each of these bunks — for such they are — is about four feet long, three feet wide, and two feet high. There is some straw or old blanket on the floor of every bunk, on which two Chinamen may be found at any time

after nightfall, smoking opium. . . . It is thus that in a space not more than fifty square feet hundreds of Chinamen may be found. And yet, in defiance of all statistics and Boards of Health promulgations relating to the increase of mortality in thickly-populated quarters, the Chinese persist in showing an extremely low death rate, and a phenomenally small amount of sickness.[23]

"Cubicle dormitories" and "cage hotels" characterized the cheapest lodging residences of other cities as well. In Chicago and New York City, landlords converted warehouses and industrial buildings into mass sleeping quarters of tiny cells. Illinois law ordered that there be at least two feet of horizontal space on each side of a bed in dormitory sleeping rooms, but, as in San Francisco, the law was seldom obeyed or enforced. Cubicle rooms could be as small as five feet by six, with as many as two hundred such rooms on a single floor, only four of which rooms would have access to outside light. Space in these lodging houses was, according to housing reformer Jacob Riis, "just enough to allow a man room to pull off his clothes."[24] There were only a few sinks on each floor and the only toilet facilities were in the basement or in the backyard.

The demand for housing that the large numbers of bachelors created offered opportunities to women, especially older unmarried or widowed women, to profit from renting rooms in their homes to boarders and lodgers. Alfred B. Wolfe studied 791 Boston females engaged in boarding and lodging occupations and found 88 percent of them to be forty-five and older. About two-thirds were widowed or divorced.[25] Though many women sustained themselves as boardinghouse keepers, the economic returns from such enterprises were not great. Renting one or two rooms would bring in a total of only two or three hundred dollars a year, excluding expenses, which sometimes left a net return of only 10 or 20 percent. And if a room went vacant for any extended period of time, the housekeeper might lose all profits. Even large boardinghouses offered only limited returns. Wolfe estimated that a typical seventeen-room boardinghouse, such as the one in the South End described above, could normally gross about $1,640 per year, taking into account vacancies. But annual expenses for coal heat, gas light, taxes, laundry, repairs, and furniture could average $1,482, leaving a net profit of only $158, or 9.6 percent of gross revenue.[26] As a result, landladies and landlords could increase their returns mostly by cramming more boarders into whatever spaces they could find.

In some instances, it was possible for landladies to charge high rents to those bachelors who could afford comfortable quarters. In an article entitled "Renting Rooms to Young Men," published in the *Ladies Home Journal* of 1908, one experienced landlady offered advice on how to get the most out of the available rental space. She recommended investing in good furnishings, decorating in dull-green and yellow-brown wallpaper, and hanging bold, well-drawn pictures on the walls. A two-quart china pitcher into which a man might throw his matches and other pocket items, a pitcher of water by the bed, and hooks and boxes for storage also were necessary. Finally, she urged the provision of a sitting room: "If one good-sized room can be set aside for a sitting room (at your own expense) it will be found to be a paying investment. The young fellows will congregate there, tell stories and fraternize. . . . And if they have some place to sit they can get along with very small bedrooms, and you will be able to rent little corners which otherwise would not be bringing you in any return."[27] John McCutcheon attested to such an attraction, noting that the presence of a sitting room relieved the oppressiveness resulting from five persons packed into one bedroom.[28] In addition, the *Ladies Home Journal* writer advised, "The best place to put young men is on the top floor. There they are by themselves and out of the way."[29]

Though discriminated against and exploited in various ways, bachelors may have had some advantages when it came to renting rooms. According to historian Joanne Meyerowitz, landladies in Chicago apparently preferred male lodgers to females, believing that men were less demanding, that they did not monopolize the bathroom, and that they more consistently obeyed house rules that prohibited cooking and laundering in the rooms.[30] Some evidence suggests otherwise, however. Bushee, for example, described common signs in Boston advertising rooms for rent as specifying "Ladies $3, Gents $3.50."[31]

Boardinghouses and rooming houses provided particular settings in which gay men might maximize their sexual freedom. The ability of tenants to have their own rooms enabled homosexuals to entertain guests without supervision. The fact that rent usually was collected weekly enabled gay men to evade long-term financial commitments to a landlord and to move when and if legal or moral difficulties threatened their privacy. Even more serviceable to gay men were the more anonymous apartment hotels, which offered more privacy because of their size. With no landlady or landlord overseeing who came and went (though some establishments employed doormen) and with general aloofness of neighbors from each other, these facilities enabled gay couples to live together in relative freedom and to entertain friends in a space reasonably secure from police harassment.[32]

Eating arrangements for boardinghouse residents had both conveniences and limitations. For men who lacked access to family meals and could not afford restaurants, boarding was an efficient means of dining, but it also restricted a boarder's independence. Virtually no boardinghouse keeper would allow residents to cook or eat meals in their own rooms, so the boarder had to adjust his eating habits to the demands of his landlady or landlord. At the common dining tables, the fare was far from elegant and the company not always amiable. Boarders usually purchased meal tickets that would be carefully punched by the housekeeper or some other dining-room monitor. Mealtime schedules were rigid, making it difficult for some workers, especially those who had irregular hours, to be present at every meal. Nevertheless, boarders had to pay for all meals, whether they ate them or not. These disadvantages, according to historian Perry Duis, contributed to the decline of boardinghouses in favor of simpler rooming houses at the end of the nineteenth century.[33] Cheap restaurants and cafeterias also arose to replace the dining facilities of boardinghouses (see chapter 4).

BACHELORS AND A FAMILY ENVIRONMENT

The relatively equal split between proportions of bachelors living with kin and those living as non-kin boarders and lodgers implies that there were two bachelor populations, each with its own subculture and behavior as well as its own living situation and life style. Further evidence suggests, however, that such a dichotomy does not hold true. Rather, a much more complex — and rich — pattern of lifestyles emerges from a closer examination of the sampled census data on bachelors when combined with literary and other sources.

Several trends indicate that as the nineteenth century faded into the twentieth, bachelors who boarded increasingly were integrated into some kind of family household environment. Figures compiled by the United States Commissioner of Labor in 1901 show that a substantial number of families — as opposed to boardinghouse proprietors — took in boarders and lodgers. In California, for example, nearly 20 percent of all family households contained boarders that year, and the proportions for Illinois and Massachusetts households were even higher: 23.4 percent for Illinois and 31.6 percent for Massachusetts.[34] These numbers are quite remarkable for a society that supposedly valued privacy.

Data derived from the census samples confirm the published aggregate figures. First, as table 3.2 shows, there was a consistent increase in all three cities over time in the proportions of boarding bachelors who lived as the only boarder or with just one other boarder in a household rather than in mass and presumably anonymous aggregations such as in boardinghouses

TABLE 3.2

Percentage of Bachelor Boarders Living in Households with 1 to 2,
3 to 4, and 5 or More Total Boarders

	1–2	*3–4*	*5 or More*	*Number*
Boston 1880	22.9	21.4	55.7	388
Boston 1900	37.5	19.6	42.8	341
Boston 1920	45.6	13.2	41.2	318
Chicago 1880	30.5	21.7	47.8	341
Chicago 1900	39.4	20.3	40.3	454
Chicago 1920	55.9	15.4	28.8	306
San Francisco 1880	16.8	13.8	69.3	882
San Francisco 1900	25.0	11.2	63.8	428
San Francisco 1920	29.7	10.0	60.4	381

Source: Sample data.

and apartment hotels. In 1880, 22.9 percent of Boston's boarding bachelors, 30.5 percent of Chicago's boarding bachelors, and 16.8 percent of San Francisco's boarding bachelors lived as the only boarder or with just one other boarder in a household. By 1920, these figures had risen significantly to 45.6 percent in Boston, 55.9 percent in Chicago, and 29.7 percent in San Francisco. (Again, the patterns in San Francisco are somewhat aberrant because of the large numbers of Chinese boarders in 1880 and of transient seamen and waterfront workers in the city in all three sample years.) Among newer immigrant groups, the number of boarders in a given household was often relatively high, yet such boarders still tended to live in a family household rather than in a more anonymous boardinghouse. Thus a survey of Polish and Lithuanian families conducted in Chicago in 1914 revealed that the average nuclear family contained slightly more than four boarders.[35]

With but a few exceptions, there was a slight tendency for white-collar bachelors who boarded to live with large numbers of other boarders and, conversely, for blue-collar boarder-bachelors to live as the sole boarder in a household. That is, clerks and salesmen resided more frequently in lodging houses and hotels that contained four or more boarders and lodgers, perhaps because they preferred or could better afford their own rooms and the amenities of privacy, the independence of taking meals at cafés and restaurants, and other advantages that would come with such a room. Blue-collar boarders, on the other hand, would have been less able to afford a hotel or lodging house, so they boarded with a family or in some other arrangement in which they shared living space and meals. Also, blue-collar boarders tended to reside in a household in which the head had the same occupation as the boarder or boarders did. This pattern did not reproduce the traditional master-journeyman-apprentice coresident arrangement of an earlier era; rather, it simply combined men who worked at the same location. Thus, the census samples show Alexander Johnson, a teamster for a certain Boston carting company, boarding in a household headed by Jeremiah Fosdike, who was also a teamster for that company. And William Temple, an employee of the Chicago gas works, boarded with Peter Slackmeyer, a household head who also worked for the gas company. The only exception was San Francisco in 1880, where Chinese working-class immigrants dominated the boarding population—they were mostly tobacco workers and laundry employees—and lived mostly in large cubicle-style boardinghouses.

More significant than the numbers of boarders in a household are the data in table 3.3, which reveal that there was a rise over time in all three cities in the proportions of boarding bachelors who lived in a family household, rather than in a boardinghouse or lodging house. In 1880, 58.5 percent of bachelor boarders in Boston, 60.7 percent in Chicago, and 29.7 percent in San Francisco lived with a family. The figures for Boston and Chicago were already impressively high in 1880, but they rose even higher in all three cities by 1920 when they reached 65.1 percent in Boston, 77.5 percent in San Francisco, and 46.2 percent in San Francisco. With the exception of San Francisco, then, a large majority of boarding bach-

TABLE 3.3
Types of Residence in Which Boarding Bachelors Lived
(by percentage)

	Family	Boardinghouse	Hotel or Other	Number
Boston 1880	58.5	34.8	6.7	388
Boston 1900	64.2	32.0	3.8	341
Boston 1920	65.1	29.6	5.3	318
Chicago 1880	60.7	33.4	5.9	341
Chicago 1900	65.2	24.7	10.3	454
Chicago 1920	77.5	10.8	11.7	306
San Francisco 1880	29.7	59.9	10.5	882
San Francisco 1900	41.8	43.7	14.4	428
San Francisco 1920	46.2	10.0	43.8	381

Source: Sample data.

elors lived in a family setting in all three sample years; when the Chinese in San Francisco are discounted, the numbers living with a family in that city were also remarkably high.[36]

One might speculate that the increasing tendency of boarders to live with families or in small groupings rather than in large boardinghouses reflected a desire to avoid the social isolation that reformers attributed to boardinghouses and lodging houses. In 1906, Alfred Benedict Wolfe, for example, observed, "There is no true social life within a lodging house. Without spiritual or intellectual reward that hermits are supposed to have for their isolation, many lodgers lead a hermit's existence."[37] Mark Peel, in his recent study of Boston lodging houses, reinforced and extended Wolfe's conclusion when he asserted that lodgers seemed to prefer social isolation, that they purposely selected residences that did not convey a "familial ethos."[38] The data presented above, however, suggest a

FIGURE 3.2. Bachelor roommates could develop special friendships and pursue common interests in recreational activities. Inside and outside their boarding-house rooms, the men could act with frivolity and flippancy that reinforced their image as happy-go-lucky fellows who were unrestrained by familial responsibilities. (State Historical Society of Wisconsin)

different conclusion: that the widespread and consistent trend toward family residence that occurred in Boston, Chicago, and San Francisco implies at least some preference on the part of boarding bachelors in these places for a family-type household rather than for a more impersonal sort of residence. The sense of quasi-family bonds was well expressed by Harry Webb Farmington, later a Methodist minister, who boarded with a woman and her six daughters in his early adulthood. He re-called, "Mrs. Charity Renshaw, the widow of a railroad man, was the fourth in the succession of my foster mothers. . . . From first to last, she registered the instincts and reactions of unadulterated motherliness. The girls became as sisters to me. . . ."[39]

Scattered qualitative evidence suggests that even those bachelors who rented rooms in supposedly isolated and asocial boardinghouses created relationships that approximated those they would have experienced in a family setting. In his autobiography, John T. McCutcheon reminisced about another time during his bachelor experiences in the early 1890s when he roomed with humorist George Ade in a Chicago boardinghouse. The two men, then in their twenties, spent almost every spare hour together, sharing adventures out on the streets and coming back to their boardinghouse room as little as possible. "We thought of ourselves as men about town," McCutcheon recalled, "and in fact we were. . . . We never went home as long as there was anything more interesting to see or any place more inviting to go, and in consequence we saw everything and every place in Chicago."[40] Harry Webb Farrington also forged close bonds of friendship with a fellow boarder after he had moved out of Mrs. Renshaw's house in the early 1900s. "It was during this second regime," Farrington recollected, "that a pale, slender, fiery, red-headed lad, by the name of Will Anderson, came into my life. . . . Will and I lived together, saw the girls together, cheated each other with all our might at croquet, and yet our souls were knit together as were David and Jonathan. The friendship [between us] was as strong and deep as it was with our girl friends."[41]

Chicago lawyer Victor Elting recalled that he shared a boardinghouse room with his bachelor cousin during the early 1890s, sleeping in "spoon fashion" to ward off the cold. Then, in his late twenties, Elting rented a small house on Huron Street with three other ambitious but not-yet-successful bachelors. Elting reminisced, "We kept house together for years, until I was married in 1904; and my friendship with my housemates was a very close one."[42]

Strong bonds of quasi kinship especially existed among those gay men who resided in urban boardinghouses. As a young man, Boston architect Ralph Adams Cram became closely linked with a group of homosexual musicians, writers, and artists, briefly including Oscar Wilde, who occupied rented rooms and rooming houses on and around Pinkney Street in the city's Bohemian section in the 1880s and 1890s. Here, the group could develop both quasi-sibling and fully romantic partnerships that their "differentness" precluded within family and heterosexual settings. Cram, for example, roomed with a music student named Guy Prescott, whom Cram sentimentally referred to as "my first and lasting boy friend."[43]

Whatever their sexual identification, there is strong evidence that in the late nineteenth century men, especially unmarried men, established intense and affectionate ties to male friends (see chapter 7). Often these attachments provided a vital emotional link as men traversed the path between the solace of the domestic hearth and the assurance of heading their own household and receiving homage from one's own wife and children.[44]

If boarding bachelors created surrogate family, or at least sibling, relationships among themselves, in a certain way adult unmarried sons who remained in their parents' household could be considered as quasi boarders whose experiences did not diverge all that much from those men who boarded with families to whom they were not related. Though it is impossible to know all the reasons why these sons remained at home into their late twenties and thirties rather than live independently, they nevertheless resembled boarders in that they led relatively independent lives and were of an age when many of their peers had left their family of origin and had married.

Just as the proportions of boarders living with a family not of their own lineage increased over time, so too did the proportions of bachelor sons living in their parents' household into relatively advanced ages. Table 3.4 shows that in each city the proportions of unmarried sons living at home in their teens and early twenties generally decreased between 1880 and 1920

TABLE 3.4

Age of Unmarried Sons Living in Parental Household
(by percentage)

	Under 20	20–24	25–29	30 +
Boston 1880	33.2	38.4	18.9	9.5
Boston 1900	29.7	35.3	19.5	15.5
Boston 1920	25.1	39.2	19.4	16.2
Chicago 1880	37.7	41.0	16.1	5.2
Chicago 1900	31.7	37.2	20.9	10.2
Chicago 1920	30.5	35.4	17.7	16.4
San Francisco 1880	41.5	41.2	12.1	5.2
San Francisco 1900	26.1	35.8	23.2	14.9
San Francisco 1920	27.8	35.4	14.4	22.4

Source: Sample data.

while the proportions living at home into their thirties and beyond rose remarkably. By 1920, one in six unmarried sons
aged thirty and older in Boston and Chicago remained in the
parental household; in San Francisco, the proportion was more
than one in five. The average age of bachelor sons living with a
parent or parents increased by two years between 1880 and
1920 in Boston and Chicago and by three and a half years in
San Francisco.

It is impossible to discern to any full degree whether or how
many unmarried sons who lived at home compensated their
parents or parent with rent money or other forms of assistance
or how many lived at home voluntarily or by force of circumstances. Compensation can exist in varied forms. Shared or do-
nated income is the most obvious type. Many scholars have
emphasized the importance of teenage and adult children's
earnings to the family economy in the industrial era, and several have observed that some children remained with their parents until more advanced ages even though they, the children,
were fully employed and presumably had enough income to
live on their own.[45] The census samples, showing significant

numbers of employed bachelors remaining within their families of origin, validate this point and suggest a heightened importance of unmarried adult sons as contributors to the family economy.

But assistance could have flowed in the other direction as well. Historian Peter Stearns has pointed out that by the late nineteenth century it was becoming increasingly difficult for young men, especially working-class men, to achieve economic independence. These men delayed leaving the parental home and continued to rely, at least partially, on their families for support and/or housing.[46] The data on coresidence between bachelors and other family members for the three cities analyzed earlier in this chapter support this view as well.

Literary evidence suggests that unmarried sons living in the parental household occupied a position of semidependence. That is, the experiences of these sons extended into later ages the transitional status between depending on parental support and achieving full adult independence and family headship, a condition that historian Joseph Kett described as characterizing late adolescence at the end of the nineteenth century. For example, in his autobiography *Dock Walloper*, Richard "Big Dick" Butler, who became an East Coast politician and labor leader in the 1920s, related that as a young bachelor he lived with and helped support his mother in New York City. At the same time, however, Butler spent most of his waking hours outside the parental home socializing with fellow longshoremen, and he even ate most of his meals at saloons and cafés.[47] Future New York governor and presidential candidate Al Smith also lived with his mother until he married.[48] Another example, vaudeville and stage entertainer Eddie Cantor, spent his bachelor youth alternately living in and out of his grandmother's house in New York City. He wrote in his autobiography that he tried living alone as a "tramp" and in a hotel, but lack of money brought him back to his grandmother's apartment where he could more easily pursue his career as an actor and his nightlife as a "rogue."[49]

TABLE 3.5
Percentages of Bachelor Sons Living
with One Parent

Boston 1880	31.8
Boston 1900	36.1
Boston 1920	34.2
Chicago 1880	22.2
Chicago 1900	28.4
Chicago 1920	29.2
San Francisco 1880	22.8
San Francisco 1900	35.0
San Francisco 1920	36.5

Source: Sample data.

Butler's, Smith's, and Cantor's experiences reflect another pattern suggested in the census analysis: the notable number of bachelor sons living in a household headed by a widowed, usually female, parent or, in the case of Cantor, grandparent. Table 3.5 reveals that in Boston and San Francisco, about one third of all unmarried sons who stayed at or returned to their family of orientation lived in a household headed by just one parent; in Chicago, the proportions were slightly lower, generally more than one-fourth.[50]

The often stereotyped phenomenon of a bachelor son, such as Dick Butler or Al Smith, remaining at home to live with and support his widowed Irish mother emerged quite strongly from the data. In each city in each sampled year, the proportions of unmarried sons living with a widowed Irish (that is, born in Ireland while the son was born either in Ireland or in the United States) mother were ten to fifteen percentage points higher than the general percentages presented in table 3.5. In general, the pattern revealed in table 3.5 reinforces conclusions about the mutual family support system linking generations that the study of family history has identified in other contexts.[51]

AN AMBIGUOUS DOMESTIC STATUS

The foregoing analysis strongly suggests that bachelors occupied an ambiguous zone between their family of orientation and an as-yet-constituted family of procreation. Some sons who coresided with a parent, such as Dick Butler, or the bachelors who lived in households headed by one of their siblings, maintained some attachment to their family of orientation but at the same time operated in a world of work and social connections where family ties could be relatively minimal. Others, such as John McCutcheon, George Ade, Harry Webb Farrington, Victor Elting, Ralph Adams Cram, and other residents of boardinghouses, were completely cut loose from their family of orientation but, through homosocial (all-male) friendships, reconstituted surrogate familial, or at least surrogate sibling, relationships. And, of course, some bachelors never completed the transition, remaining confirmed, or never married, for all of their lives. Just as the proportions of bachelors who were heads of households rose in all three cities, so too did the proportions in all family-status categories who were aged forty and older, most of whom had apparently avoided marriage altogether.

Gender historian E. Anthony Rotundo has noted that in the nineteenth century young men making the transition to adulthood were often searching for a sense of self, a set of values to sustain them in their passage from dependence to independence. Some men, while pursuing economic and social autonomy, still retained bonds of dependence or participated in the mutuality of a family setting. Dick Butler and Al Smith, who apparently helped to support their mothers while living in their mothers' abode, might have fit this model. Others, such as George Ade and Ralph Adams Cram, turned for emotional support to men like themselves, and they formed quasi-familial groups of peers who shared their same experiences and fears with each other. "At no other time in life," Rotundo observes, "were males so likely to seek help and reassurance from male peers as during these turbulent years of transition."[52] These peer interactions often involved intimate friendships. Close male relationships were cultivated both informally as well as institutionally in clubs, gangs, secret societies, lodges, and fraternities whose members used familiar and familial terms such as "brother" and "house." (see chapter 4)[53] By the dawn of the twentieth century, says Rotundo, the search for self expression and freedom from authority became linked to the new consumer culture, especially for middle-class men.[54] The close friendship of John McCutcheon and George Ade, who reveled in being "men about town" going to "every place in Chicago," and the homosexual intimacies of Ralph Adams Cram in Boston's Bohemia on Beacon Hill lend credence to Rotundo's contention.

In his analysis of nineteenth century American family law, legal scholar Milton Regan has identified a tension in family life between two kinds of individual identity. He describes one identity as that of *status*, in which an individual experiences rights and expectations stemming from a family role such as husband, wife, parent, and the like. On the other hand, Regan identifies the contrasting *acontextual self*, in which the individual stands apart from family relationships and pursues her or his individual needs and desires with maximum independence. The concept of family status, to Regan, implies communal obligation, responsibilities that comprise a fundamental part of a person's sense of belonging. The acontextual self, in contrast, is characterized by nascent individualism, the quest for independent self-realization in which family roles are shouldered by choice rather than obligation.[55]

Bachelors, it is apparent, represented the epitome of the acontextual self. The acontextuality of their lives helps to explain what made bachelors a feared, subcultural group. Bachelors consistently defied long-standing social conventions: by avoiding marriage, by remaining in their parental households while their peers were establishing their own families, by living alone, by residing in and frequenting disreputable places (see chapter 4), by violating taboos in their sexual relationships, and by engaging in other supposedly inappropriate behavior. And if, as Regan claims, Victorian family law was concerned with reinforcing the roles and obligations of statused family members (see chapter 5), bachelors were to be particularly feared because of their subversive individuality, a lifestyle that freed them from communal responsibility. Here, of course, lay what may be the most important origin of the boarder problem.

A closer look at the domestic life of bachelors, however, seems to reveal that many of these men led lives that included the possibilities for kin or quasi-kin relationships rather than simply sinking into lonely isolation. These possibilities, which would have tempered the acontextuality of their lives, existed to an extent unrecognized by contemporary social analysts who viewed unmarried men only in terms of their dysfunctional roles and behaviors. As historian Jules Tygiel has noted with regard to those myriad bachelors in San Francisco who boarded with families rather than in boardinghouses and lodging houses, the affiliation with a family that these men experienced limited their independence in a way so as to provide "a subtle means of social control for a potentially unruly segment of the population . . . [and] elements of familiarity in an otherwise alien environment."[56] In their ties of "familiarity in an otherwise alien environment," then, bachelors constituted a subcultural, rather than a countercultural, population.

There might have existed more intricate class, racial, and ethnic variations than the preceding analysis has been able to perceive and that might have complicated the above observations and interpretations. Nevertheless, the patterns that I have identified retain suggestive importance. The large numbers and proportions of unmarried men who resided in American cities, and especially in the three cities I examined, in the late nineteenth century and early twentieth appear to have reflected a variety of instrumental, calculative choices involving their independence and residential relationships. Bachelors sustained familial bonds or sought out environments that enabled them to nurture their individual freedom yet retain some quality of social support. They may still have been acontextual in their actions, roles, and relationships, but they used functional methods to ease the anxieties about their condition and to combat the social ostracism propounded by their critics.

Institutional Life

Between November 1912 and February 1913, a group of college students working under the auspices of the Social Service of the Home Mission Board of the Presbyterian Church fanned out across New York City to survey workingmen on how they spent their spare time. The students collected questionnaires from over one thousand subjects representing 164 different occupations. Some of the men who were interviewed worked eight hours a day while others worked more than eleven, and their salaries varied from a subsistence level of ten dollars per week to a relatively comfortable thirty-five dollars per week. The surveyed men also came from seven major nationality groups. In spite of their differences, however, virtually all of the workingmen devoted their leisure time to a wide variety of activities, ranging from attending motion pictures, art galleries, and libraries to reading magazines, playing cards, and shooting pool.

George Esdras Bevans, who compiled the surveys for his doctoral dissertation in political science at Columbia University, subtitled one of his chapters, "Ways in Which Single and Married Men Differ in Their Use of Spare Time."[1] Bevans offered no analytical insights, but the data he tabulated certainly substantiated distinctions by marital status. While the most common leisure activity among married men was time spent with family, single men tended to devote many more hours with friends and in active, commercial amusements. Thus, while married men responded that just over half of their spare time was occupied by family and just under 20 percent by the combined pursuits of social clubs, movies, theater, dance, saloons, pool halls, and friends, single men expended about 23 percent of their time to family and over 35 percent to extra-family activities. (Other pastimes included labor unions, religious organizations, educational pursuits, and newspaper- and magazine-reading.)[2]

The behavioral differences in men's leisure-time activities by marital status make intuitive sense; married men naturally would be expected to devote more time than unmarried men to family activities. But the data also open revealing insights into some of the most important constituent features of the bachelor subculture. During the late nineteenth century and into the twentieth, American urban society underwent a commercial and consumer revolution as new public amusements were created and all classes of people quested for leisure time.[3] At the same time, burgeoning numbers of unmarried men, especially in cities, created demands for entertainment and a variety of other services, demands upon which opportunistic entrepreneurs could capitalize. As a result, cities fostered a number of institutions that catered to specific, and often unique, bachelor needs. Together, the population of single men and the commercial services of the city altered urban culture. This chapter surveys those institutions and services that were especially linked to the lives of single men, leaving for the next chapter a discussion of the social interactions in which the men who patronized those institutions engaged.

THE SALOON

Called by one scholar the "poor man's club,"[4] the saloon, along with the boardinghouse, stood at the forefront of bachelor society. The nondomestic, mobile lifestyle of single men fit the amiable, service-oriented environment of public drinking establishments, and it is no surprise that those urban areas where bachelors were heavily concentrated contained high numbers of saloons. In 1889, for example, there were seventeen bars along one five-block stretch of Chicago's North Clark Street in the mostly working-class, rooming-house district between Elm Street and North Avenue. In 1890, a saloon graced nearly every corner in Denver's core district, especially in low-rent areas where unattached workingmen tended to gather and reside.[5] Other cities harbored similar concentrations.

Nor were saloons exclusively the retreat of working-class bachelors. After business hours, unmarried middle-class clerks and salesmen frequented downtown drinking establishments and bars along transportation routes between where they worked and where they lived. Charles Oliver, a bank clerk, testified that in his bachelor days "after work each day you go to the pub and 'bum' around until seven o'clock. By the time you get done then you get a couple of more on Second Street. By the time you get home it's time to go to bed."[6] There were wide variations in saloons, ranging from run-down skid row and waterfront bars, to no-frills neighborhood gathering places surrounding major commercial intersections, to elegant establishments in hotels and converted mansions catering to political and sporting clienteles, to concert saloons offering formal entertainment along with libation.

By the end of the nineteenth century, the numbers of saloons had reached an impressive magnitude, to say the least. An 1895 survey of ninety-five American cities found an average of one licensed saloon for every 317 residents (including all people, minors as well as adults). In Chicago and San Francisco, where license fees were low, the ratios were one for every 232 persons and one for every 218 respectively. The ratio in the frontier city of Denver was the same, one to 223. In working class neighborhoods of New York and Chicago, the ratios were one to 129 and one to 127 respectively. In Boston, where the license fee was relatively high, there were fewer legal saloons: one per 716 people. These proportions are deceptively conservative, however, because the number of unlicensed "blind pigs" and kitchen saloons in every city was uncountable. These illegal watering places were perhaps as numerous as, if not more numerous than, the legal establishments, especially in working-class neighborhoods.[7]

According to historian Jon Kingsdale, the typical urban saloon was located on a busy street corner, accessible to public transportation as well as to pedestrians. Inside, the bar/counter usually ran the length of the room, with occasional tables and chairs scattered about the sawdust-covered floor. A mirror was often mounted behind the bar, and sports posters and prints of seminude women covered the walls. The potables were simple and cheap. A glass of beer cost a nickel; whiskey, ten or fifteen cents, sometimes including a water or milk chaser. Business districts housing various financial and commercial services supported more well-appointed establishments. Bars in these places were made of mahogany instead of simple pine, and the artwork was more respectable. There were other varieties of drinking establishments as well, ranging from the foul, furnitureless dives and "wine dumps" of the slums to the cheerful German beer gardens and suburban roadhouses.[8] The self-proclaimed tramp and ne'er-do-well Jack Black described the cheap wine dumps of San Francisco as consisting of "long, dark, dirty rooms with rows of rickety tables and a long bar behind which were barrels of the deadly 'foot juice' or 'red ink' (cheap wine). . . . The most disreputable wine dump in the city was in Clay Street, below Kearney, and I never failed to visit it when in the neighborhood."[9]

To be sure, not every saloon patron was a bachelor; indeed, saloons functioned as strong components of *male* culture, whether the male was married or not. (Before the 1920s, few respectable women of any social class would likely be caught in such a place.) But most saloons, especially those located in or near boardinghouse and cheap-rent neighborhoods, provided services, in addition to libation, that bachelors needed and could obtain nowhere else. As quasi banks, they cashed checks, held savings on account, and extended credit. As business exchanges, they acted as mail rooms, message centers, and clearinghouses for employers and job seekers. As organizational centers, they provided meeting rooms for fraternal orders, labor unions, benevolent associations and political organizations. As operators of quasi health-centers, many a barkeeper dispensed whiskey and alcoholic concoctions as medicinal treatment for a wide variety of ailments, ranging from snake bites to impotence. Many saloons also contained rooms for temporary or more permanent lodging. They often were the only establishments that offered free public toilets, and some of them provided watering troughs for horses. As well, of course, saloons were the location for much of a city's vice, especially gambling and prostitution.[10]

Many urban saloons also offered an important supplemental service: free lunches. In fact in some cities, such as Boston, local law required licensed drinking establishments to provide food gratis. This repast, which proprietors hoped would be consumed as accompaniment to a glass of beer or whiskey, was vital sustenance to many a bachelor who otherwise had restricted means of securing meals. The food found at these saloons was not at all lacking in quality or quantity. In the opinion of reformer Raymond Calkins, who surveyed saloons in 1901 in a somewhat futile search of a means to replace them, "The best free lunches to be found anywhere in the country are in [saloons in] Chicago, St. Louis, and San Francisco."[11] According to one contemporary report, a saloon on Chicago's northwest side spent between thirty and forty dollars a day on foodstuffs, including "150–200 pounds of meat, 1 1/2–2 bu. potatoes, 50 loaves of bread, 35 pounds of beans, 45 dozens of eggs, . . . 10 dozen ears of sweet corn, $1.50–$2 worth of vegetables."[12]

Saloon food particularly fed men who lacked family and monetary resources by which to feed themselves. German immigrant Oscar Ameringer recalled that when he lived as an unemployed bachelor in Cincinnati during the late 1880s, he subsisted by sleeping in abandoned buildings and eating at the free-lunch table in saloons. "By investing five cents in a schooner of beer and holding on to the evidence of purchase," he wrote in his autobiography, "one could eat one's fill of such delicacies as rye bread, cheese, hams, sausages, pickled and

FIGURE 4.1. The saloon and its lunch table (seen on the right of this photograph) served a special function for all men, but particularly for bachelors. The bartender acted as host to a gathering of informal sociability, and the food — mostly salty varieties of crackers, sausages, and eggs — provided purposeful accompaniment to the beer consumed by most patrons. (Culver Pictures, Inc.)

smoked herring, sardines, onions, radishes, and pumpernickel."
Ameringer also revealed a common ploy to obtain food even
when he was flat broke. "It is true I did not always have the
required nickel," he wrote. "But by patronizing only the large
saloons through the rush hours one could always commandeer
a partially filled glass some absent-minded cash customer had
left unguarded, and by doing so escape the suspicion of being a
deadbeat."[13] Even the lowest ranking saloons served free food.
In addition to what the winos called foot juice or red ink, the
libation that was served by San Francisco's "wine dumps,"
there also was, as one patron recollected, "a small lunch counter in the back where the winos could buy for a nickel a big
plate of something that looked like stew, and a hunk of stale
bread. . . ."[14]

While they drank and ate, saloon patrons could often view
or partake in a variety of amusements, some of which evinced
the pretense of high culture. In Denver, Cheney's saloon exhibited original paintings on its walls, well before the city had an
art museum. A few places offered dramatic and musical presentations. Henry Hill's saloon, called by some moralists the
"most dangerous and demoralizing place in New York," offered, according to one historian, "(p)ainted chorus girls in
tights, minstrel shows, sparring matches, female boxers, suggestive dancing, and the finest liquors. . . ."[15] Probably the
most common active entertainment among imbibers was card
playing, especially in working-class bars. Varieties of whist,
rummy, and, of course, poker were the most common games.
Sometimes also a billiard or pool table attracted interest,
though, in an attempt to stifle gambling, ordinances in some
cities prohibited such tables.

In addition to its function as a center for entertainment and
games, the saloon was an important disseminator of current
events and, especially, sporting news. Many establishments
provided ticker-tape machines, telegraph lines, or other means
of reporting up-to-date scores. Books and music, however,
were not often found in big-city saloons. Even though the establishments furnished local newspapers and male-oriented

journals, such as *The National Police Gazette* (see chapter 6), reading was too individual, too antisocial an activity to occupy saloon patrons' time. With the exception of places like Henry Hill's, most proprietors could not afford live music, and patrons did not demand it. Occasionally an establishment would provide a gramophone or other mechanical music device, but such entertainment was the exception. Whatever music existed more commonly resulted from the spontaneous—and often discordant—singing done by patrons themselves.[16]

Most of all, the saloon provided an all-male environment of amiable sociability. Here, aided by the inhibition-releasing effect of beer and liquor, men could escape from the pressures of both their work and domestic lives, find camaraderie with others who shared the same situation, call each other by nicknames, and reinforce class, ethnic, and, perhaps most importantly, gender identities. Drinking was sustained not only by food but also by the custom of treating. According to this practice, each man—at least each man who hoped to be accepted by the group—was expected to buy a round of drinks for his fellows and in turn expected to be treated to drinks by the others. Occasionally, when the process lagged, the saloon keeper himself would contribute a round on the house.[17] This ritual provided continuity and momentum to saloon culture.

The conversation that surrounded the drinking rituals was steeped in coarse language and profanity, which served, in Leon Ellis's terms, as the "motif of man-to-man friendship."[18] Joking, hassling, complaining, posturing, and out-and-out ribaldry permeated most discussions. But, as Ellis points out, such vernacular, though strongly personal and sexist, was not pernicious or misogynous. The teasing and braggadocio seem to have been part of a "vital folk culture that poked fun at the relationships of the sexes."[19] Likewise, the nude and seductive images of women on the saloon walls and the bawdy songs sung by patrons represented a claim to "male space and male freedom" rather than unqualified salaciousness or strict anti-female hostility. All of these features served to put women at a distance and to give the saloon an extramarital quality, reinforcing its alternative, but not necessarily oppositional, status with regard to family and home. Likewise, saloons were homosocial (all male) but not homosexual. Men, often under the influence of drink, hugged and kissed each other, sang sentimental songs, and cried. Most likely, liquor broke down inhibitions and helped to create a fellowship that freed men to express a kind of uninhibited sentimentality that differed from homosexual love.[20]

Some saloons nevertheless acted as important centers of rendezvous and interaction for those men who desired homosexual encounters. As historian George Chanucey has shown, men known as fairies (men who acted as and sometimes dressed as women) who offered themselves as sexual partners for the "rough trade," as well as "normal" (straight or usually heterosexual) men who sought casual, episodic sex with other men often could be found in saloons. Indeed, certain saloons acquired reputations as centers for homosexual activity, and some establishments rented their back or upstairs rooms, which also could be used by female prostitutes, to fairies and their partners. For example, in 1901, investigators of the Sharon Hotel bar on New York's Third Avenue near Fourteenth Street found men having sex together in a back room. A report on Billy's Place nearby in the same year noted that the establishment's patrons included seventy-five "fairies . . . dressed as women [with] low-neck dresses, short skirts, [and] blond wigs."[21]

As Chauncey has pointed out, however, for gay men (most of whom were unmarried) saloons functioned as more than just places of sexual assignation. Just as they did for straight men, saloons provided gay men with sites for social contact where individuals of like identity could meet and socialize. The saloons acted as community centers, where gay men could organize and hold club meetings, sponsor dances and parties, share information about police activity and upcoming events, and find solace in each other. In a society that ostracized them, homosexual men used the saloon to build their own private community. In New York, for example, a club of gay men called the Cercle Hermaphrodite rented a room above the Paresis Hall bar. Here members could safely meet and pursue the other half of their double lives, changing into women's clothing and engaging in entertainment that they otherwise had to hide from the outside world. As gathering places for gay men, saloons also provided targets for police raids and the tirades of moral reformers, but, especially for those gay men of limited means, the saloons served as a private place for socializing that in their public lives was unavailable.[22]

Whatever their sexual identity, men of all sorts used saloons as a functional institution of their culture, and bachelors particularly found saloons to be useful social centers. The Rumanian immigrant physician M. E. Ravage, who frequented numerous barrooms during his bachelor days, expressed vividly and appreciatively the appeal these watering places had.

> A barroom — even an East Side barroom — is not, as some good people suppose, a mere hang-out for the indolent and the degenerate. It is, whether you like it or not, one of the central meeting places of humanity. It is an institution where all the classes congregate in all their modes — the bestial and the generous, the morose and the convivial. Thither . . . the merchant will resort with his customer when both are jovial over a particularly satisfactory bargain. A bum will shuffle in to dry his rags by the stove or to snatch a morsel from the free-lunch counter. . . . And if your mind is built to receive impressions, and if your heart is attuned to beat in harmony with other human hearts, your apprenticeship in a saloon will serve for as good a start toward a well-rounded education as you could desire.[23]

POOL HALLS, BARBER SHOPS, AND OTHER BACHELOR "HANG-OUTS"

Within both male culture and bachelor subculture, the billiard parlor played a role similar to that of the saloon. Indeed, in many instances their functions were almost identical. Reformer

Raymond Calkins concluded in his 1901 report that "[a] discussion of the value of billiard and pool rooms as social centers is simplified somewhat by the discovery that the opportunity to indulge in this pastime is generally inseparable from the sale of intoxicating liquors."[24] Calkins found that of Denver's seventy-six billiard rooms, sixty were licensed as adjuncts of saloons or clubs (though, as noted above, still separate from saloons), and only a few of the 140 billiard halls in Chicago did not sell liquor and drinks. In most cities, even pool halls[25] that were not adjuncts of a saloon (in Philadelphia and Boston, saloon keepers were prohibited by law from operating billiard and pool facilities) were located near a saloon so that, according to Calkins, the billiard room proprietor could attract saloon patrons after or between drinks and vice versa.[26] The setting of most billiard parlors prompted Calkins to conclude, "It is doubtful if the 'atmosphere' of the ordinary billiard room is appreciably different from that of the saloon, or if it really encourages patrons to any higher standard of conduct."[27]

The activities of billiards and pool playing, however, functioned somewhat differently from the social drinking of the saloon. As a physical activity and a competitive game, billiards not only required skill but also encouraged gambling and partisan support from onlookers. It provided a specific, rather than general, topic for conversation, and, because of the wagering by both players and spectators, it furnished some men with a means of earning income—and others of losing it. But like the saloon, the billiard hall acted as a center of male amusement and escape, even without the gambling. As social reformer Alfred B. Wolfe observed in the early twentieth century, pool halls "undoubtedly afford welcome relief to many a male lodger from the weary evening hours in which he does not know what to do with himself."[28]

The game also furnished a daytime diversion. Billiard champion Willie Hoppe recalled in his autobiography the case of a young bank clerk who used to disappear from his office for two hours in the middle of every day. When asked where he went, the man replied,

> Well, it's this way. I come down here [the bank] every morning at 8:30 and work over the books for three hours and a half. When noon comes my head is all cluttered up with figures. Sixes and sevens and naughts are all whirling around before my eyes, and I'm pretty well fogged out wrestling with them. I go over to the hotel billiard room and get a sandwich and a glass of milk and for two hours I play billiards. I don't bet on the games. I only play for the fun of the thing and get all those figures out of my head. When I get back to the bank in the afternoon, I feel able to tackle the books again.[29]

According to Leonard Ellis, the pool and billiard halls of major cities divided into two types: downtown establishments, whose function was primarily high-stakes gambling; and neighborhood rooms, where casual gambling took place but entertainment and sociability were more important.[30] Those facilities that were located in the central business district rented play at their pool and billiard tables on an hourly basis, usually for fifty cents an hour. Housed in buildings situated above street level, these establishments were fairly clean and ornate. They catered to businessmen and hustlers, and they attracted most of their business around lunchtime. Several such places acquired notable reputations. According to sports historian Steven Riess, in the early twentieth century Detroit's Recreation Room was the largest billiard parlor in the country, with 142 tables, but Graney's in San Francisco was probably the most famous, for both its decor and for the high caliber of its competition. Places such as these and the matches they sponsored attracted true aficionados, hustlers, politicians, and remnants of the male sporting crowd that had arisen before the Civil War (see chapter 1). Major tournaments and matches, sometimes involving wagers of five hundred dollars or more, took place at these establishments.[31]

Pool halls in slum neighborhoods provoked some of the

FIGURE 4.2. Pool halls assumed various sizes and styles, but all were also vital institutions of bachelor subculture. This fairly large and elegant pool hall was located in a respectable commercial area of New York City and offered over a dozen tables, renting them by the hour. (Museum of the City of New York)

loudest public protest. Located in dingy basements and primitively furnished, they attracted transient and local working-class bachelors (and a few married men) who engaged in a cruder and lower-stakes variety of game than the one that occurred in the fancier downtown establishments. In neighborhood halls, drinking accompanied sociable gambling on matches, and activities sometimes included poker and dice games as well as pool and billiards.[32] Critics objected not so much to the competition of pool itself but rather to the wagering that it inspired and to other allegedly related immorality, such as drinking and prostitution, that seemed to surround it. Attention of moralists focused especially on the negative effects pool and billiards had on young men. Municipalities passed ordinances to prevent pool halls from opening near schools and churches, levied high license fees on pool halls, and limited the number of tables any one establishment could possess.

Secluded, open at all hours, inexpensive, and vaguely dangerous, the pool hall had a lurid attractiveness to young unmarried men, and pool was sometimes popularly referred to as the young man's game.[33] But older men frequented the halls as well, and there was no real age segregation involved in the patrons' activities. In fact, as Ellis notes, the pool hall often became the setting for a common ritual in which young men were introduced to and accepted into adult male society. For working-class bachelors especially, social acceptance into the saloon and the pool hall society constituted a rite of passage from street-corner gang to a new kind of camaraderie of competitors.[34]

The one quality that pool halls and billiard parlors did not include, regardless of where they were located, was the presence and influence of women. Like the saloon, the pool hall served as an all-male retreat. Legendary pool champion "Wimpy" Lassiter nostalgically looked back to his youth in the early twentieth century and recollected, "A long time ago I used to stand there and peek over the lattice work into that cool-looking darkness of the City Billiards in Elizabeth, North Carolina. . . . And it seemed as though the place had a special sort of *smell* to it that you could breathe. Like old green felt tables and brass spittoons and those dark polished woods. Then a bluish haze of smoke and sweet pool chalk, and, strongest of all, a kind of *manliness*."[35] Vaudevillian Eddie Cantor recalled being awestruck when he first encountered the corner poolroom of his youth. There, he watched "fellows who could put English on the ball, reverse, draw, shoot at any angle, and make the little ivory sphere behave like [it was] charged with life."[36]

In addition to the games themselves, the absence of salutary female influence in pool halls resulted in the same kinds of all-male features as the saloons: drinking, semipornographic decorations, and profanity-filled conversation. According to one observer of Chicago pool halls, "Women not being present and there being no restraint of any kind, often the lowest and foulest expressions are heard. Obscene stories are related by small groups who do not engage in the game, but congregate in the corners and smoke cigarettes."[37] To this and other observers, an environment without women lured men down the path of dissipation.

The gambling that occurred in pool halls and billiard parlors illustrated both the subcultural and countercultural aspects of the institution. In the minds of moralists, persons who gambled were at war with society and with the family. Thus reformers targeted pool-hall patrons as candidates for rehabilitation, dissolute people who posed a danger to themselves and to others. To be sure, many a bachelor and married pool player lost money that could have been, and needed to be, put to better use. But in a world in which competitive economic activity and the pressures of their jobs distanced workers from control over their occupational lives, wagering at the pool hall gave men opportunity for what Ellis calls "self-directed and consequential activity for agency, mirroring that which the economic world offered in theory to all but so often in reality denied them."[38] The high-stakes games that characterized competition among the sporting class were the exceptions; more common was the competitive camaraderie of the neighborhood pool hall where a contest involved playing for the price of the game itself or at most for a round of drinks. In these instances, the game provided the means for rewarding individual accomplishment. And in this regard, pool halls and pool-hall gambling were not necessarily adversarial to the outside world; instead of being strictly countercultural, they mainly provided subcultural alternatives to a man's work and family life in which monetary and psychological rewards reinforced the system of male sociability.[39]

As keystones of a homosocial culture, of what journalist Ned Polsky called "the greatest and most determinedly all-male institution in American social life," pool halls represented an ideological expression of permanent bachelorhood, regardless of whether the patrons were single or married.[40] Whether the pool halls were alternative or oppositional cultural institutions depends on who was experiencing them and who was observing them. Some contemporaries would have preferred that men choose other pastimes, but some of these critics believed pool rooms to be acceptable diversions for bachelors who lived alone and had few social activities. Thus the City Club of Chicago reported in 1913, "Dingy, unattractive [boardinghouse] rooms, often cold and unsanitary, do not tempt young men to stay at home evenings. Cheer and good fellowship may be found in the pool room, dance hall, and saloon."[41] Others, however, such as a member of the Georgia Anti-Poolroom League, charged that the pool hall "divert[ed] man power" and encouraged "idleness . . . dissipation . . . intoxicants . . . profanity . . . lascivious stories . . . [and] the love of chance. . . ."[42] Perhaps most indicative was the statement offered by Hickey Hickman in Eugene O'Neill's play "The Iceman Cometh": "Well, anyway, as I said, home was like jail, and so was school, and so was the damned town. . . . The only place I liked was the pool rooms, where I could smoke Sweet Caporals, and mop up a couple of beers, thinking I was one hell-on-wheels sport."[43]

If urban entrepreneurs, such as saloon keepers and pool-hall proprietors, found that they could capitalize on the social and personal needs of the bachelor population, the barbershop surely represents one of the clearest types of such capitalization. Perhaps even more than the saloon and pool hall, the barbershop was an exclusively male retreat. Until well into the twentieth century, barbers provided haircuts and, especially, shaves to all classes of men. Women, of course, did not need to shave their faces, and they were culturally conditioned to avoid — and were not welcome to partake of — the haircutting and other tonsorial services available at barbershops. Women developed and frequented their own hairdressing and beauty shop establishments, making these places central to their own homosocial subculture. Moreover, husbands, who inhabited the domestic environment of their own household, needed barbershops less than did men who lived in rented rooms where they usually lacked a basin and hot water necessary for shaving. Thus barbershops were more vital to unmarried men than they were to married men.

A history of hair styles is beyond the scope of this study, but suffice it to say here that even though beards, mustaches, and other types of facial hair of various sorts moved in and out of favor in the late nineteenth century and early twentieth, most men of that era shaved at least part, if not all, of their faces. Shaving requires particular equipage, namely a sharp razor or knife, water that usually is steamy hot, and a mirror. The razor and mirror could be purchased by anyone wishing to perform self-barbering, but hot water was not readily available because very few domiciles of any social rank had the technology for providing hot water out of a faucet. Gas- or oil-fired hot water heaters still loomed in the future; hot water had to be obtained by taking time to heat it on a stove or in a fireplace. A man living in his own or his parents' home could have access to water heated in this way and thereby shave himself; a man living in a boardinghouse had a harder time getting such access. Instead, he went to a professional who shaved him for a price. (Men who lived in their own home used barbers for shaving as well, but they usually did so more for convenience than out of necessity.) An experienced professional barber could shave a man in just over one minute and thereby service numerous customers very expeditiously. Because a close shave, applied by a skilled barber, could last for a week, even working-class men could afford the ten cents or so that the service

FIGURE 4.3. One of the most masculine of all establishments, the barbershop was a fixture of city neighborhoods, providing needed services to unmarried men. The cabinet of shaving mugs and the supine position of the customers testify to the importance of shaving, even more than haircutting, as a barber's major function. (Joseph J. Pennell Collection, Kansas Collection, University of Kansas Libraries)

cost. Similarly, a male living in a domestic setting could engage a wife, sister, or mother to trim his hair every month or two; such accessible and dependable service did not exist for the unmarried boarder and lodger.

Understandably, then, as a city's population of unmarried men increased, so too did the number of barbering establishments. In just six years, between 1905 and 1911, the number of barbershops in Boston increased 14 percent, from 925 to

1,051. Chicago harbored just 308 barbering establishments in 1880, but the number grew to 1,885 in 1896 and 2,993 in 1917. The number of barbershops in San Francisco doubled from 272 in 1885 to 540 in 1900 and increased by half again to 734 in 1915.[44] In Chicago's rooming-house district in the early twentieth century, nearly every block housed at least one barbershop; some had two or three.[45] And as one would expect, each ethnic and racial group had its own barbering establishments, usually in a location known for the commercial and social institutions patronized by that particular group. For example, barbershops were important gathering places for African Americans who lived in Chicago's South Side and West Side, and some black barbers achieved status as community leaders.[46] In San Francisco's Chinatown, Chinese barbers offered both social and tonsorial services to that city's large community of Chinese immigrant men.[47]

Barbershops also provided services other than shaving and haircutting. From ancient and medieval times, barbers had applied medical treatments to customers, acting as heelers and physical therapists, and in some cases even performing minor surgical procedures. The memoir of one barber who practiced his craft in Portland, Maine, in the late nineteenth century and early twentieth listed folk formulas for various tonsorial remedies that he regularly used, including hair oil, aqua vita, cough drops (made from powdered sugar, paregoric, water, checkerberry, and sugar), a cure for ringworms (acetic acid plus tincture of iron), and hair dye.[48] According to one historian, by the early twentieth century many barbershops were deriving up to 50 percent of their revenues from massages and other facial treatments as well as from manicuring services.[49] Equally if not more important, the barbershop, like the saloon and pool hall, offered an environment of affable male sociability, a gathering place where a man could find friends and talk about common male interests. The availability of newspapers and male-oriented publications such as *The National Police Gazette* reinforced the sense of a masculine outpost (see chapter 6). The *Police Gazette* in fact catered to barbershops and their clientele, who were the main subscribers, publishing in every issue a feature article on the tonsorialist of the week. The publication also included a column titled "Tonsorial Notes," which printed recipes for hair care products such as camphorated oil tonic and rosemary hair tonic designed to prevent "falling hair."[50] Before queues were abolished in 1902, San Francisco's Chinese barbers braided queues for their customers, again providing a service that otherwise would have been available only if the man had a home and family of his own and could have his wife or children perform the task for him.[51]

A few other establishments besides saloons, pool halls, and barbershops functioned as recreational hangout sites for unmarried men. The candy store provided adolescent males with an initiation to the sociability of bachelor subculture. This type of commercial establishment dotted the inner city and attracted youths of both sexes, offering a variety of sweets, cigars, and cigarettes, and often a soda fountain. One survey of the Tenth Ward on New York City's Lower East Side counted some fifty candy stores. Expanding beyond retail trade, such shops sometimes contained a partitioned back room where clubs held meetings and social functions.[52]

Paralleling the candy store was the cigar store, a hangout for somewhat older males. One journal claimed that in 1906 there were 20,000 places in Chicago that sold cigars, though some of these establishments were not known as cigar stores per se. Many shops sold both candy and smoking materials, but pure cigar stores included tables and chairs where customers could converse and play checkers, dominoes, or cards as well as indulge in a nickel smoke and peruse erotic pictures that occasionally were sold under the counter. Some cigar stores, like pool halls, even sponsored competitions, such as championship matches in checkers and other board and card games. Though eliciting fewer complaints than other hangouts, the cigar store nonetheless played a role in the social subculture of urban bachelors.[53]

When they were not condemning saloons and pool halls, social reformers fired critical blasts at candy and cigar stores. In spite of their innocent appearance, candy stores evoked sharp warnings that boys and young men spent too much time there and that such shops encouraged dangerous pursuits such as gambling and smoking. The implication, often made explicit, was that boys who hung out at candy stores became schooled in aimless loafing and that when these youths became adults, they would have already received indoctrination into bachelor habits that would lead them into the pool hall and the saloon.[54] Such freedom from domestic restraint, which reformers interpreted as wanderlust and irresponsibility, thus derived from the simple patronage of commercial establishments that had originated to serve growing numbers of unattached men in the city.

RESTAURANTS AND CAFÉS

Unmarried men who were without family—and even some who lived with kin—could not dine continuously at the saloon's lunch table, nor was it convenient or pleasant to take every meal at a boardinghouse (see chapter 3). More frequently, these bachelors patronized one of the burgeoning number of commercial eating establishments that every city offered. Indeed, many such places specialized in catering to the gustatory needs of unattached men and even, as noted in the case of men like Dick Butler mentioned in chapter 3, those bachelors who lived with a parent. Especially in a city's rooming-house district, a wide selection of cheap restaurants, cafés, bakeries, and delicatessens sold and served bachelors cooked and precooked meals. In 1912, for example, a survey of Chicago's North Side rooming-house district found ninety-three restaurants and sixty-two bakeries in an area just two miles long and one-half mile wide.[55] These places can be credited with creating the kind of fare that would appeal to single men, such specialties as the blue-plate special and the three-for-two. The former is of unknown origin but consisted of an inexpensive meal, usually cooked in bulk, and served on cheap (i.e., blue rather than white) dinnerware. The latter arrangement apparently originated in San Francisco and consisted of three dishes — usually soup, meat, and dessert — for two bits (a quarter). In the more deluxe three-for-two establishments, a glass of wine could be substituted for dessert or ordered for an extra ten cents.[56]

The eating houses that attracted single men varied widely according to the customers' economic resources. At the top of the line were downtown restaurants such as San Francisco's Bismark Café in the Pacific Building at the corner of Market and Fourth streets. Offering a twenty-two-page menu, it especially boasted of its private section reserved "For the Gentlemen." Here, heralded the restaurant's management, "Our Beefsteak Rooms afford an opportunity for novel entertainment, which must appeal to the gentlemen who contemplate bachelor dinners or like functions. Here you may entertain your friends under the rafters and feel assured that the surroundings will aid materially in the success of your entertainment."[57] Another such eatery was Normann's Café, located under San Francisco's Baldwin Hotel at Market and Powell streets. Normann's featured male-oriented decor, including a fifty-foot bar of polished oak, a backroom adorned with insignias of Bacchus, an oak and marble cigar stand, and "a patent appliance by which two hundred and forty oyster stews can be made in one hour, thereby causing no delay no matter how great the rush may be."[58]

Most restaurants that attracted single male customers were not so elaborate, but they did seem to provide quantity and quality victuals for economically-pressed middle-class and working-class bachelors. Author Albert Payson Terhune described such establishments that he frequented when he lived the bachelor life in New York City.

On fifteen or twenty dollars a week, one does not live in guilty
splendor. But in the mid-1890s, a lot of us had plenty of fun on
such wages. There were restaurants—Marias's, The Black Cat,
Duquesne's, Morelli's, and a hundred others—where one could
get a really well-cooked *table d'hote* dinner and gulp a pint of
vin ordinaire, red or white, for anywhere from thirty cents to
fifty cents. . . . [F]ifty cents at Jack's would buy a porterhouse
steak weighing a pound, and with it all the rolls and butter one
could eat, as well as a high-piled side dish of French or German
fried potatoes and a saucer of piccalilli. All this for a half dollar;
and at a ten cent tip. . . .[59]

The fare at Jack's might still have exceeded the budget of a
man earning only fifteen dollars a week, but for those clerks
and salesmen making twenty or more per week, such an establishment would have proven quite satisfactory, even if only on
an occasional basis.

A few of these establishments provided opportunities for satisfying more than one's appetite. Journalist H. L. Mencken described a place called Tommy McPherson's Eating House in
Baltimore which, during Mencken's bachelor years in the early
1900s, boasted a certain notoriety. Mencken recalled in his autobiography, "Tommy's place was arranged in two layers, with
tables for men only alongside the bar downstairs, and a series
of small rooms upstairs to which ladies [prostitutes] might be
invited. The cops, goaded by vice crusaders, had forced [Tommy]
to take the doors off these rooms, but he had substituted heavy
portieres, and his colored waiters were instructed to make a
noise as they shuffled down the hall, and to enter every room
backward."[60]

Men subsisting on smaller incomes could eat at any number
of cheap restaurants, or hash houses, though the fare at such
places was not as palatable or varied as at a restaurant such as
Jack's or Tommy's. According to one investigator, the only
worthwhile cheap restaurant in San Francisco was the New
Economy, "which probably deserves the distinction of offering

FIGURE 4.4. As important as the saloon, the café provided unmarried men with the sustenance they needed when living away from their families. In this scene, a mother and son preside over a workingman's café—perhaps in the basement of a boardinghouse—where simple, inexpensive, and regularly scheduled meals were served. (Chicago Historical Society)

more good food for the money than any other restaurant in San Francisco, if not in America." For just five cents, a diner at the New Economy could be served a main dish of either a small steak or hamburger, pork and beans, corned beef hash, or ham plus a beverage of coffee, tea, or milk.[61] In his less heady bachelor days, journalist Ray Stannard Baker sometimes was forced to pawn his silver watch, the proceeds of which would enable him to eat at Burky and Milan's, which Baker believed to be the most famous of Chicago's hash houses. There he could be served "a heaping plate of potato salad, a roll, and a cup of coffee, all for ten cents. It was momentarily filling—and that is about all that could be said for it. I even tried eating it twice a day, until the odor, to say nothing of the taste, of the purported 'olive' oil in the salad became nauseatingly unbearable."[62]

At the bottom of the order were the penny lunchrooms and dives that served the cheapest food to the lowest working-class laborers, transients, and homeless men. In Chicago, the Hobohemia restaurants on West Madison Street displayed food in their windows and did their cooking in the sight of the street to attract customers for their low-priced meals. Advertising "Home Cooking" and "Home-Made Bread and Coffee," they often served seemingly tantalizing dishes that were usually made with low-quality, spoiled, or doctored ingredients. The menu of a typical cheap restaurant, Gus's Place on South Halsted in Chicago, included pig snouts and cabbage, liver and onions, and sausage and mashed potatoes, all for fifteen cents each.[63] Another Chicago establishment was Mother and Father Greenstein's on South State Street, known as Mother's. According to one investigator, Mother's was one of the few places in Hobohemia that could legitimately write "Home Cooking" on its window, and it had a high reputation even among reformers. Chicago also had penny lunchrooms operated by charitable societies. One such dining hall, sponsored by the St. Luke's Society, provided wholesome meals for a penny to a nickel apiece, and had the expressed goal of "reclaiming men and women addicted to liquor, or drug habit."[64]

In spite of their importance to the bachelor subculture, however, restaurants, lunchrooms, and cafés could not compete with saloons and pool halls as places of entertainment for urban bachelors. Because they needed to turn over customers quickly in order to make a profit, the eating establishments did not furnish facilities that could sustain the same sociability as the saloon or pool hall. There were a few exceptions, however. The most expensive restaurants such as the Bismark or Normann's, with their separate men's sections and well-appointed furnishings, acted as private club rooms for bachelors of means. Also, ethnic restaurants, such as Italian lunchrooms and German bakeries often included large back rooms with numerous chairs and nonalcoholic drinks (they usually lacked liquor licenses) in addition to food. These places served as social centers and, at times, alternatives to the saloon.[65] The Rumanian immigrant M. E. Ravage worked as a peddler during his bachelor youth in New York City and fondly recalled his daily visits to the same ethnic restaurant. "It was a great comfort," he wrote in his autobiography, "after a day spent out in the cold, to go into a cozy room, and have a warm meal, and hear my native Rumanian spoken. Now and then a musician would wander in and gladden our hearts with a touching melody of home, and we would all join in until the tears drowned our voices."[66] As well, certain restaurants took on special significance for homosexual bachelors. A few restaurants in New York, for example, catered to a gay clientele, while others allowed gay men to take over and make the establishment a center where their society could meet and eat in privacy and safety. According to George Chauncey, these restaurants often provided a setting of acceptance for men just developing their gay identity, as well as serving men with more deeply ingrained homosexual identities as centers of information on police activity, social affairs, and cultural events.[67] For all unmarried men, male-oriented restaurants and cafés functioned as a part of the bachelor subculture that existed as an alternative to the domestic life absent from their daily routine.

THEATERS, DANCE HALLS, AND OTHER COMMERCIAL AMUSEMENTS

American cities at the turn of the century offered a wide variety of commercial amusements that attracted and developed to serve single men of all social classes. Some, such as the candy store, the penny arcade, and the dance hall, were patronized mostly by adolescents and young adults. Others, such as the concert saloon, the dime museum, vaudeville, and the ballpark, appealed to men of all ages. Women and married men also could be found at most of these entertainment centers, but commercial recreation played a special role in the lives of bachelors, helping to create as well as to reinforce both the alternative and, on occasion, the countercultural aspects of their lives.

A number of commercial spectator amusements entertained single men. Penny arcades, dime museums, and nickelodeons were especially popular among working-class males. The penny arcade was probably the cheapest of the cheap amusements, providing viewing machines which, for a penny dropped into the slot, presented a variety of scenic pictures and musical selections. Sometimes an arcade also included a shooting gallery, a knife stand, or other attraction, which, for a few cents, enabled customers to throw at a target and win prizes. An arcade also might include a photograph exhibit, which displayed images of scenery and animals. Ostensibly innocent, penny arcades nevertheless roused criticism from reformers. Most objectionable to opponents of these establishments was the almost universal special section, which advertised itself as designated for men only and which featured more salacious offerings than those available in ordinary peephole machines. A popular illustrated rendering in a New York City arcade, for example, was titled "How Girls Undress."[68] According to a contemporary commentator, the sexually-oriented picture machines accounted for from 30 to 60 percent of all those included in a particular arcade.[69]

Dime museums, made popular before the Civil War by entrepreneurs such as P. T. Barnum and other impresarios, provided what one observer described as "a kind of middle ground between the circus and the playhouse. It is here that the three-legged boy or double-headed woman, the orang-outang, [sic] and sea serpent can be seen. It is here that Madame Bosa swallows live snakes . . . that the Indian rubber-man turns himself inside out."[70] Sites such as Austin and Stone's Museum and the

Grand Dime Museum, both in Boston, offered these kinds of bizarre attractions plus lurid tragedy and coarse comedy for evening audiences comprised chiefly of males.[71] Dramatic presentations usually consisted of standards such as "Dr. Jeckyl and Mr. Hyde" (though embellished with gags and asides) or scenes to satisfy specifically male tastes such as "the vagaries of a drunken man, the follies of an Irish servant girl, the exploits of a policeman, and other scenes from street and tenement life."[72]

Concert saloons and cheap theaters also drew a clientele of older boys and young men.[73] These entertainments originated in the United States in the 1850s and evolved out of antecedents in England and on the European continent. A concert saloon usually contained a bar in the front and performing space amid chairs and tables in the back, situated in such a way that facilitated interaction between performers and the audience. Theaters sometimes advertised themselves as being for men only, and their acts boasted of "classy girls," "bathing beauties," or "fancy dancing." Cheap theaters, sometimes called music halls, provided female entertainers who, after performing on stage, circulated among the audience and solicited drinks and sex. So-called waiter girls provided the same services. Labeled by reformers as the lowest type of entertainment and satisfying the most depraved taste, these amusements thrived not only on the growing population of unmarried men but also on the toleration for commercial sex that had already begun in cities before the Civil War.[74]

The program of acts from a well-known Chicago saloon-theater from August 14, 1899, illustrates the kinds of entertainment fare that made these establishments popular among single men. Most of the acts emphasized physical feats and conflict, including many that involved female performers (who probably used the theme as a pretense for displaying a scantily-clad body, though this theme of fighting and physical exploits by women was a common one in the popular culture of late-nineteenth and early-twentieth-century bachelor society. See chapter 6.). For example, one Bessie Raymond performed a routine titled, "She is Handy With Her Mitts," and Miss Topsy Turvy offered "In Training for a Rough House." The show also included in its finale an act titled "A Grand Wrestling Match," in which George Wilson "Will Meet a Different Man Each Evening." An act earlier in the show, also featuring Wilson, was advertised as "The Modern Atlas in Feats of Heavy Lifting." In between were performances by Mr. Fred Hawley on "Jeffries' Next Opponent" (probably a dramatic reading alluding to the heavyweight boxer James Jeffries, later to be known as "The Great White Hope," who fought and lost to the black champion Jack Johnson in 1910) and Annie Leslie performing "The Unknown and Undefeated."[75] With such a bill of fare, it is easy to see how reformers and commentators concluded that these establishments catered to aimless, "degraded" bachelors and that "[t]he very men that frequent these places . . . are men that most need decent recreation."[76]

The bawdy nature of the entertainment and the suggestion of prostitution that characterized cheap theaters and concert saloons kept respectable women away. By the end of the nineteenth century, vaudeville houses began to seek a broader, family-oriented clientele, and by the early twentieth century, motion pictures further made live and photographic entertainment respectable for both sexes. Still, single men remained the major patrons of even these amusements. The racy, ribald nature of many early vaudeville acts attracted working-class men, and though some surveys reported that one-third of vaudeville audiences were women, the majority still were probably unmarried men.

Early movie audiences also consisted largely of males. Places called kinetoscope parlors that formed a bridge between penny arcade peepshows and motion picture theaters offered five-to-ten-minute coin-operated shows to male-only audiences. Similar fare was presented when the Biograph Company began showing presentations from its mutoscope machine just before the turn of the century.[77] Even after modern motion pictures became common, men constituted the majority of audiences. George Bevans's study of leisure-time pursuits calculated that young, mostly single workingmen spent an average of fifteen cents a week on movies, at a time when tickets cost between five and ten cents apiece.[78] Sounding like a critic of the cheap theater, one observer asserted that the content of movies consisted of "trashy and lurid . . . ridiculous melodrama; [motion pictures] are . . . the twentieth century substitute for dime novels and nickelodeons."[79]

Active—as opposed to spectator—amusements also expanded in late-nineteenth and early-twentieth century cities and, in the process, reacted to the needs of the growing numbers of single people. The rise and functions of one such amusement, the commercial dance hall, have been detailed in other studies.[80] Suffice it to say here that by the early 1900s, dance halls were immensely popular among all classes of unmarried (and some married) people of both sexes. For example, a study undertaken by the Chicago Juvenile Protective Association estimated that in 1911, eighty-six thousand young people danced nightly in Chicago's public dance halls and academies.[81] Usually, both the male and female patrons came to the dance hall in single-sex groups and found their partners at the hall. Except in those instances, sometimes exaggerated by moralists, in which a man picked up a female partner and she left with him to exchange sexual favors, at the end of the evening a woman usually departed with her female friends and a man left with his male friends. Cabarets and dance resorts that catered to middle-class patrons more closely regulated relations between the sexes by prohibiting unescorted women, suggestive dancing, and sexual contact off the dance floor. The less expensive dance halls with working-class customers permitted, or at least ignored, more unruly behavior such as sexual contact and drinking.[82]

One dancing establishment that was unique to bachelor subculture was the taxi-dance hall. A public dancing place designed explicitly for male patrons only, the taxi-dance hall employed women who sold tickets that entitled purchasers to the privilege of dancing with them. Each female employee was expected to accept any man who selected her for as many dances as he was willing to buy, and she was paid on a commission basis, depending on how many tickets she sold. Paul Cressey, the University of Chicago sociologist whose study of taxi-dance halls in the 1920s remains one of the few ever focusing on that institution, claimed that taxi-dance establishments were "the dominant type of dance hall in the business centers of our largest cities."[83]

The taxi-dance hall derived from the Forty-Nine Camps of San Francisco's Barbary Coast and the dancing academies that existed in many cities at the end of the nineteenth century. The Forty-Nine Camps combined the functions of both the saloon and the dance hall by hiring female hostesses to induce patrons to purchase drinks and then paying the employees according to the revenue generated by their inducements. Dance academies were ostensibly places where a patron could go to learn how to dance. But in New York City one academy owner, who was a former proprietor of a Forty Nine Camp, began attracting male "students" by providing female instructors who worked on a ticket-a-dance basis. Operators of other dance academies and public ballrooms soon adopted this practice, and when campaigns to close down segregated vice districts achieved broad success in major cities during World War I, taxi-dance halls and other ticket-a-dance operations became an acceptable legal alternative for men seeking female companionship.[84]

The taxi-dance hall attracted a variety of unmarried male customers. It functioned primarily as a means for immigrants and social outcasts to attain, however tenuously and temporarily, female companionship, with the sexuality hinted at by dancing, free from the risk of rejection. According to Cressey, inside the halls "[t]he brown-skinned Filipino rubs elbows with the stolid European Slav. The Chinese chop-suey waiter comes into his own alongside the Greek from the Mediterranean. The newly-industrialized Mexican peon finds a place in the same crowd with the 'bad boys' of some of Chicago's first families. The rural visitor seeking a thrill achieves his purpose in the company of a globe-trotter from Australia." Significantly, according to Cressey, "The American Negro remains the only racial type excluded from the taxi-dance hall."[85] Cressey also noted that in every establishment one could find "a few men, handicapped by physical disabilities, for whom the taxi-dancer's obligation to accept all-comers makes the establishment a haven of refuge." Most of all, the greatest number of patrons were "of marriageable age" for whom "in the impersonal contacts of city life [the taxi-dance halls] play an . . . obvious role."[86] That role exclusively benefited the bachelor.

The taxi-dance hall seems to have been especially important in the social lives of Filipino and other Asian immigrant bachelors in cities such as San Francisco and Chicago. According to some observers, Filipino men, newly arrived and anxious to become American, went to taxi-dance halls to escape the close supervision of courtship that they had endured in their homeland. In addition to seeking the thrill and excitement that the taxi-dance hall offered, Filipino men, observers noted, naively believed that a taxi-dancer conformed to their simplistic moral ideal of an American woman who was sweet, pure, and eager to please a man. At the same time, however, case studies undertaken by reformers led them to believe that naive Asian immigrants were easy prey for designing taxi-dancers who took advantage of them financially and emotionally. There were a few instances of Filipino men actually marrying Anglo taxi-dancers, though often the marriages were annulled at the insistence of the woman's parents. Other marriages, however, having been contracted from "highest romantic idealism," seem to have lasted.[87]

Not unexpectedly, in a large and culturally diverse city such as Chicago, most taxi-dance halls were located in or near the lodging-house districts, especially those along transit lines that operated late at night. These sites made the halls accessible to their most regular customers. A sample of one hundred taxi-hall patrons analyzed by Cressey revealed that while the majority lived within the city's rooming-house sections, a number did come from family-type homes. Though Cressey concluded that these men were either immigrants, "slummers," or the physically handicapped, those with domestic backgrounds reinforce the finding outlined in chapter 3 that unmarried men who lived in their parents' household did partake of a city's bachelor subculture.[88]

Reformers often considered taxi-dance halls to be countercultural threats to moral order. They lamented the "disorganizing" influence that these places exerted on both the male patrons, whose presumed loneliness and marginality prompted them to frequent the halls, and on the female dancers, who were willing to expose themselves to intimate approaches of a questionable nature and who were forced to feign affection for their paying partners. But rather than abolish taxi-dance halls, most city officials grudgingly accepted them and tried to regulate them or convince their operators to police themselves. San Francisco, for example, did not prohibit taxi-halls but instead exercised its police power to supervise them as a means of preventing prostitution and protecting the dancers from exploitation. In Chicago, the police were not involved in any type of regulation; instead, proprietors formed the Ballroom Managers' Association and established standards and practices that all members agreed to uphold.[89]

As much as reformers railed, however, taxi-dance halls normally were not headquarters of prostitution. As one thirty-year-old bachelor informed Cressey, "Whenever I want to dance I come to a place like this (taxi-hall) but when I feel I want to get relief (sex) I go to a place where I can feel more sure of getting it." More important was the temptation and the commercial value and profit that could be derived from it. The same respondent told Cressey, "(The dancers) fool around with a fellow so much that they get him half crazy, and he is bound to go and buy some more tickets."[90]

Occasionally, recreation reformers encouraged the establishment of alternatives to allegedly immoral and antisocial places such as cheap theaters, concert saloons, and taxi-dance halls. One such attempt involved the creation of Chicago's Lonesome Club—symbolically named—established in 1915 as a place where unmarried individuals could find wholesome social contact. Its motto bespoke the founders' assumptions about the need for such a social institution: "A Bright Spot in a Blue World." The club was run by social reformer-chaperones who called themselves hosts and hostesses. These individuals organized social events and once the event was underway, circulated around the room introducing attendees to each other. The Lonesome Club spawned various imitators, such as the Get-Acquainted Club, the West Side Social Dancing Club, and the Middle-Aged Dancing Club. These supposedly clean establishments, however, could not truly compete with the commercial dance hall or the taxi-dance hall. They might attract a lone and lonely individual once or twice, but the tight supervision that they imposed on patrons did not interest most independent-minded young people, and those "not at ease in a social gathering or not possessing social graces" found the Lonesome Club lacking.[91]

As demoralizing as he found taxi-dance halls to be, Cressey admitted that they were easily more tolerable than brothels and thus served some useful functions in the lives of unmarried men. In Cressey's mind, the taxi-halls could conceivably facilitate the emotional adjustment of certain men by providing their "only opportunity for affectional ties of a heterosexual character." Moreover, he grudgingly speculated that the taxi-halls represented an important example of how the city's new commercial amusements were responding to the needs of the unmarried, unassimilated male population. The era of the early twentieth century, he observed, was one in which "even romance is sold on the bargain counter," and taxi-dance halls were satisfying a demand for such romance. To Cressey, the rise of taxi-dance halls and their resistance to regulation furnished evidence that the institutions of the impersonal city made the problem of social control especially difficult. On the other hand, these establishments also highlight how the patronage by the large populations of urban bachelors could and did influence the course of commercial amusement.[92]

SATISFYING A DEMAND FOR SERVICES

The market demand created by single men also spurred the development of numerous other urban commercial establishments. Public bathhouses, though like other services not specifically designed for bachelors, attracted patrons primarily from the unmarried male population. Just as lack of access to copious hot water had provided a market for barbers' services, so too did the unavailability of sufficient water in working-class residences and boardinghouses create a demand for bathhouses. At the end of the nineteenth century, social reformers, concerned about hygiene, convinced governments in several cities to construct free public baths for poor people as a means of health protection. Boston built its first indoor public bath on Dover Street in 1898, and within a year the facility was attracting more than 18,000 men and boys per month and more than 8,000 women and girls. At the same time, Chicago had its own indoor bathhouses (promoted in part by the notorious machine politician "Bath-House" John Coughlin); by 1917, the Windy City boasted fifty-one such establishments. At the turn of the century, one survey counted total daily bathhouse patronage by Chicago men at 25,450.[93]

In addition to these facilities, which served mostly the bathing needs of the working class, entrepreneurs in several cities opened elegant private bathhouses, often called Turkish, Roman, or Electric baths, and attracted paying customers from wealthier groups. Among San Francisco's twenty-one bathhouses in 1915 were two large indoor bathing establishments, which charged as much as twenty-five cents a visit, a price beyond the means of the working-class or lower middle-class bachelor. Private facilities of this sort also operated in places such as New York, Chicago, Boston, and Philadelphia. Offering a range of services, including massages and other treatments, these fashionable and respectable establishments fed the upper middle and elite class's increasing preoccupation with health and the body at the turn of the century.[94]

One of these higher-class San Francisco establishments, Sutro's Turkish Baths, became a gathering place for gay men. Similar establishments existed for gay men in other large cities, including Chicago and New York, and they functioned as meeting places as well as locations for homosexual encounters and assignations. Private bathhouses frequented by gay men usually were of two types: gay-tolerant, in which management permitted homosexual activity but catered to a general male clientele; and gay-only, which explicitly excluded nonhomosexual patrons. At gay-tolerant bathhouses, management allowed sexual encounters between men so long as they were mostly hidden inside dark spaces such as dressing areas and the steam room. In gay-only bathhouses, such the Ariston Bath in New York's Ariston apartment hotel on West 57th Street, the management sought to bar straight men because of the potential for angry reaction and reprisal they might initiate. Safer than parks and public rest rooms, bathhouses provided gay men, married as well as unmarried, with the opportunity to appropriate their own private space where they could not only find sexual pleasure but also cultivate their own subculture.[95]

Whatever their clientele, bathhouses fit into the range of services that characterized bachelor subculture. Novelist and journalist Homer Croy summarized the wide appeal when he recollected that a bath, located behind a New York barbershop that he often frequented, offered an "enchanting white tub" for twenty-five cents. He wrote in his autobiography, "The bath was patronized by the men who lived in the rooming houses, by drummers (traveling salesmen), by the men who worked in the livery stables, and by the men who worked at the coal pockets and at the wheat elevator."[96]

FIGURE 4.5. Urban bathhouses often offered the only bathing facilities available to bachelors who resided in boardinghouses and rooming houses. With their private dressing rooms, these establishments sometimes became haunts for men seeking homosexual encounters, but mostly the bathhouses provided inexpensive ablution. (Museum of the City of New York)

Gymnasiums also served important functions for urban bachelors. Often adjuncts to the YMCA and similar young men's organizations in many cities (see chapter 5), gymnasiums inspired enthusiastic support from reformers who saw them as alternatives to the saloon and pool hall. At the turn of the century, the San Francisco *City Directory* listed eight gymnasiums; the Chicago *City Directory* listed seven. Boston had seventeen indoor gyms in 1905, some privately funded, some municipal. The East Boston Gymnasium was the Massachusetts city's first; the gift of a local philanthropist, it opened in 1897. Two years later, the city of Boston began operation of the country's first large municipal gymnasium in South Boston. These establishments, plus several outdoor gymnasiums, all stayed open in the evening and used extensive electric lighting for the benefit of nighttime patrons. Charging minimal or no fees, they offered instruction in calisthenics, games, and sports and held special hours for different sex and age groups. Young, mostly unmarried men, however, were their most numerous habitués.[97]

Critical to middle-class and even some working-class bachelors who lacked access to the domestic aids that a family could provide, tailor shops comprised another service that flourished in many urban boardinghouse districts. In Boston in the early 1900s, for example, there were some seventy such establishments. Their services were necessary but not cheap. Operators usually pressed trousers for ten or fifteen cents and sponged and pressed a suit for fifty to seventy-five cents, but they also often sold men's clothing for bargain prices. Laundries provided the same services; in 1915, Boston housed 161 nonChinese laundries plus 30 establishments separately listed as clothes-cleaners. The same year San Francisco had 177 non-Chinese laundries. Chinese laundries, which originated as social as well as commercial services for Chinese immigrant communities, found ready clientele among the broader urban public — especially its bachelors — in most large cities. Housing reformer Alfred B. Wolfe remarked that in Boston, "seemingly every other corner is occupied by a Chinese laundry."[98]

Working-class bachelors also found benefits from pawn shop services. A person in financial need utilized pawn shops to obtain a quick loan by depositing an article of some value as collateral and receiving in return cash that was equivalent to a small percentage of the article's market worth. In more prosperous times, the person could redeem the pawned article (assuming it had not been sold) by paying the broker a sum in excess of the amount received when the article was pawned, thereby allowing the pawnbroker to profit from the exchange. Even though less than one-third of pawned articles were ever redeemed, pawn shops usually held the articles for slightly over a year before selling them retail or to secondhand, junk, and antique dealers. San Francisco's *City Directory* included thirty-eight dealers of "second-hand goods" in 1912, and Chicago's *City Directory* listed sixty-eight pawnbrokers in 1904, most of them located in areas housing large numbers of working-class bachelors. One pawnbroker on Chicago's North Clark Street testified that more than 60 percent of pawned articles in his store came from men. Married as well as unmarried people used such a service, but it appears that pawn shops thrived on their bachelor clientele.[99]

That same bachelor clientele constituted a ready demand for many other urban services. Boston's lodging-house district in the early twentieth century housed some 175 physicians, who ranged from the highly competent to "the most dissipated quacks and criminal operators." Numerous drug stores, whose proprietors dispensed various tonics and remedies, fulfilled medical needs as well, though Wolfe observed that it was "doubtful if many of [the drug stores proprietors] would live but for their cigar, soda, and candy sales." Wolfe also took a cynical stance toward the "many palmists, card-readers, business mediums, trance-artists, astrologers, and the like" who operated in Boston's South End, where they constituted "an unpleasant feature of the district." Because these occult services often operated out of rooms in lodging houses, Wolfe and others suspected them of actually conducting prostitution.[100]

By the 1920s, the growth rate of the bachelor population had slowed as marriage rates rose and marriage age declined, but the numerous institutions that arose to serve the needs of single men had become fixtures of the urban environment. Evi-

dence abounded that a specialized bachelor commercial economy was thriving. Some institutions of this economy, such as
the saloons and restaurants that catered to a clientele of unmarried men, had evolved from types that existed well before
the expansion and visibility of their customers had occurred in
the late nineteenth century. Others, such as the taxi-dance hall,
provided new services to those who had a special demand. For
all the apprehension that these institutions raised among the
rest of the population, what went on inside them was, for the
most part, tame. Mostly, they simply reflected new opportunities for some to partake of a rising service-oriented economy
and for others to profit from a large and willing cohort of
customers.

Associations: Formal and Interpersonal

CRITICS AND social commentators have long indicted the urban environment for its atomizing and impersonal effects on the human character. Such insinuation carried enhanced meaning when applied to bachelors. A representative reform group, the Committee of Fifteen, an antivice society established in New York City in 1900, summarized the city's relevance to the presumed aimless lives of unmarried men by asserting that "the main external check upon a man's conduct, the opinion of his neighbors, which has such a powerful influence in the country or small town, tends to disappear. In a great city one has no neighbors. No man knows the doings of even his close friends; few men care what the secret life of their friends may be. . . . (T)he young man is left free to follow his own inclinations."[1] The Committee of Fifteen and other such organizations promoted the assumption that bachelorhood was a lonely time, an existence without anchor or inspiration.

For the most part, however, the evidence indicates that the years of a man's bachelorhood did not necessarily constitute a time of loneliness. Rather, bachelorhood was a period in which single men were torn between a desire for independence, which often involved release from family restraints and obligations on the one hand, and a need for social interaction along with the emotional and financial support that, on the other hand, kinship could provide. In a search to satisfy both sets of needs, unmarried men formed a network of individual relationships and group connections. Those attachments of a private and interpersonal nature are difficult to uncover; some of my research into autobiographies sheds light on these relationships, but the complexity and diversity of the personal life of any individual who lived a century ago make full understanding elusive at best. Bachelors, however, compensated at least in part for their social isolation by joining a variety of organizations, and this associational behavior can offer insights into the ways in which these men coped with their condition and with the society in which they lived.

Though individuals harbored different ideas of and reactions to what it meant to be independent and/or alone in the city, and the same individuals maintained a variety of interactions with others, the number and scope of actual associations suggest that bachelors could experience, and usually did experience, some kind of meaningful community and organizational life. Whether in street gangs, school classes, social and fraternal clubs, religious organizations, literary and debate societies, sports teams, work groups, or political organizations, bachelors found social outlets that helped them to evade potential isolation. Some of these relationships even replicated kin networks, while others ran bachelors afoul of the law. Occasionally associations included both men and women or mingled unmarried with married men. Most organizations under analysis in this chapter, however, were created by and for bachelors and underscore the richness of a bachelor subculture in American cities in the late nineteenth century and early twentieth.

Gangs, Clubs, and Fraternal Orders

For many urban working-class men, a gang provided the first experience of organizational affiliation, one that could continue beyond youth, in refashioned form, for many years after the onset of adulthood and married life. In other ways, however, the gang acted as an institution unique to the independent or semi-independent bachelor stage between childhood, when a boy remained tightly incorporated within a family structure, and marriage, when the man became reincorporated into a family of his own creation.[2] This time of life, usually in the late teens and early twenties, marked a period when there was nearly universal coincidence between working-class males and public spaces in the nineteenth- and early-twentieth-century American city. Informal associations of males that gathered on street corners and in pool halls, candy stores, smoke shops, and other commercial establishments (see chapter 4) became a prominent means of socialization for young men, and more formalized groups evolved out of these gatherings to constitute the infamous youth gangs that pervaded working-class neighborhoods. Though notorious for its seeming commitment to crime and violence, a gang more often was, as one analyst has observed, simply "just a bunch of boys in it for amusement, hanging out on a corner, waiting for 'something doin'."[3]

The turn-of-the-century American city offered a fertile environment for the rise of gang culture because of the ways in which social and economic shifts affected the lives of young working-class males. By the late nineteenth century, male-oriented activities that formerly had integrated young men with older counterparts now excluded older boys and younger men. Apprenticeship had faded, leaving many youths deprived of formal work settings and the intergenerational exchanges that had existed in such settings. Fire companies had professionalized, replacing the volunteer agencies that once had integrated boys and young men into an all-male social organization. Politics too had professionalized, excluding males who were too young to vote and too inexperienced to participate meaningfully in a party organization. Even criminal practices such as thievery had become more sophisticated and professional, and the enhanced business orientation of crime — hierarchical organization, emphasis on planning, use of modern technology — often excluded youths. These and other similar changes left only the street gang as a means by which young working-class men could achieve and articulate their male identity and blaze their own path into public space.[4]

The size of a street gang could fluctuate daily, depending on the activities taking place. Just hanging out on the corner or in the pool hall could include as few as four or five individuals, either loosely or tightly affiliated. In a battle with a rival group, a gang might mobilize forty or more youths. In practice, virtually every boy in a particular neighborhood was automatically a potential member of the gang that prevailed in that district.[5] In a social-psychological sense, the gang provided the young male with a needed sense of identity, one to which the individual laid claim through the thrill-seeking and competitive behavior that the gang promoted. Conflicts with the police and with other gangs represented expressions of territorial prerogatives and personal character, and included a means of rejecting primary identification with one's mother. According to sociologist Leon Ellis, the gang did not serve as a surrogate for more mature forms of male social participation; rather, the street-corner tie was in and of itself "a practically valuable and socially valued mode of organizing and participating in social life."[6]

Frederic Thrasher, the University of Chicago sociologist who undertook a detailed study of Windy City gang life in the 1920s, described a group of male youths that he contended was a typical gang. He called it the Dirty Dozen. Thrasher related that the Dirty Dozen had spontaneous origins, resulting from the casual meeting of a dozen or more fellows aged sixteen to twenty-two on a street corner at the entrance to a neighborhood park. Later, the group moved its gathering place to a pool hall a short distance away. The members were all unmarried, mostly unemployed, and they spent their time playing sports, gambling, and mostly just sitting around and talking. Each gang member, Thrasher asserted, thirsted for physical conflict and was able to satisfy this craving with less risk by pursuing it with the protection of his fellow gang members rather than by starting hostilities on his own. Thrasher admitted that the gang was largely an adolescent phenomenon and that marriage was one of the most potent causes for the disintegration of a gang such as the Dirty Dozen, but he observed also that certain qualities of gang style could be retained by a man as he aged.[7]

At the other end of the socioeconomic spectrum, young (as well as older) unmarried men of elite society had their own opportunities for socialization in men's clubs. Originating in the antebellum period, elite men's clubs reached full flower after the Civil War, pervading high society in every major city by the 1890s. Each man's listing in blue books and social registers included his club affiliations, and every true patrician was expected to become a member of at least one, if not several, of these clubs. The lodging and eating facilities of these establishments were discussed in chapter 4; these functions as well as the more general social atmosphere of the club and club rooms contributed to the inculcation of both gender and class values in young elite bachelors. Though club members undoubtedly considered their organizations far more refined than working-class gangs, the clubs provided functions for single youths of high social standing that resembled those experienced by working-class men in gangs. Like gangs, clubs existed as all-male affiliations in which men could define and reinforce their identity as men. The exclusivity of membership, though based on different criteria than those for gangs, effected a similar result of constructing and reinforcing certain values and behavior through participation by and in the all-male body.[8]

Elite social clubs and associations seldom existed solely for bachelors, but a number of them, such as the Penn Club of Philadelphia, supported junior divisions for younger, almost exclusively single men, usually between the ages of twenty-one and thirty. Members in this division paid reduced dues and had their initiation fees waived, presumably because they could not afford higher costs. When they reached their thirtieth birthday, they had to pay full dues, though the initiation fee remained forgiven. Members of all divisions regardless of age or marital status, however, were expected to abide by the same set of club rules and decorum.[9]

In spite of such provisions, contemporary critics frequently charged that the presumably dissipated habits that were nurtured in elite clubs attracted primarily incorrigible bachelors,

AT THE CLUB.

Gay Bachelor: Do you think there is anything in the theory that married men live longer than unmarried ones?

Henpecked Friend (wearily): Oh, I don't know—seems longer.

FIGURE 5.1. Men's clubs furnished a homosocial retreat from the burdens and responsibilities of domesticated family life. They also provided one of many venues in which antimarriage and probachelor ideology, often expressed humorously, was cultivated. This cartoon, from an 1891 edition of *Life* represents a typical form of bachelor—and antimarriage—humor. The term "gay" in this instance signifies carefree rather than homosexual. (*Life* vol. 18, no. 464, November 19, 1891).

forcing apologists to contend otherwise. Francis Gerry Fairfield, in his early history of the clubs of New York, declaimed, "It has been alleged in some quarters that the rolls of these associations are mostly recruited from the ranks of unmarried men. It would be natural to suppose so, but an examination of the facts disproves the proposition, which is one of those a priori conclusions that people are apt to indulge in out of respect for what they conceive to be the fitness of things."[10] It appears that though clubs provided a privileged space where men could, if they wanted, indulge in certain pleasures that the rest of society would hold in disrepute, little of men's participation in elite clubs involved the purposeful pursuit of such pleasures. Gambling and billiards were mainly forms of male sociability for both married and unmarried men. In fact, Fairfield asserted that three-fourths of club membership in New York consisted of married men. Nevertheless, the intensity of disclaimers such as Fairfield's bespeaks of the strong link between formal male associations and elite bachelor subculture.[11]

Middle-class men's organizations consisted mostly of fraternal orders. These organizations served a variety of purposes: mutual benefit (enabling members to purchase burial and life insurance), religious (holding prayer meetings and Bible classes), didactic (offering lectures and classes on a multitude of topics), humanitarian (sponsoring various charitable projects), as well as social (parties and dances as well as spontaneous conviviality). Fraternal orders were especially prominent in the United States during the peak years of urban-industrial growth. One observer labeled the period surrounding the turn of the century as the Golden Age of Fraternity, a time in which more than three hundred different fraternal orders existed nationally, encompassing a membership of some 5.5 million American men, the majority of whom were most likely to be solid middle-class white-collar men of all ages and both marital statuses.

If such figures are accurate, one-fourth of all adult males belonged to at least one of these orders, including 810,000 Odd Fellows, 750,000 Freemasons, 475,000 Knights of Pythias, and dozens of other organizations that met in the 70,000 lodges and meeting halls scattered around the nation, especially in the cities. At regularly held meetings, initiations occurred, incorporating new members and raising existing members to a higher level of the order, officers presented reports and organized service projects, and members received some sort of program, often consisting of a didactic lecture. But, as sociologist Michael Kimmel has pointed out, the most important function of these organizations was their encouragement to middle-class males to enjoy the company of other men like themselves, away from domestic pressures and responsibilities. Yet at the same time, Kimmel adds, a fraternal order offered its members the stimulation of economic, cultural and domestic life. It was "alternately the artisan guild, the church, or the home — or all three simultaneously."[12]

The use of ritual gave fraternal orders a singular male quality. Applying mystical terms and rites to their activities and offices, these organizations attempted to make their fellowship unique, substituting what Kimmel refers to as a wifeless, motherless, band of brothers for the biological family and creating a secretive sanctuary where men could experience an intimacy that was all their own.[13] The initiation ritual stood at the center of fraternalism. Modeled on baptism, it symbolized a rebirth into the family of brethren as well as a rite of passage, rewarding a man's worthiness for membership. Like warriors in a tribe, initiates achieved their identities to become full-fledged Knights, Red Men, Woodmen, and Eagles. Married men as well as bachelors participated in these ceremonies, but the rituals held different meanings for the two groups. Among married men, the bogus medieval hocus-pocus provided a countering force to the feminized home — though unmarried men who had continued to live in the parental home would have felt the same effect also. For bachelors away from their family of origin, the ceremonial aspects of fraternal orders offered a structured source of fellowship and camaraderie, a substitute for, rather than an alternative to, the family. Thus members called each other "brother" and sometimes referred to their organization as a family.[14]

Social clubs among gay men served similar functions, with the addition of sustaining a distinctive gay subculture in various unique ways. Clubs organized in New York and other big cities sponsored dances and provided information on cultural events. Initiates were acculturated into the dress and behavioral styles of "fairy" life. Like straight men's clubs, gay clubs strengthened bonds of quasi kinship, not only furnishing support for individuals otherwise ostracized from society but also enabling them to relate to each other by calling other members "sister" and using terms not recognized by the outside world.[15]

The extent and importance of fraternal orders seems to have declined after the 1890s, though bachelors remained a valued component of many organizations long after that date. Many memberships dwindled simply because formal insurance arrangements developed to replace those that once had been central to a fraternal order's functions. For example, like many such orders, the B'nai B'rith, an organization of Jewish men, initially had offered members a program in which, for regular monthly payments, the order would provide a cash payment and monthly stipend to the widow of a member upon that member's death. This program, as would be expected, mostly attracted married men. But after the 1890s, when married men began purchasing life insurance policies from corporate insurance companies rather than from B'nai B'rith, the order's membership dropped by more than one third. In response, the organization opened its rolls to unmarried men under the age of thirty who did not wish, or believed they had no need, to participate in its insurance program but could still be active in the organization's charitable and educational activities.[16]

Perhaps more importantly, by the late nineteenth century, men could find the fellowship they craved in other realms, such as the world of leisure, especially participant and spectator sports. In heterosexual contexts, males of all social classes often tried to display their prowess in acts such as picking up unattached women and prostitutes, fathering children, and dominating female family members. But, as several scholars have pointed out, men more frequently sought confirmation of their maleness in the exclusive company of other men.[17] The interactions within saloons, pool halls, clubs, and other male retreats reinforced this search, but so also did the physical competition — active and witnessed — of sports. Though married as well as unmarried men engaged in athletic pursuits, the sporting institution itself held greater meaning for bachelors because it furnished a refuge from loneliness and isolation, a substitute for a conjugal family, and an opportunity for social cohesion that otherwise might not have existed. Moreover, the competitive physical nature of sports encouraged and glorified the so-called manly activities of drinking and betting that distinguished the bachelor subculture.[18]

Participation in sports such as bowling and cycling (in addition to pool and billiards — see chapter 4) typified some of the active sporting activities that consumed bachelors' interests in the late nineteenth century. Cheap and accessible in some saloons as well as in separate establishments, the sport of bowling became a standard feature of the male bachelor subculture in the late nineteenth century. By 1920, Chicago boasted 230 licensed bowling alleys, most of which served as hangouts where men could socialize and prove their physical skills.[19] Though, like pool, the sport abetted gambling and drinking, it retained higher respectability than pool and therefore attracted middle-class as well as working-class participants.

As well, cycling became a national craze in the 1880s and 1890s and this prompted the formation of bicycle clubs that often included only men. Such clubs sponsored activities that bolstered bachelor sociability and connectedness. Presidential candidate and New York governor Al Smith, for example, had joined a cycling organization called the Century Club in his bachelor youth during the late 1880s. Membership in this club, he recalled, meant that "you had ridden a hundred miles in a single day." Smith described a typical club activity: "With a number of young men from my neighborhood, I left Oliver and Madison Streets at nine o'clock on Sunday morning and wheeled to Far Rockaway. We went in swimming, had our dinner there, and wheeled back."[20]

Spectator sports such as baseball and boxing also tightened male bonds, especially among bachelors. Both sports, with their special qualities of tense drama interspersed with lapses of action, gave spectators frequent opportunities to discuss the game and make bets — activities that enabled them to show off their expertise to male companions as well as to identify vicariously with the physical contest that they were watching. The shared witnessing of a commercial spectacle provoked passionate conversation beyond the ball field and boxing ring and served as a vehicle for social contact and conversational engagement. As Leon Ellis has asserted, however, the bonds created by these contacts did not lead to substantial formal social organization; rather, because of the temporary and tenuous nature of their origin, they reflected "a bond of an audience and nothing more."[21] Yet, as Ellis admits, the development of the spectacle of commercial spectator sports did create a "mass masculine culture," which existed as "a new way in which men [were] linked in social life," a place where the all-male peer group that characterized bachelor subculture nurtured itself.[22]

The YMCA and Its Imitators

Probably the most well-known and well-populated formal organization for middle-class and some working-class bachelors was the Young Men's Christian Association (YMCA or the Y). Founded in England in 1844 as a vehicle for providing moral guidance to young drapers and other urban tradesmen, the YMCA was brought to North America (Boston and Montreal) in 1851. Its sponsors in the United States intended the organization particularly to attract unmarried clerks and other middle-class men seemingly adrift in the city. The Y's early activities included the establishment of libraries and literary societies along with prayer meetings and Bible classes, all with the aim of nurturing a young man's Christian faith and guarding that faith against the corrupting temptations that surrounded the otherwise morally vulnerable male. Aided by concerned benefactors, the Ys in the largest cities constructed imposing buildings that contained not only meeting rooms and lecture halls but also low-cost residential and dining facilities — all meant to tend to a young man's worldly as well as spiritual needs. In addition, in the 1860s a number of local branches, such as those in San Francisco, Washington, D.C., and New York City, built gymnasiums as a means of offering "wholesome" recreation for members. Within a few years, the organization began fitting its various functions into a neat package called the fourfold program of services: spiritual, mental, social, and physical.[23]

Explicitly designed for the average young bachelor — meaning one who was self-sustaining and not poor — the YMCA's fourfold program aimed to counter the allurement of the political boss and the saloon by providing a meeting place for sociability, an outlet for youthful recreational cravings, and a hothouse for the cultivation of piety and self-discipline. The goal, asserted Luther Gulick, the organization's first international secretary for physical work, was to train "the whole man" in a balanced way. To symbolize this balance, in 1895 Gulick proposed a red triangle, with each side representing a different component of a man's healthy nature: physical, spiritual, and mental.[24] As time passed, the number and intensity of religious activities, such as street preaching and noon-day prayer services, declined while the number of secular activities, such as education and athletics, increased. The Chicago association, for example, increased its expenditures for social activities (dances, concerts, and other such events) from $875 in 1900 to $8,614 in 1909; its budget for physical activities (mostly held in the gymnasium) swelled from $2,679 in 1900 to $26,625 in 1909. In both cases, the expenditures rose to ten times their previous level in less than a decade.[25]

The Y also engaged in activities expressly intended to aid young bachelors entering a city for the first time. For example, according to one account published in 1915, the San Francisco YMCA was involved in "the meeting of trains and boats, thereby protecting the unsophisticated [young bachelors] from taxicab men, the sending of men to good rooming houses, thereby helping them to avoid moral difficulties, the housing of about two hundred men in the YMCA Building, and the conducting of an employment department through which permanent and temporary employment for many hundreds of men is secured."[26] More often, the Y served simply as a familiar oasis for migrants seeking housing and social connections. Journalist and novelist Homer Croy, for example, sought out the YMCA as soon as he got his first job as reporter for an urban newspaper.[27]

The Y buildings themselves offered an ever-expanding range of amenities. Facilities at the huge Central YMCA in Chicago in the early twentieth century included, in addition to a gymnasium: four parlors and reception rooms; a game room; a 200-seat assembly room; a 1,000-seat restaurant; a barber shop; an emergency hospital; a correspondence room; a 1,500-volume library; a reading room; ten classrooms; three laboratories; a darkroom; a locker room with 2,500 lockers, seventy-five dressing rooms, forty-five showers, and seven bathtubs; a natatorium; a steam room; and a handball court. The main building of the San Francisco YMCA, which opened at Mason and Ellis streets in 1895, contained almost exactly the same facilities as the Chicago Y, with the addition of a bowling alley and shooting gallery.[28] Activities at these places focused on education rather than leisure. The list of daytime classes taught at the Central Chicago Y encompassed a wide variety of subjects, including mathematics, law, business, government, languages, drawing, physics, chemistry, history, rhetoric, and carpentry.[29]

For the use of its facilities and enrollment in its classes, the association in each city sold annual memberships. In 1903, a one-year full membership at the Chicago Central YMCA cost

$15 (raised to $17 in 1905) and entitled a member to full use of all facilities, including the gym, baths, and handball court. For $7.50, a man could buy a limited membership, entitling him to access to the reading rooms, library, and parlors, entrance to all evening classes and clubs (upon payment of tuition and club fees), two tickets to entertainments (usually concerts and lectures) and use of the baths, employment bureau, and bicycle storage. In 1905, limited members also received a discount at the barbershop plus free Bible classes.[30]

Membership fees usually did not strain the budgets of middle-class young men, whose incomes normally ranged between seven hundred and one thousand dollars a year. But extra services, such as educational courses at the Y, added to the expense of membership. Tuition for day classes ranged from $10.00 for one month to $65.00 for nine months, though tuition also covered full membership in the association. Those who already were members received discounts on tuition. Rates for evening classes ranged from $2.00 to $5.00 per course. Other special charges included $1.50 to $3.00 per year for a locker, $8.00 to $13.00 for a dressing room, towel rentals for $0.01 each, and $0.25 to $1.00 for a treatment from a masseur. There also were individual and package charges for the entertainments, which included concerts by bands and singers, illustrated lectures on exotic places and animals, and dramatic presentations. Membership fees at the San Francisco YMCA duplicated those in Chicago almost exactly, except that the San Francisco Y also had a $25 fee for businessmen.[31]

YMCA hotels, which operated in most major cities, furnished a service that bachelors may have welcomed and utilized as much as the Y's classes, gymnasiums, and other facilities. Early in their existence, some Ys had constructed dormitory rooms in their buildings as an inducement to membership and as an additional service to men already established with a job. The San Francisco YMCA building at Mason and Ellis streets, for example, contained 140 "sleeping rooms with hot and cold water . . . in every room."[32] But dormitory rooms carried rules

FIGURE 5.2. The YMCA, initially organized as a spiritual haven for unmarried men leaving their families for the city, quickly developed secular activities in sports, education, and entertainment that made it one of the most popular bachelor-oriented organizations. This locker room at a Chicago YMCA represents just one of many facilities that the Y offered. (Chicago Historical Society)

and restrictions that distinguished them from more private quarters. At the San Francisco Y, for example, use of dorm rooms was restricted to men aged twenty to thirty-five, and, according to an association report, "all shall be given to understand that the dormitory is not an hotel or a club, and that some variety of service is expected of each person."[33] Having established programs for young men once they had arrived in the city, the Y in the early twentieth century turned to finding a way to house these men more conveniently and prevent them from becoming victims of the dreary world of flophouses and cheap hotels. The YMCA hotel acted as a place of healthful temporary abode until the man could find a suitable permanent place to live.

The Chicago YMCA Hotel provides a good example of how such an establishment operated. Opened in 1916 on Wabash Street on the city's Near South Side, the hotel contained 1,821 tiny bedrooms (mostly six-by-eight feet), all without running water (bathrooms were in the hall), and renting for thirty to fifty cents per night. (By contrast, rates at a cheap rooming house averaged ten to fifteen cents per night.) The hotel had a clear purpose: "The YMCA of Chicago will serve in this hotel the self-respecting man at the threshold of his city life; men of moderate means passing through the city, and those temporarily out of work. Its design is to protect men from the dangerous environment which is frequently found in cheap hotels and lodging houses in and near the loop district; to assist men in securing employment and later to locate them in regular Association dormitories, or carefully chosen homes."[34] The building included a cafeteria and lunch counter, plus a checkroom, barbershop, shoe-shine stand, laundry room, writing room, telephone service, employment and vocational bureau, and newsstand. Like the regular Y building, the hotel offered musical entertainment and lectures in the evening, and it also provided games such as checkers, chess, and billiard tables. A doorman screened visitors and potential guests for good character. "On Sunday guides [were] provided to direct men to the churches of their choice, and everything possible [was] done . . . to meet their religious needs."[35] The hotel proved to be a great success; occupancy rates in the first years averaged between 90 and 95 percent.[36]

Ironically, though the YMCA intended its activities to protect men from the supposed moral dangers to be found in the lodging houses, in New York and in other big cities the YMCA and its hotels became centers of homosexual social life. According to George Chauncey, gay men sometimes appropriated

161

YMCA facilities for their own sexual testing grounds and used them to introduce willing members and hotel residents to a new world of homosexual counterculture. Men in this subset of bachelors could find others with similar sexual identification in the protected environment of the Y's rented rooms, baths, restaurants, and meeting halls. In these environments as well, men who did not necessarily identify themselves as homosexual could learn about the existence of gay culture and experiment with sexual alternatives. A number of men, however, came to the Y specifically to find sex partners. The association management usually denied that such sexual activity was taking place in their establishments, while at the same time creating restrictions, such as prohibiting dormitory and hotel residents from bringing outsiders into their rooms, to prevent it. But how freely gay men could operate inside YMCA establishments depended chiefly on the toleration of local managers, security personnel, and desk clerks, who sometimes were homosexual themselves. As a result, several Y's acquired reputations, both among gay and straight men, as headquarters for gay society.[37]

In addition to their main buildings and hotels, YMCAs in large cities established branches to serve individual neighborhoods and special groups of men. Mostly, these satellite branches provided miniature versions of the services offered in the main branch. The San Francisco YMCA, for example, supported branches in the Mission and Presidio districts as well as special branches for members of the army and navy.[38] During the 1890s, the Canadian-born African-American William A. Hunton and black minister Jesse E. Moorland established several YMCA branches for black men, and in Chicago, philanthropist Julius Rosenwald, a major contributor to YMCA programs, helped fund construction of a separate building for African Americans on South Wabash Street in 1913.[39]

The so-called Chinese YMCA in San Francisco was both a representative and unique branch operation. Created at the turn of the century to bring the predominantly bachelor Chinese population into Christian fellowship, the Chinese Y at first sponsored lectures on health, education, and religion but quickly developed social events and recreational activities that emphasized the secular side of life. When the association opened a new building on Stockton Street in Chinatown in 1912, it included a game room and classrooms for courses in topics ranging from mechanical drawing to English. A newer Chinatown Y opened just three years later on Stockton Street; it included a large reading room with books in both English and Chinese and a machine shop for classes in mechanics and woodworking. At the same time, the association organized a Chinese YMCA Orchestra, and members began to participate increasingly in sports activities.[40]

Patterned in part after the YMCA, the Young Men's Hebrew Association (YMHA), primarily for Jewish bachelors, was founded in the 1850s and flourished after the Civil War in both large and medium-sized American cities. By 1880, YMHA branches existed in twenty-eight cities, located in every major geographical region, and hundreds more opened in the next decade.[41] The YMHA emphasized educational activities even more than the YMCA, but like its Christian counterpart, the YMHA aimed to protect and provide for young bachelors alone in the city. An early report from the Newark, New Jersey, YMHA expressed the association's goals: "Our Jewish young men of this city must have a place where, after the toilsome labor of the day, they can seek recreation in literary pursuits, in reading and listening from time to time to eminent lecturers, whose discourses are to enrich their minds with all that history can teach, with all that human experience can suggest, and with all that science can establish. And if in time to come our houses of worship shall not crumble into dust and our congregations dwindle away, the young men must also be made familiar with our history, our literature and philosophy. . . ."[42]

YMHAs generally de-emphasized social events and prohibited cardplaying, gambling, drinking, and sometimes smoking in an effort to distinguish themselves from secular social clubs. Nevertheless, they did not omit recreational functions altogether, and their buildings included gymnasiums and swimming pools in addition to libraries and auditoriums. In the early 1900s, the Philadelphia YMHA, for example, sponsored informal social nights, men's nights with vaudeville-type entertainment, musical performances, a Bachelors' Ball, and chess and checkers tournaments.[43] The YMHA did not offer residential facilities, preferring instead to establish community centers that included meeting rooms for educational organizations, such as literary and debate clubs, and philanthropic activities, such as tending to the needs of new Jewish immigrants. Frequently, these YMHA centers, originally intended for young men, were transformed into general Jewish community centers, a circumstance that, when combined with the heavy influx of immigrants and the diversion of commercial amusements, contributed to the decline of the YMHA in the second decade of the twentieth century.[44]

All of the YMCA services and facilities, and to a slightly lesser extent those of the YMHA, attempted to create a family-type environment for middle-class bachelors. The YMCA's motto of "A home away from home" reinforced the goal of creating a domestic place for unattached men, what Ward Adair, a leader of the New York City Y in the early twentieth century, defined as "a substitute for a man's home while he . . . might be several hundred miles from his own dwelling place."[45] Attempting to blend the religious with the social, the Ys also cultivated fellowship in a supportive environment. Ideally, Adair reflected, "If one fellow happened to be down, all the others would give a lift. If one were sick the others would visit or write him. If one were out of work the others would pull for him to get him a job. If a fellow wanted to talk with somebody about some problem, he could make an appointment with the man of his choice."[46] Thus the YMCA and YMHA attempted to infuse the bachelor subculture with values and institutions derived from the dominant domestic culture, and they tried to counter the disorientation, loneliness, and temptations that respectable bachelors presumably encountered in the city by offering them alternatives to the saloon, the pool hall, and the boardinghouse. Significantly, however, the YMCA indirectly endorsed bachelor subculture because, unlike the Young Women's Christian Association, which viewed the independent status of a woman in the city as only a temporary condition before she was restored to a home environment, the YMCA did not encourage the independent man to return to his family.[47]

Though the YMCA was predominantly a Protestant agency, the Catholic hierarchy generally accepted it, and Catholic bachelors could be counted among the Y membership in most cities. Early in the twentieth century, however, a few bishops and priests urged Catholics to establish their own organizations for young men. In this vein, Rt. Rev. Charles E. Baden of Cincinnati founded the Fenwick Club in that city in 1915. Named after Edward L. Fenwick, the city's first bishop, the club adopted most of the rationale and functions characteristic of a YMCA. As one Fenwick Club member wrote in 1922, "The need of a Catholic institution possessing all features of, and equal to the YMCA, plus a Catholic environment, has been recognized for years. The absence of home influences, the associations formed with frequenters of cheap hotels and go-as-you-please rooming houses, are responsible, to a great extent, for the neglect of religious duties which eventually lead to indifference and frequently result in complete loss of faith by many young men."[48]

In 1917 the Fenwick Club opened a nine-story building in the heart of Cincinnati's downtown. Like most central YMCA buildings, the Fenwick Club boasted a gymnasium and swimming pool on the first floor, a lobby room and libraries on the second floor, offices for a chaplain and other staff personnel on the third floor, a cafeteria on the fourth floor, a kitchen and storerooms on the fifth floor, and private rooms on the remaining floors. The club also sponsored regular lectures, entertainments, dances, and athletic contests. The Fenwick Club expanded so rapidly that it purchased land for a building annex in 1921 and planned to construct "the finest 'Gym' in the city."[49] In other cities, the National Council of Catholic Men and other Catholic societies sponsored similar men's clubs, but though the Fenwick Club seems to have been the most successful, none of the strictly Catholic clubs ever grew to the extent that the YMCA did.

The YMCA and its imitators were only partially successful in their efforts to service any city's bachelors. Reformer Raymond Calkins warranted that although YMCAs provided invaluable services to single men, they reached only a tiny fraction of the male population. He estimated that in cities such as Chicago and Boston, only about 1 percent of men of all ages were members of the YMCA. Moreover, as Calkins also pointed out, Ys failed to attract most working-class and foreign-born men. He found that of the 3,547 members of Chicago's Central YMCA in 1900, 2,517 worked in mercantile pursuits, 557 in professions, 402 in skilled labor, and only 71 in unskilled jobs. In addition, though 58 percent of all Chicago wage earners were foreign-born in 1900, only about 23 percent of Chicago's YMCA members were foreign-born or native-born of foreign parents.[50] The YMCA and its imitators thus remained as middle-class bachelor organizations well into the twentieth century.

The Company of Women

Though they led their lives in the mostly homosocial male environments of commercial establishments (saloons, pool halls, ballparks) and social organizations (gangs, clubs, fraternal associations), bachelors certainly did not and could not ignore women. Those living with kin inevitably interacted with female relatives. As chapter 3 noted, a number of bachelors lived with and helped support widowed mothers. Others shared residential space with unmarried (and sometimes married) sisters and engaged in forms of mutual exchange, such as sharing housing costs, doing favors for each other, or providing emotional support. More importantly, however, those bachelors—indeed probably the majority—who viewed their unmarried condition as temporary sought the companionship of "outside" women, individuals who could serve as potential marriage partners or sex objects—or both.

The growing numbers of independent or semi-independent unmarried people, both men and women, in American cities at the end of the nineteenth century undermined traditional courting rituals and chaperonage (see chapter 2). At the same time, the growth of commercial amusements and public leisure space in the cities expanded the possibilities of indiscriminate assemblies and contact between strangers that enhanced opportunities for heterosocial interaction. The institution of dating had not yet formally developed to regulate these contacts, and thus a bachelor's social life had a somewhat disparate quality.[51] Assessing the leisure time of young men in the city, reformer Raymond Calkins observed,

> (T)he necessity for some sort of wholesome social opportunity becomes very apparent. Thousands of [unmarried men] are condemned to the boarding-house in the evening, for they will not (patronize) religious institutions, nor can they afford the better class of amusements. Many walk the streets; many patronize cheap amusements; many have little sociables at home; some belong to bicycle clubs; some to lodges; some take advantage of what is offered in night schools and free lectures.[52]

Many bachelors did find wholesome entertainment in the company of a respectable female companion. As author Albert Payson Terhune recollected from his bachelor days when he worked as a *New York Post* reporter, "In the mid-1890s, one could take a girl to the theater and to supper afterward—I am speaking of The Kind of Girl One Marries—for incredibly little money. Theater seats were $1.50 each. A cab could be chartered for the evening, by arrangement for $3.00. Another $3.00 bought a big bunch of violets. At Delmonico's, a delicious after-theater supper for two came well under $5.00, including the tip."[53] The nearly $15 that Terhune might have spent in one evening on a female companion, however, represented a week's earnings to many bachelors, and as the title of a Chicago *Tribune* article announced: "Man Getting Eighteen Dollars a Week Dares Not Fall in Love." The writer grumbled that a young man "could not even buy a young lady an ice cream cone," not to mention theater and dinner.[54] Less expensive were the kinds of experiences recalled by New York investment banker and insurance agent Roger Babson, who wrote, "I usually went around with only one girl at a time. . . . Skating, sliding, and sleigh-riding provided good times in winter; while hayrack rides, swimming, and picnics were the rule in summer."[55]

Terhune and undoubtedly many other bachelors quickly distinguished between two kinds of women, the reputable and the not-so-reputable. The former type could not be coaxed into drinking a bottle of wine with supper, nor could she be taken to a dance hall. The latter type offered other possibilities. As Terhune observed, "If it were a matter of The Kind of Girl One Doesn't Marry, a marvelous after-theater supper at Jack's or at Burn's could be bought for incredibly little. Canvas-back ducks . . . cost only $3.00; and Jack's chef knew how to cook them. Champagne was only $3.50 a quart—champagne of any of a half dozen good brands. . . ."[56] Increasingly as the twentieth century dawned and passed, this type of female, "The Kind of Girl One Doesn't Marry," occupied the social life of bachelors, even outnumbering or becoming confounded with the formerly respectable "Kind of Girl One Marries." Historians of amusement parks, dance halls, and cabarets have shown that by 1910 these establishments were attracting large numbers of unescorted women out on the town with only the desire to have fun and willing to be picked up by an acceptable man. Some of these women became "charity girls," individuals who offered themselves, including sexual favors, to strangers in return for gifts, attention, or simple pleasure.[57]

These women often forced bachelors to balance between temptation and the ultimate consequence of indulgence: marriage. Several autobiographers noted that as much as they relished going out with women they picked up, they also learned to avoid committing themselves because they believed marriage would hamper their career. Abe Hollandersky, an aspiring boxer, told of how he believed a wife would be dangerous to his ambitions and that his closest call occurred when he almost let himself submit to a beautiful woman he had briefly known. "Of course I got out of the clinch with pretty Carlotta Puertos," he wrote, "but not without damage to myself, as I learned the next morning when I started for Panama. Senorita Puertos informed the whole island that I had promised to marry her after the fight."[58] Vaudevillian George Jessel reported that he was constantly having crushes on women he picked up and that only timely intervention by his friend, Eddie Cantor, saved him. Jessel remembered, "The elder and wiser Cantor told me, 'Forget about such things; only your career is worthwhile. In our work you will meet the most beautiful women in the world. We must think only of getting an act by ourselves that will get us in a Broadway show.'"[59]

In addition to indulging charity girls, whose provision of sexual favors was casual and occasional, bachelors also patronized professional prostitutes. From the late-eighteenth century onward, American cities sustained a sexual service establishment that catered to a market consisting primarily of single men. By the end of the nineteenth century, as a growing web of commercial amusements spread across the urban landscape, sexuality accompanied it, whether in the form of the imaginary titillation of erotic literature, picture cards, and theater or the direct access to prostitutes on the streets and in dance halls and brothels.[60] By the turn of the century, most Americans assumed that prostitution was a common part of urban life, but from there the assumption forked. One group, the segregationists, were willing to tolerate the carnal vice, allowing brothels and other institutions of commercialized sex to concentrate in redlight districts that could be avoided or frequented according to taste.[61] A more moralistic contingent, the abolitionists, waged fervent campaigns to eliminate the "social evil" altogether, seeing it as disruptive to community and family life, a threat to public and individual health, a means to enslave and debauch innocent young women, and a corrupter of men.[62]

Though most historians would agree that prostitution pervaded American cities at the turn of the century,[63] the sparseness of the historical record prevents an analysis of the men who purchased the sexual labor of prostitutes. Scholars, as well as contemporaries, have concluded that the most likely customers of prostitutes and brothels were transient, unattached men.[64] These individuals allegedly had the most lascivious appetites and, because they lacked family restraints (see chapter 4) were most susceptible to sexual temptations. Homer Croy was one such man, who recalled in his autobiography, "One night, instead of going directly home, I turned out of my regular course and into a very gay street. The door of each house was set back into a kind of vestibule; inside was a doorbell button. The window curtains were closely drawn, but from inside came the sound of music and laughter. Now and then a door would open and a man would come out and dart hurriedly away. I longed with all my soul to go in and be a part of this gaiety and laughter. But my conscience would not let me."[65] The simple availability of such temptation to bachelors like Croy roused widespread moralistic fears. Thus an article in *Forum* magazine in 1888 claimed that "men's matrimonial discouragements and bachelor compensations are many; they can have more pleasures outside marriage; they are almost chartered libertines, so lax is sentiment."[66]

As Croy's recollection reveals, few men ever explicitly admitted to hiring a prostitute, though some did indirectly confess to such activity when they alluded to their attending a house or district of ill repute in order to satisfy their curiosity. George Jessel, for example, described visiting a red light district and brothel in New Orleans in 1910 when he was a

young bachelor working in an acting troupe. "I had been looking forward," he recalled, "to this first visit to the famous old
Southern city. Not only was the weather balmy, the food different, but I was to see for the first time in my life, the famous
'over the tracks.' New Orleans at that time had the largest
sporting-house district of any city in the world. There were
hundreds of cribs as well as huge palaces, such as Lulu White's
and Lesse Arlington's, with mirrored bedrooms and girls from
all over the world." Jessel stopped short of relating what he
did in such an establishment, but he did express some empathy
for the women who enlisted into "the life." During the year
before his visit to New Orleans, Jessel wrote in his autobiography, "I had been reading and found myself seriously interested
in how girls came to that sort of life. Each one, I thought,
would have a sad story of white slavery and tear-jerking experiences. These soiled madonnas were, however, the happiest
group of women I have ever met."[67]

In a few cities, segregationists convinced the local government to experiment with legalizing and regulating prostitution
within special districts, notably New Orleans's Storyville and
San Francisco's Barbary Coast. Sentiment for regulating prostitution existed in San Francisco well before the twentieth century and had focused chiefly on the interaction between prostitutes and the city's large bachelor population. In the early
1900s, Dr. Julius Rosenstirn, one of San Francisco's leading
proponents of legalized prostitution, asserted that prostitution
was a necessary evil that served the useful purpose of allowing
unmarried men to satisfy their sexual desires. Rosenstirn believed that even though many of these men could not afford to
marry, they still deserved access to sexual pleasure. He therefore lobbied the city council to provide for licensing and
strictly regulating prostitution and to establish a municipal venereal disease clinic.[68]

The crusade by Rosenstirn and his allies reached fruition in
1911 with a city ordinance that required all prostitutes to con-
fine themselves to a designated district in the city's China-

FIGURE 5.3. Bachelors seeking sexual adventure often patronized "tenderloin" districts, where prostitution, gambling, and other vices received unofficial, and sometimes official, sanction from city officials. The attractions of New Orleans's Storyville district, the city's "official" vice district between 1897 and 1917, were described in Blue Books that listed prostitutes by name, address, and special features such as physical characteristics and ethnicity. Though undoubtedly used by married as well as unmarried men, the Blue Books formed a special genre of bachelor literature. (Historic New Orleans Collections)

town—the so-called Barbary Coast—and to submit at least twice every year to a medical examination carried out by a city-appointed physician. Any woman found to be free of venereal disease received a booklet containing her photograph and record of her medical examinations. She was required to produce this booklet on demand by a police officer. If a medical check found her to be diseased, she had to surrender her booklet and would receive free medical treatment until cured, at which time the authorities would return her booklet.[69]

This de facto licensing seemed to work well at first but then encountered determined opposition from William Randolph Hearst's *San Francisco Examiner* and from prohibitionist clergymen, doctors, and businessmen. Mayor James Rolph, Jr., was able to draw on these forces in his effort to withdraw police cooperation with the clinic in 1913, thereby canceling enforcement of the quasi licensing. The next year the California legislature passed the Redlight Abatement Law, making brothels a public nuisance and formally ending the San Francisco licensing experiment. Then, early in 1917, police blockaded the Barbary Coast and closed down its remaining dance halls, prostitution cribs, and parlor houses. Abolition had unanticipated consequences, however. After 1913, San Francisco's prostitutes began haunting a greater variety of locations, hoping that their dispersion away from the Barbary Coast and other known zones of vice would make them less visible to the police.[70]

It appears that by the early twentieth century, the ascendancy of prohibitionists over segregationists caused brothels as the locus of prostitution to decline. The laws and raids did not eradicate the oldest profession, however. Instead, prostitutes began working more frequently out of boardinghouses and hotels where they could more directly service their bachelor clientele, either meeting them there without prelude or inviting them there from the dance halls, cabarets, and streets. Historian Timothy Gilfoyle has cited statistics from New York City showing that while 25 percent of the city's prostitutes operated outside of brothels in the 1870s, more than 85 percent did so by the 1910s.[71] Albert Wolfe, in his study of Boston lodging houses, claimed that the public knew altogether too little about the prostitution rampant in the lodging houses. "It seems safe to say," he maintained, "that there are few lodging houses which may not at some time come under moral suspicion."[72] Wolfe described two types of lodging-house keepers, both of whom usually were women: those who operated a brothel in the guise of a lodging house; and, more frequently, those who tacitly consented to the use of rooms for the purposes of prostitution.[73] Nevertheless, the incidence of prostitution itself likely declined in the half century after the 1920s. Though roadhouses, the streets, and private rooms continued to sustain commercial sexual activity, the success of police crackdowns, the reduction of immigration, and, most of all, the decrease in the proportions of unmarried men diminished the demand for prostitutes in cities across the country.[74]

In the Lap of the Law

As pointed out in chapter 1, American society had aimed a legal finger at bachelors since the earliest days of the republic. Fearing the potentially destructive effects of their "rogue elephants," communities had attempted to regulate both the behavior of their unmarried men and the operations of those institutions that bachelors presumably most frequented. Moreover, states and localities sought to encourage "the single to become whole" by legislating inducements to marry and penalties for evading matrimony. Consequently, the opportunities for a bachelor to directly confront the criminal and civil legal systems multiplied, and court dockets filled with cases involving men whose unmarried status somehow related to their alleged offense. Though not always, a bachelor's uncomfortable position in the lap of the law often resulted from his relationship with a woman.

Men in general often found it difficult to abide by society's ideals for orderly and moral conduct. In any city, the most common arrests were for drunkenness, vagrancy, and disorderly or suspicious behavior, and men constituted the overwhelming majority of those who ran afoul of the laws defining these offenses. For example, in Boston, where there was one arrest for every 496 local inhabitants in 1891, 83 percent of all persons arrested were males.[75] In 1900, 87 percent of all those arrested were males, and in 1910 the proportion reached 90 percent.[76] As one would expect, young men comprised the largest component of males arrested; a quarter of the males arrested in Boston in 1900 and 1901 were between the ages of fifteen and twenty-five, and undoubtedly most of them were unmarried. More importantly, bachelors dominated the cohorts of males who allegedly offended public order. In an attempt to understand the sources of public drunkenness, Stephen O'Meara, the Boston police commissioner, undertook a study of those arrested for drunkenness on Saturday, March 27, 1910, the day of that year boasting the largest number of apprehensions for that crime. Of the 327 persons arrested for drunkenness that Saturday, 310 were male, but 218, or nearly 70 percent, of those men were unmarried, almost all of them aged twenty-one or older.[77] Similar studies in other cities would likely have produced the same outcome.

Indirect evidence suggests that bachelors numbered heavily among violators of other public codes of criminal conduct. In San Francisco, a city with extraordinarily high proportions of men who were single, arrests for vagrancy climbed from 1,407 in 1890 to 3,481 in 1910, and those for disorderly conduct rose from 191 in 1890 to 1,306 in 1920. Though arrests for larceny tripled during the same twenty-year period, those for crimes against person, such as assault and battery, and crimes against property, such as burglary and robbery, remained constant.[78] In Boston between 1890 and 1910, males between ages fifteen and twenty, most of whom presumably were unmarried, continued to account for relatively high proportions of perpetrators of crimes against person and property as well as against public order. In 1890, for example, young males constituted over 40 percent of arrests of adult men for such offenses.[79]

Records on bachelors' criminal misbehavior are somewhat obscure, but their confrontations with societal norms emerge more visibly in civil cases. In these instances, courts often reckoned marital status—or, more accurately, lack thereof—as an exacerbating factor, especially when a case involved a romantic relationship with a woman. Chapter 1 of this book outlines some of the legal distinctions that courts and legislative bodies applied to single men in the period before the late nineteenth century. In those early years, communities endeavored to uphold the patriarchal family and encourage marriage by penalizing those who incorrigibly remained unmarried and by offering inducements to change the minds of those hesitant about undertaking the matrimonial plunge. Most of the statutes and prosecutions pertained to land holding and sexual behavior. As late as the 1850s, for example, federal land law for Oregon Territory declaimed that a single man was entitled to but half the amount of public land purchase that a man and wife could claim. And once a man had married, the law made it very difficult for him to untie the knot. An early commentator on domestic law echoed social values in 1852 when he wrote, "Marriage is in every view the most important institution of human society, it involved the most valued interests of every class; awakens the thoughts and engages the care of nearly every individual; and how it may be entered into, or how dissolved, or what is the collateral effect of a dissolution, is a matter of almost constant legal inquiry and litigation."[80]

By the mid- and late-nineteenth century, fears over moral excess and threats to social cohesion (resulting from rapid social and economic change), fostered a growing concern over threats to the orthodox republican family. As a result, the state increasingly intruded into formerly private domestic matters, and the law, rather than clergy or community, became a principle instrument for settling family conflicts, determining an in-

dividual's legal status, and protecting patriarchal authority. To
be sure, most families evaded contact with the legal system; for
the most part, when judges intervened into the internal work-
ings of a family, they focused on selected features of domestic
relations, usually disputes over property or custody arising
from a family member's death.

But also, courts increasingly concerned themselves with conflicts occurring outside of but closely related to family life,
most particularly the formal rituals that preceded and supposedly led to the creation of family: that is, the implicit or
explicit exchange of matrimonial pledges. Here is where bachelors most frequently fell into a web of legal perplexity. What
obligations did a man incur when he pursued and won a
woman's affections? What, if anything, did he owe her if, having won her devotion, he were to withdraw his attention and
presumed pledge of marriage? Did a man who successfully
wooed a woman enter into a tacit but powerful contractual
relationship with her that could not be broken without recompense? These questions and others related to them brought
many a bachelor into court during the late nineteenth century,
with far-reaching consequences for the battle of the sexes.

A Chicago bachelor named Darius Greenup confronted the
severity of these questions when in 1846 the Illinois Supreme
Court rejected his explanation that his estranged lover, Nancy
Stoker, had misconstrued his attentions. He had never meant
Miss Stoker to interpret his advances as representing an intention to marry her, Greenup argued; he merely wished to express his admiration for her. The judge disagreed and awarded
the jilted complainant monetary damages. The judge also plied
Darius Greenup with a lesson in nuptial etiquette, admonish-
ing him that in "the common language of the country, to court
or to pay attention to a lady are synonymous. The latter is but
a method slightly more refined and genteel of expressing the
same thing."[81] A bachelor, so it seemed, whose words and attentions appeared to take advantage of a woman while he
stubbornly persevered in defending his unmarried status could

not escape judicial as well as moral liability if the alienated maiden should complain. As a result, throughout the nineteenth century, courts manifested a consistent willingness to intervene into the private relationships between lovers on the assumption that a jilted lover had as much right to damages under breach of contract as did a merchant who broke a contract to purchase or deliver merchandise.

Before the nineteenth century, most judges had applied a *caveat emptor* principle to courtship. That is, they concluded that the parties to a romantic or premarital relationship entered their attachment out of mutual consent and therefore were to suffer the consequences of their own decisions if the romance soured. As the case of *Greenup v. Stoker* illustrates, however, courts soon began to sustain and protect the moral position of women, treating breach of promise as a violation against female purity, and ascribing, in the words of legal scholar Michael Grossberg, to the "Victorian belief in women as victims of the uncontrollable passions of men."[82] Judges also allowed such breaches to be considered as torts, subject to awards for damages. Thus, in an 1880 Michigan court ruling, a man named Bennett had to compensate Mary Beam for recanting on his pledge to wed her as soon as he had completed building some buggies. For what Beam claimed was a hypocritical seduction, Bennett received a lecture from the judge:

> In many cases, the loss sustained for a breach of the agreement to marry may be but slight indeed; but never can this be the case where the life-long blight which seduction entails enters the case. Respectable society inflicts upon the unfortunate female a severe punishment for her too confiding indiscretion, and which the marriage would largely if not wholly removed her from. The fact of seduction should therefore go a great way in fixing the damages, as in no other way could amends be made to the plaintiff for the injury she sustained, or the defendant properly punished for his aggravated offence."[83]

Only very young men, usually those under the age of twenty-one, received exemption from these responsibilities, with judges allowing minors to reconsider their youthful indiscretions.[84]

Suits claiming breach of promise targeted many a bachelor during the nineteenth century. Ironically, in settling these cases, courts simultaneously punished male suitors for their insolence toward women while at the same time expressing less concern about a man's unmarried status than a woman's. This split attitude revealed itself as early as 1818 in *Wightman v. Coates*, a landmark case that established breach of promise as actionable under both contract and tort law. In this case, which reached the Massachusetts Supreme Court, Maria Wightman, frustrated by a long engagement, charged Joshua Coates with refusing to honor his marriage promise. Coates denied that he ever asked Wightman for her hand, but Wightman carried the day by producing love letters that convinced the court that her claim was legitimate. But also, in awarding damages to Wightman, Chief Judge Isaac Parker specified a gender distinction that placed bachelors in a precarious position. "When the female is the injured party," Parker wrote, "there is generally more reason for a resort to the law than when the man is the sufferer. . . . A deserted female, whose prospects in life may be materially affected by the treachery of the man to whom she had pledged her vows, will always receive from a jury the attention which her situation requires. . . ."[85] By implication, according to Judge Parker, a jilted man needed no recompense because he was more marriageable—that is, he still had better prospects of future marriage—than a jilted woman, whose continued unmarried state would be more a cause of suffering.

In addition to their vulnerability to breach-of-promise suits, bachelors (and married men as well) faced more serious prosecution when charged with the offense of seduction. Breach of promise involved civil action; seduction could be criminal. Thus, according to Section 268 of the California Penal Code, which presumably was representative of most states, "Every person who, under a promise of marriage, seduces and has sexual intercourse with an unmarried female of previous chaste character, is punishable by imprisonment in the state prison for not more than five years, or by a fine of not more than five thousand dollars, or by both. . . ."[86] Like breach-of-promise settlements, however, decisions in seduction cases also devolved from a need, expressed by the court, to protect women from the designs of men. As a Michigan judge observed with regard to the intentions of seduction laws, "[W)henever it shall be true of any country that the women as a general fact are not chaste, the foundations of civil society will be broken up."[87]

The only consolation a bachelor might have had was that a married man charged with seduction could incur greater wrath from the court. Judges articulated this wrath in two ways. First, as the Massachusetts Supreme Court determined in a 1911 judgment, a married man faced double indictment. In this case, a married man named Morris Rosenthal appealed his guilty verdict, claiming that his convictions for both the crime of abduction of a young woman for the purpose of unlawful sexual intercourse and the offense of adultery were patently and constitutionally unfair because an unmarried seducer could never be found guilty of the second offense. The court denied his appeal.[88] Second, as the Virginia Supreme Court asserted in a similar case, a married man deserved heavier penalty for seduction because he had betrayed more critical obligations than an unmarried seducer might betray. According to the Virginia court,

> If there can be degrees in a crime so shocking in its consequences as the seduction of an innocent woman, the greater guilt would seem to attach to the married man rather than to the unmarried man. His age, his experience, the duty he owes to his wife, all conspire to darken the offense, and he is unable to make reparation by marriage, as an unmarried man may do. From its inception, his effort to win the affection of a woman other than his wife is criminal and infamous. Of necessity, therefore, it is as far

as possible concealed from every eye, and if courts and juries are required to follow the "trail of the serpent" throughout his dark and devious course, truly the path of the seducer would be made easy.[89]

By the late nineteenth century, courts began to modify and moderate their approach to breach-of-promise cases. Lawyers had increasingly objected to the harsh settlements of these cases, especially to the provisions that excused a defendant bachelor from the court's wrath only if such defendant married the offended party. Such a resolution, the lawyers complained, demeaned rather than consecrated marriage and threatened the family solidarity that courts generally wished to strengthen. Treating a marital promise as a contractual and tort matter, they said, commercialized family life. An aptly named legal writer, George Lawyer, contended in 1894, "The maintenance of [judgments against those who jilted potential spouses] for the breach of the marriage contract so belittles and degrades the relation itself that the public is coming to look upon it as a matter of business alone. . . . The divine purpose is destroyed."[90] Fearing the consequences of the already rising divorce rate, experts on marriage urged, and judges seemed at least to begin to agree, that in order to ensure successful marriages courtship should be considered experimental, not contractually binding, and that the incompatibility of lovers, signified by broken engagements and reneged marital promises, should be the purview of agencies other than the courts.[91]

As a consequence, the judicial system began yielding bachelors some slack in their amatory behavior. According to Michael Grossberg, judges aided defendants by trying to distinguish between consequential espousals and mere courtship, insisting that a marital pledge required clear proof. Thus, in 1872, the Illinois Supreme Court remanded back to a lower court a case in which a woman's claim to breach of promise consisted only of her own statements to her sister. In this instance, the court allowed that if such flimsy evidence could be

made grounds for damages, "it would be dangerous for an unmarried man to pay attention to any unmarried woman."[92]
Fourteen years later, the Michigan Supreme Court affirmed this
opinion when it rejected a woman's statements to her friends
as admissible evidence of an alleged suitor's marital pledge. Re-
iterating the Illinois judge's opinion, the Michigan jurist stated,
"The plaintiff . . . has certain advantages . . . of fabricating by
her acts and declarations, without [the defendant's] consent of
knowledge, evidence to make a case against him. It would
place almost every man at the mercy of an evilly disposed and
designing woman. . . ."[93] From this time forward, courts continued to rule that evidence such as wedding preparations and
statements from the plaintiff's family could not alone constitute proof of a defendant's promise to marry. At the same time,
Grossberg has added, judges made damage awards in successful breach-of-promise suits based on actual, rather than imagined, injuries.[94] Finally, judges released male defendants from
liability for damages in breach-of-promise cases when it could
be proved that the female plaintiff had had sexual relations
with another man prior to the defendant's relationship with
her.[95]

In this rethinking of what to do when a party to a proposed
or implied marriage backed out, bachelors who wished to remain unmarried benefited because courts made prosecution of
them more difficult than it previously had been. Moreover, as
Grossberg has suggested, the dwindling support for a woman's
right to be compensated for breach of nuptial promise may
also have reflected the emerging status of women in the public
sphere. That is, as women gained greater social freedom and
legal rights in the marketplace, Grossberg asserts, "loss of an
initial suitor posed less of a threat to her future happiness than
it might have earlier in the nineteenth century."[96] Women's special legal protection diminished and so did their favorable position in breach-of-promise cases.

The new attitude, however, may also have simply reflected
recognition of the growing numbers of bachelors in American
society and represented the intentions of some reformers to

make marriage a more protected institution out of fear that marriage had become not only more rigidly contractual but also less common. An understanding of this reversion requires a return to legal scholar Milton Regan's distinction between *status* and *acontextualism* introduced in chapter 3. According to Regan, family law in the early and mid-nineteenth century had reinforced notions of status, meaning that individuals received their identity from the interdependent roles assigned to them in society. These roles carried legal responsibilities as well as hierarchical position, and pertained to the family as well as to society. Thus the status of father, son, brother, and so on carried prescribed social expectations reinforced by family law. The rise of what Regan calls modernism included a revolt against what were deemed to be restrictive roles of family law and replaced them with notions of individual self-realization. The resulting acontextual self could claim legal protection through provisions of contract law.[97]

In the 1880s, jurists, apparently fearful of rising individualism and its effects on family cohesion, began to restore attention to the importance of status. The U.S. Supreme Court expressed such sentiment when it asserted in 1888 that "[m]arriage is more than a mere contract. The consent of the parties is of course essential, but when the contract to marry is executed by the marriage, a relation is created between the parties which they cannot change."[98] A new edition of the standard text on marriage law voiced further sentiments for retaining status roles, contending that "marriage confers on the husband the right to companionship and services of a wife" and a wife could expect her husband "to protect and support her while in the substantial discharge of her duties."[99] Bachelors, in this light, evaded status-based responsibilities, and therefore marriage had to be protected from the attitudes and lifestyles inherent in their unattached condition.

The influence of bachelors in loosening the constraints of courtship by separating it from presumptions of marriage did not subside as time passed. Nor did the ire of disappointed objects of bachelor attentions. Breach-of-promise suits continued to clog court dockets well into the twentieth century. In several instances, bachelors learned, or were advised, how to protect themselves from such litigation. In 1925, for example, one writer noted that because of the "recent epidemic" of breach-of-promise suits, "many lawyers are advising their wealthy clients to use the telephone instead of the pen, as the bases of most of these suits is the ardent love letters written between the two parties."[100] Only in the 1930s did a few states begin to diminish the incidence of such suits by passing what were called heart balm statutes, which essentially eliminated the right to bring breach-of-promise suits. Nevertheless, lawyers still were able to find ways to initiate litigation on behalf of injured clients, keeping bachelors under the scrutiny of legal vigilance.[101]

In their subculture of institutions, organizations, and interpersonal associations, bachelors in the late nineteenth century and early twentieth occupied an anomalous position between the public sphere of the street and the marketplace on one hand and the private sphere of personal and familial life on the other. Even among those many bachelors who lived with kin, a bachelor's life was less than full in both spheres. In the public sphere, single men encountered discrimination, legal anomalies, and other disadvantages resulting from their condition. In the private sphere, their lives were, in the minds of the prevailing culture, incomplete because bachelors had failed to form a family of procreation. But also, bachelors, more than married people, blended the two spheres by making their public, non-familial peer group and other associations into quasi families and by carrying on their personal affairs in mostly public or semipublic places such as boardinghouses, saloons, the streets, clubhouses, and the like. Without a home that they themselves headed and could call their own, bachelors created a world for themselves that counteracted the potentialities for social isolation. They also attracted the attention of the creators of popular culture, the topic of the next chapter.

The Popular Culture
of Bachelorhood

JACK BLACK was the kind of bachelor that turn-of-the-century American society feared the most. Jack was born in the 1870s, and his mother died when he was a child, leaving him in the tutelage of his scoundrel father and without the presumably moderating influence of female nurture. He grew up fast, roaming the countryside with his father, and never married. Before he finally reformed when he was about fifty, he had lived a full and notorious career as a tramp and professional criminal. He drifted from one city to another, served several prison sentences, and frequented the deviant underworld of low-life bars, disreputable boardinghouses, and cheap playhouses.

As a young adult living in Kansas City in the 1890s, Black entered the bachelor subculture when he shared quarters with his father in a hotel filled with single men. At first, Black later recalled, "everything was new and strange to me. Men coming and going all day, eating and drinking. Everything was noise and bustle, and it took me a few days to get used to this new life." But then, young Jack began not only to partake of the environment of bachelor subculture but also to consume the products and literature that sustained that subculture. He recalled, "I found lots of papers lying around — some cheap novels, *Police Gazettes*, etc. — and I read them all, everything I could get hold of." And in this way, Jack learned what it meant to be a bachelor.[1]

In 1922, a few years before Jack Black penned his autobiography, humorist George Ade noted how American media and consumerism seemed to "aid and abet the bachelors" when he wrote,

Newspapers, magazines, picture plays, novels, current anec-
dotes — all have fallen into the easy habit of making it appear
that the bachelor is a devil of a fellow; that the spirit of youth
abides with him after it has deserted the stoop-shouldered [mar-
ried] slave commonly depicted as mowing lawns and feeding fur-
naces. The bachelor, as an individual, may sell very low in his
immediate precinct; but the bachelor, as a type, has become fic-
tionalized into a fascinating combination of Romeo and Mephis-
topheles.[2]

Ade used his verbal acrobatics to satirize both marriage
and bachelorhood, but like Jack Black he had come to recognize that American entrepreneurs had awakened to the existence of the manifold unmarried men in the urban population. The purveyors of popular culture in the late-nineteenth
and early-twentieth-century city not only commented upon
the bachelor subgroups in their midst but also courted their
patronage by plying them with sympathetic and/or particularly appealing features as a means to tempt them to patronize their newspapers, magazines, plays, and other products
and services.

This chapter uses two types of representative popular publications to illuminate the bachelor subculture that Jack Black
and George Ade experienced, and to suggest means by which a
variety of entrepreneurs attempted to respond to an apparently
lucrative market for goods and services created by the burgeoning numbers of bachelors. The following analysis features
The National Police Gazette, which for half a century served
not only as one of the nation's most popular and unique journals published exclusively for men but also functioned as the
unofficial scripture of the bachelor subculture. Secondarily, I
discuss two other types of publications, one a journal and the
other a literary genre, both of which directed their content almost exclusively at unmarried men.

A PINK PERIODICAL OF SENSATION AND SPORTS

The National Police Gazette could arguably proclaim to have been one of the country's most sensational — and influential — journals of the late nineteenth century and early twentieth. By the 1880s and 1890s, just a few decades after its founding, the *Police Gazette's* subscriptions exceeded 150,000, and a few special issues required printings of 400,000. More importantly, the *Police Gazette's* regular readership included an estimated half million or more men. On sale at most urban newsstands and available to be read gratis in almost every barbershop, hotel, pool hall, fire company, and street-corner saloon, each issue passed through dozens of hands, virtually all of them male.[3] *The National Police Gazette* appealed to such a large number of men because it catered to all of the idiosyncracies of working-class and middle-class male culture and made special overtures to the bachelor subculture.[4]

The journal itself derived from two types of antecedents: the "sporting press" that began to flourish in major cities during the 1830s and 1840s and that catered to the sporting male culture discussed in chapter 1, and the cheap paperback publications sold by so-called sex and crime sensation mongers that spread throughout the country in the 1850s and 1860s. (To a lesser but still important extent, it also received a boost from the so-called penny press publications of lurid adventure accounts, also beginning in the antebellum era.)

The sporting press dates its origin to December of 1831, when William Trotter Porter, a country journalist who left Vermont to seek his fortune in New York City, began publication of the *Spirit of the Times*, a newspaper dedicated to reporting on sports such as horse racing, cricket, rowing, foot racing, yachting, and later, but especially, baseball. During the 1840s, a panoply of similar publications entered the same market as Porter's *Spirit*, including Thaddeus W. Meighan's *The Rake*, George Woolbridge's *The Whip*, and *The Flash*, jointly operated by Charles G. Scott, John Vanderwater, and William Snelling.[5] Though a few of the early sporting journals, such as *Billiard Cue* and *Chess Monthly*, continued to focus on a specific segment of competitive activity, by the 1860s several of the sporting press publications were also giving extensive coverage to salacious new stories involving crime and sex. Culling information from newspaper reports and criminal trials around the country, these journals often added titillating woodcut engravings to provide illustrated drama to the sensationalism. Publishers justified this coverage by expressing sentiments of moral righteousness and by posing as crusaders against crime. Thus *The Rake's* editor could claim, at the same time that he published sensational stories, that "We loathe, detest, abhor, condemn, and abjure licentiousness in every form and shape." Nevertheless, by presenting such lurid accounts, the sporting press boosted sales and succeeded in glamorizing the lewd and the lurid in daily life.[6]

No journal succeeded in purveying the lure of lubricity more shamelessly than did *The National Police Gazette*. George Wilkes, a journalist already steeped in sensational publications, and Enoch Camp, a New York lawyer, founded *The National Police Gazette* in 1845. Patterning their medium after British police bulletins, Wilkes and Camp claimed that they published their journal with the intention to help the police (whose functions and professionalism were only just developing in the mid-nineteenth century) to recognize actual or likely criminals and to facilitate the arrest of perpetrators and the prevention of crime. (With as yet no provisions for detecting wrongdoers, victims and/or witnesses had to identify an offender in order for the police to make an arrest.) Early issues of the *Police Gazette* presented detailed narratives of malfeasance and misbehavior, including the means by which miscreants were apprehended and brought to justice, plus information about alleged offenders, including their names, aliases, physical descriptions, career histories, places of residence, and current movements. Weekly issues of the newspaper also printed notices listing

stolen property along with advertisements for patent medicines, sporting goods, and insurance. Distributed by mail nationally, Wilkes and Camp claimed a circulation of forty thousand by 1850.[7] Camp retired shortly thereafter, leaving Wilkes
as full owner.

In 1856, Wilkes bought Porter's *Spirit of the Times*, renam-
ing it *Wilkes's Spirit of the Times* and continuing to develop it
into the nation's premier sporting publication. At the same
time, he sold *The National Police Gazette* to George Washington Matsell. A former New York City police chief who at one
time had been the target of Wilkes's criticism for his laxity in
law enforcement, Matsell catered even more directly to the *Police Gazette's* male readership by expanding coverage of crime
and sex stories, and adding more racy woodcuts. The journal's
classified ad section also expanded, listing notices for products
such as photographic cards for gentlemen and nostrums to restore manhood. Matsell compiled his material from a corps of
correspondents scattered across the nation who sent in reports
of nefarious misdeeds and scandals, preferably those involving
a love triangle. But by the time the Civil War had ended, a host
of competing sensational newspapers had arisen and Matsell
found his operation losing money from declining subscriptions
and its costly commitment to extensive illustrations. So in
1866 he sold out to his engravers, and *The National Police
Gazette* entered a brief period of remission.[8]

A decade of doldrums ended in 1877 when Richard Kyle
Fox became publisher and self-styled proprietor of *The National Police Gazette*. A journalist who had begun his career in
Belfast, Ireland, Fox had arrived in New York in 1874 penni-
less but full of ideas and ambition. Hired by *The National Police Gazette* to sell advertisements, he succeeded so well that he
became business manager in 1875. Using borrowed funds, Fox
bought the paper two years later, hired a staff of experienced
writers, and offered reduced subscription rates to saloon
keepers, barbers, and hotel managers — places where male
readers would most likely pick up his publication. In 1878, he

FIGURE 6.1. A premier feature of both male culture and bachelor subculture, *The National Police Gazette* had a readership well beyond its subscription numbers. In saloons across the country, as this woodcut depicts, it was the most popular form of reading material and was passed from one reader to another. (Corbis-Bettmann)

expanded the weekly tabloid publication from eight to sixteen pages by increasing its coverage of sex and sin, and he differentiated his editions from competitors by printing his pages on pink paper. Fox also increased the number of illustrations, especially featuring buxom burlesque dancers and soubrettes (young female performers, usually of the vaudeville or burlesque stage) in revealing poses. In 1879, Fox assembled the nation's first full journalistic sports department and began extensive coverage of prize fighting contests, even though the sport remained illegal in many states. He also initiated the practice of publishing sports and entertainment gossip columns, and he used screaming headlines on every page.[9]

Fox's success was meteoric. He tripled the paper's circulation from what it had been under Matsell and constructed a new quarter-million-dollar headquarters for the journal in central Manhattan. By 1885 the publication was receiving one dollar per agate line from advertisers, the same price charged by such popular national organs as *Ladies Home Journal* and *Godey's Ladies Book*. By this time as well, Fox's trademark silk hat and Prince Albert coat had made him a celebrated personality on the streets of New York. Apparently obsessed with crude titillation, Fox started publishing other scandal sheets, including *Fox's Illustrated Weekly Doings*, begun in 1883 with the purpose of serving as "the spiciest dramatic and best story paper in America," and *Illustrated Day's Doings and Sporting World*, which he founded in 1885 and used as a vehicle to print horror stories of lynchings, tortures, assassinations, and bizarre tales such as that of a woman who gave birth in her coffin after she had been buried alive. No other Fox publication matched the success of *The National Police Gazette*, however; *Fox's Illustrated Weekly Doings* lasted only one year, and *Illustrated Day's Doings and Sporting World* survived for only five.[10]

Fox's *National Police Gazette* swiftly situated itself at the center of bachelor subculture. By the 1880s and 1890s, its exploitation of women and crime, luridly illustrated, attracted unmarried male readers who frequented the boardinghouses, saloons, and barbershops across the country. Writer and editor Franklin P. Adams recalled that "one of the first jokes I ever heard . . . was 'Seen the Police Gazette?' 'No, I shave myself.' " Adams found the explicit illustrations especially enticing. "I would gaze at a picture a long time. Usually it was a picture of a woman, or of many women. Sometimes they were pursuers, sometimes pursued. Occasionally somebody had a revolver. . . . But it was the ankles and legs that really got me. . . . And these pictures showed some women's skirts — thousands of skirts — in

abandoned disarray. Women were running, and were osten-
tatiously careless whether they displayed their legs almost to the
knee."[11] There were, then, no shortages of female skin and dam-
sels in distress.

The National Police Gazette offered a particular sort of vul-
garity, an illicitness that matched the bachelor's position at the
edge of acceptability but not quite beyond the pale and not too
iniquitous. In addition to the gory and distressing tales of murder and revenge, the low life described in *Police Gazette* pages
challenged Victorian propriety and represented a reality that
existed below — but not too far below — prevailing standards of
respectability. Fox and his staff seemed to take pleasure in
leading their readers slightly off the primrose path into a dusky
world where brutal, manly pursuits, such as dogfights, cock-
fights, and demonstrations of human strength or unusual skills
in water drinking and haircutting masqueraded as sport. The
denizens of this world, titillating characters such as Beefsteak
Mike, the champion opium smoker of Colorado, and Minerva,
the San Antonio, Texas, strongwoman who could catch balls
fired from a cannon, graced every issue. And the lingo of this
world, common slang terms such as "dizzy blond," "racket,"
(swindle), "fancy," (boxing aficionado), and "fly" (sporting
gentry), entered bachelor vernacular nationwide through the
pages of *The National Police Gazette* and its imitators.[12]

Times change, however, and popularity is fleeting. As in the
1860s, in the early 1900s *The National Police Gazette* became
a victim of its own success, and its dominance in providing
both scandal and sports news succumbed to a series of challenges. Seizing an opportunity to satisfy an ever more curious
public, enterprising publishers began printing daily tabloids
and confession magazines that exceeded *The National Police
Gazette* in disseminating news of sin, scandal, and sensation.
Capitalizing on new frankness in the discussion of sexual matters, Sunday newspaper magazines also began to print similar
sensational stories. As well, legitimate metropolitan daily
newspapers, such as those in the Hearst and Pulitzer empires,

began to include separate sports sections that surpassed Fox's ability to offer full coverage, especially because he had invested his major commitments to boxing, to the neglect of most other sports.[13]

Then, after the First World War, passage of the Eighteenth Amendment, which closed down saloons, undercut both subscriptions and readership. At the same time, many barbershops had to make themselves more respectable in order to reap business from flapper female patrons seeking to bob their hair, a development that also dented *Police Gazette* sales and subscriptions. The final blows came with Fox's death in 1922 and the bankruptcy sale of *The National Police Gazette* in 1932. Several publishers tried to sustain the publication into the 1940s, capitalizing on the revived interest in the manly sport of boxing, but the paper's old zest and semipornographic appeal belonged to a bygone age. With the rise of glossier publications, such as *Playboy* and *Sports Illustrated* by the mid-twentieth century, one of the nation's most unique journals had lost its notoriety.[14]

Prurience and Pugilism: Contents of *The National Police Gazette*

A survey of *The National Police Gazette's* contents from the beginning of Richard K. Fox's editorship until the early twentieth century illuminates the ways in which the journal both created and responded to the bachelor subculture. I do not claim that *The National Police Gazette* exclusively directed itself to, or was read only by, bachelors; certainly it attracted a married male as well as a single male readership. I do contend, however, that the *Police Gazette's* general characteristics and specific features, including its advertising as well as its text and illustrations, situated it squarely within bachelor society and reflected the influence that unmarried men wielded on popular consumer culture during the years in which their proportions in the total adult population peaked. Richard K. Fox and his writers manifested a peculiar combination of attitudes and values: intensely narrow and bigoted on the one hand, openly permissive and tolerant on the other. Sometimes falsely moralistic, at other times genuinely humanitarian, *The National Police Gazette* promulgated virtues that blended the modern with the antimodern, while at the same time serving up tasty morsels to satisfy bachelor male hunger for vicarious entertainment.

In the half century during which *The National Police Gazette* flourished under Fox's management, the journal evolved in several directions. Shortly after he assumed ownership, Fox expanded the publication from eight to sixteen pages and announced in his inaugural issue that he harbored a "determination to place the *Gazette* ahead of all competition as a live, illustrated journal of the sensational and striking occurrences of the day." And lest readers doubt the certitude and quality of his enterprise, Fox added, "With its numerous, able, and trustworthy correspondents in all parts of the country and full corps of artists and first-class talent, its readers may always rely upon the authenticity of its reports of events and the accuracy of its illustrations and portraits."[15]

In accordance with this pronouncement, during Fox's first years as publisher, the journal focused almost exclusively on crime. In 1878, for example, the only major sporting event on which the *Police Gazette* reported in any detail was Tom Hyer's defense of his heavyweight prizefighting championship. During that year, the crime stories fell into a small number of categories. Most numerous were love crimes, usually resulting from jealousy amid a romantic triangle and/or revenge for theft of a lover or from being jilted. Fox seemed particularly fascinated with gruesome killings, presenting a digest of these crimes in columns with such titles as "Homicide Harvest," "Murder Mania," and "Epidemic Evil." He also was quick to report homicides of police officers and murders of whites by African Americans — and the inevitable lynching that followed in retribution. Other news stories reported on such phenomena as the seduction of women and resultant loss of virtue, abortions gone wrong, notorious urban vice dens, and women who impersonated men.

At the outset of his reign as proprietor, Fox also announced that "All the striking criminal and sensational affairs of the day will be accurately illustrated . . . by a corps of artists of first-class talent, who will be detailed, as occasion may demand, to sketch such events at the scene of their occurrence."[16] In actuality, however, the illustrations chiefly enhanced the prurience of the prose. For example, in July of 1878 the story of a ferocious cat that invaded a bathhouse in St. Louis provided a *Police Gazette* artist with an opportunity to present a half-page illustration that featured bare-breasted young women cowering from the feline threat to their ablutions. Other illustrations depicted titillating scenes of abductions, with the victim's clothing falling off her shoulders or riding up her thigh, and the aftermath of a crime — usually a victim lying in a pool of blood while the alleged perpetrator stood nearby holding a dripping knife or smoking pistol.

Under Fox, the classified advertisement section, which financed the *Police Gazette* as much as, or more than, subscriptions did, developed slowly. During his years as business manager prior to ownership of the journal, Fox had solicited ads from a number of concerns who catered to a male and bachelor clientele: concert saloons, physicians and surgeons who specialized in male problems, playing card manufacturers, divorce lawyers, and foreign lotteries. During Fox's first years as publisher, the number of classified advertisements temporarily decreased, but their character both showed continuity with the past and signaled the direction of the future. A *Police Gazette* edition from May 1878, for example, included the usual ads from concert saloons and playing-card companies but also listings from manufacturers of tapeworm cures and other patent medicines plus several mail-order outfits promoting photographs of young actresses.

In 1879, Fox initiated a new and consequential direction for

BOUND AND CHLOROFORMED.

MRS. MACHA TIED DOWN, HER HUSBAND PUT TO SLEEP, AND THEIR HOME SET FIRE TO BY A DESPERATE GANG OF BURGLARS IN CHICAGO.

FIGURE 6.2. Sensational crime was the first and foremost staple of *Police Gazette* news. Practically every front page depicted some lurid, supposedly true, crime scene. In this typical cover from 1887, a highlighted and pretty woman (attired provocatively in only her nightgown and with bare feet) has been bound by burglars who have rendered her husband unconscious and set her house on fire while her dazed son looks on. (Collection of Howard P. Chudacoff)

The National Police Gazette. In addition to sensational crime news, the publication began extensive coverage of sporting events. Each weekly edition featured one major sports story, often of a prizefight but also including horse races, pedestrian races, Greco-Roman wrestling events, rowing and sculling competitions, a swimming tournament, and an exhibition of a brutal British sport called a kicking match. At the end of that year, Fox also instituted a weekly column titled "Sporting Notes," which presented tidbits of sporting news such as race results, challenges such as that by a strongman offering $125 to anyone who could beat him at pulling a heavy stone and throwing a hammer, and brief baseball news — the last type presented mainly in the summer. Illustrators depicted many of these events, especially the prizefights and foot races. Nevertheless, the *Police Gazette* still remained far from a sporting journal. Most pages dripped with tales of felonious behavior (including a significant number of crimes against whites perpetrated by blacks, Chinese, and Indians), titillating sexual misdeeds (including bigamy, seduction of innocent country boys and girls, and scandalous behavior by clergymen), and crimes of jealousy (including wives who killed their husbands' mistresses) along with numerous salacious drawings that sometimes included women's naked breasts.

In 1880, Fox developed the third major dimension of *The National Police Gazette* in addition to the illustrated crime and sports stories. In October of that year, the journal introduced a feature called "Footlight Favorites," a collection of portraits of young, coquettish females, often referred to as soubrettes. These illustrations usually depicted stage and burlesque performers in costume or high fashion. Though the "Footlight Favorites" occasionally revealed bare arms, ankles, and/or breast cleavage, the poses were formal and the drawing were considerably less risqué than those accompanying the crime stories. That same year, 1880, Fox also began publishing weekly picture portraits of prominent athletes, mostly prizefighters (including a dignified portrait of the African American, George

Taylor, "the colored light-weight champion pugilist") but also pedestrian champions, jockeys, and cyclists. Occasionally, a fighting dog, racing dog, or race horse would be pictured. One issue even presented the combative pose of Libbie Ross, the "champion female boxer of America," the caption to which announced, "There is probably no woman in the world who can compare with her in this line, and Miss Ross evidently is firm in this belief, and she boldly challenges anyone of her sex to try the issues as to her skill with the gloves."[17]

Throughout the 1880s, the *Police Gazette* adjusted but changed little. Fox began using larger typefaces and added more pictorial features, such as the weekly Gallery of Footlight Favorites, featuring individual soubrettes. Woodcut drawings continued to accompany sensational news and crime stories, but the bare-breasted maidens who occasionally had appeared in earlier issues disappeared as the treatment of female subjects became suggestive rather than explicit. Sporting events received somewhat increased coverage, in keeping with Fox's expressed belief that sports were becoming central to male interests. Fox also cultivated a fascination, perhaps even a fetishistic fascination, for reporting about females who behaved in "unwomanly" ways, such as a woman who created her own militia company, a female pastor who conducted baptisms, a lady bicyclist who raced against horses, and an occasional column of news tidbits titled "Woman's Pranks: Latest Eccentricities and Peccadilloes of the Fast and Loose of the Fair Sex." More intriguingly, the *Police Gazette* often—sometimes almost weekly—featured news stories about women who engaged in fistic battles with each other or who wreaked revenge on a man or men through physical violence that ranged from spankings to beatings to murder (see below).

Early in the 1880s, *The National Police Gazette* began its long and stormy relationship with one of the era's major male—and bachelor—heroes: prize-fighter John L. Sullivan. (For more on Sullivan's manly image, see chapter 7.) For reasons that remain unclear, Sullivan early in his career seems to

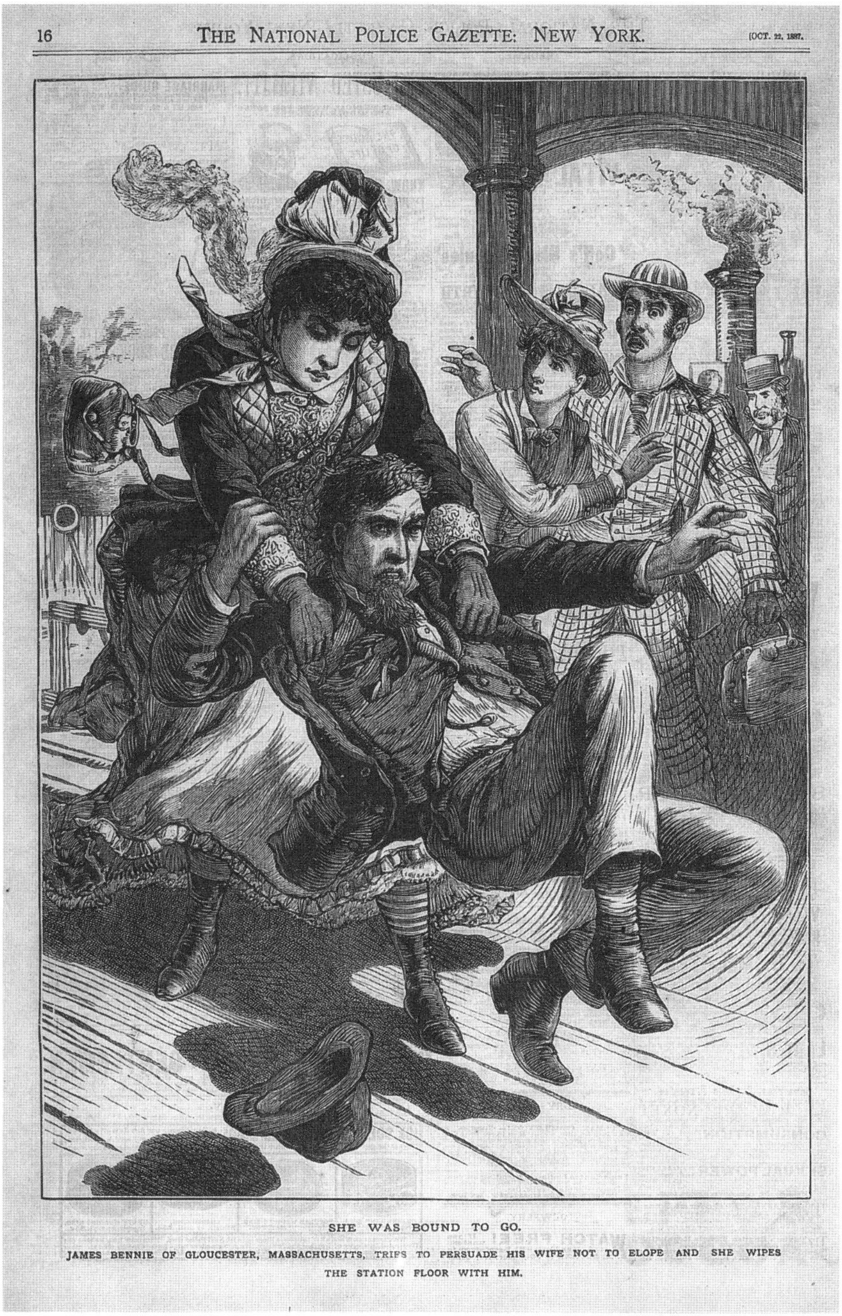
16 THE NATIONAL POLICE GAZETTE: NEW YORK. [OCT. 22, 1887.
SHE WAS BOUND TO GO.
JAMES BENNIE OF GLOUCESTER, MASSACHUSETTS, TRIES TO PERSUADE HIS WIFE NOT TO ELOPE AND SHE WIPES THE STATION FLOOR WITH HIM.

FIGURE 6.3. One consistent and unusual feature of *Police Gazette* illustrations involved a woman's aggressive and "unfeminine" physical assault upon a man or another woman. Here a rebellious wife resists her husband's attempt to prevent her from running away by "wiping the floor" with him. (Collection of Howard P. Chudacoff)

have won Fox's enmity, probably because of a clash between the strong personalities of both men.[18] Whatever the source of the discord, from 1881 onward, the *Police Gazette* consistently and explicitly backed Sullivan's opponents and only grudgingly reported Sullivan's victories. In January of 1881, for example, the *Police Gazette* focused intently on the pre-fight buildup to a title match between Sullivan and the then heavyweight champion Paddy Ryan. When Sullivan knocked out Ryan after "nine terrible rounds," the *Police Gazette* eagerly published Fox's telegram to Ryan which read "Dear Paddy—Am sorry you lost the fight. Can I do anything for you? Am willing to back you again for $5,000." Fox also telegraphed his representative in New Orleans to give Ryan "all the comforts money can buy."[19] Sullivan received no such acknowledgement. A year and a half later, Fox announced that he was backing the English boxer Tug Wilson in a championship match against Sullivan. When Sullivan won but forfeited a big stake by failing to knock Wilson out, Fox declared Wilson the *Police Gazette* champion.[20]

The *Police Gazette* publisher could be fickle and shift loyalties when the situation suited him. Early in 1883, a prizefighter named Slade, who was then *Police Gazette* champion, dumped Fox as his manager in favor of a former opponent. Fox felt so betrayed that he gloated when Sullivan knocked out Slade the following August.[21] Throughout Sullivan's boxing career, however, Fox and the *Police Gazette* continuously published disparaging remarks about the "Boston Strong Boy," especially his drinking and rowdy lifestyle. Yet the journal's coverage of Sullivan's matches, in print as well as in drawings and photographs, was so extensive that it almost appears as if Fox actually was shrewdly promoting Sullivan—and, simultaneously, *The National Police Gazette*—by purposely antagonizing Sullivan's myriad and loyal supporters.

During the decade of the 1880s, Fox also began to enhance his publication's visibility by sponsoring various nonboxing sporting contests and offering "diamond" belts and cash prizes, often reaching several hundred dollars, to contest winners. In turn, these contests, including the training and preparation that participants endured as well as detailed descriptions of the contests' actual occurrence and outcomes, became major news features of the *Police Gazette*. In 1882, for example, the *Police Gazette* sponsored cycling and pedestrian races, wrestling matches, and prize fights, with Fox awarding a special medal to each new *Police Gazette* champion.

The success of the *Police Gazette* during Richard Fox's first decade as publisher revealed itself in several ways. Late in 1883, Fox boasted that the journal had "1,000,000 Readers Every Week!"[22] Even though subscriptions totaled only about one-sixth of that number, given the newspaper's circulation throughout the commercial institutions of urban bachelor subculture, the claim may not have been all that exaggerated. Perhaps more indicative was Fox's ability to finance the construction of an elaborate new headquarters for the publication, built on New York City's Franklin Street early in 1883. The structure stood seven stories tall and included a relatively new technological advance: elevators. By the mid-1880s as well, the journal must have been benefiting from enhanced advertising revenues. Over the previous ten years, the classified section had expanded from a few columns to almost an entire page—always page 15, the next-to-last page. This page included notices for real estate, men's jewelry, how-to books (especially so-called marriage guides), and special *Police Gazette* publications, such as accounts and illustrations of prominent prizefights—chiefly those promoted by the *Police Gazette*—along with the usual listings for consumer products of the male culture and bachelor subculture: sporting goods, photographs of young actresses, and patent medicines, especially those making the claims "Manhood restored."

As he entered his second decade as proprietor, Fox refined *The National Police Gazette* further, adding more gossip news about stage and sports personalities and publishing a larger number and variety of sports stories. Crime news still screamed

FIGURE 6.4. Classified advertisements formed another unique feature of *The National Police Gazette*, listing products and services that would appeal especially to bachelors. Note the listings for male medical products (many of them offering promise of physical and sexual vitality), photographs and cards (often semipornographic), and potential marriage mates. (Collection of Howard P. Chudacoff)

from several pages of each weekly issue, but increasingly it shared space with other features. Editions included numerous news anthologies that presented short, human interest tidbits, sometimes amusing but more often lurid. A column titled "Masks and Faces," for example, reported gossip of the theatrical world, and another labeled "This Wicked World: A Few Samples of Man's Duplicity and Woman's Worse Than Weakness" digested oddities of human behavior. By 1890, fully half of the journal's sixteen pages were devoted to illustrations and photographs, including sensation-seeking drawings on both the cover and on the back page plus portraits of stage and sports personalities on pages 4 and 5. Four other pages presented a mixture of portraits and action drawings. Regular features, such as a column entitled "Before the Bar: News and Gossip in the Wine, Liquor, and Beer Trade," catered to barkeepers and the saloon crowd, who may well have become the core of *Police Gazette* readers and subscribers. And classified ads, which by 1887 covered six columns over one and one-half pages, targeted more than ever the publication's bachelor readership. This section now included personal ads listing "eligible" women supposedly looking for lonely single men who might be interested in marriage, plus advertisements for sex publications and for manuals of advice on how to win at gambling. One typical advertisement in 1887 announced: "Gents: If you are single and want to marry, send 10 cents for a list of lady correspondents, confidential circulars &c. Photos of marriageable ladies furnished. Mention this paper. Mutual Friend, Brighton Park, Illinois."[23]

Fox's obsession with pugilism caused him to tout prizefighting over all other sports in the late 1880s. The *Police Gazette* publisher fashioned himself and his publication as the main arbiters of the sport, often referring to the ornate Police Gazette Diamond Belt that was awarded to the individual whom Fox himself selected as world champion. Fox crowed that he had spent over $50,000 to promote high-quality sporting events and to award prizes to champions, and he heaped credit upon himself for legitimizing the "well-behaved and manly pugilist [and] the reliable and skillful oarsman. . . ."[24] In 1887 *The National Police Gazette* began an intensive idolizing series of articles on heavyweight boxer Jake Killrain, who had beaten the British champion Jem Smith the previous December. Killrain quickly became the next in a long line of *Police Gazette* heroes groomed to beat the mighty John L. Sullivan. Killrain's victory over Sullivan in June of that year was followed by a rash of adulatory *Police Gazette* stories rehashing the event and venerating Killrain at Sullivan's expense. When Sullivan knocked out Killrain in a return match in 1889, however, the *Police Gazette* rationalized that Killrain lost the seventy-five round, two-hour-and-sixteen-minute marathon because he was ill and therefore had decided to "succumb gracefully."[25]

By the end of the 1880s, the content of a typical *National Police Gazette* sixteen-page tabloid issue consisted of the following format: The cover page continued to feature a sensational illustration, often but not always of some crime described in the inside pages. Page 2 included a long editorial from Fox, brief tidbits of news, and the long-lasting "Masks and Faces" column of stage gossip. Page 3 presented brief crime reports and other human interest stories, usually of bizarre events. Pages 4 and 5 presented photographic portraits of female stage performers and male sports personalities. Page 6 featured the edition's major crime story and other lesser new items of human interest. Page 7 was devoted to an extended article on a particular sport, such as dog fighting or cock fighting, as well as boxing. In earlier years, more crime stories would have dominated this page, but they diminished as the journal turned increasingly to sports news. Pages 8 and 9, the middle pages, were totally devoted to illustrations, often a two-page woodcut depicting a crime scene. Pages 10 and 11 included most of the sports columns, such as "Pugilistic News," "Sporting Notes," "Baseball Notes," and "Whip and Spur" (horse racing). The titles of these columns varied weekly rather than consistently representing the same subjects. Pages

12 and 13 offered more photographs and drawings. Page 14 included a column of brief sports items, but most of pages 14 and 15 printed classified advertisements, now including numerous listings for products that supposedly cured venereal disease and "self abuse." Page 16 presented another full-page sensational illustration.

As *The National Police Gazette* neared the completion of its second decade under Fox's administration, it continued to represent women in three peculiar ways, all of which involved some form of objectification but which also included other more subtle messages. First, the number of photographs of soubrettes multiplied. Usually these photos presented full-length poses of attractive young women, often identified as French or British performers, dressed in high fashion. Second, illustrations of crime stories inevitably included well-proportioned young females garbed only in lingerie or with clothing falling off (or being torn off) their shoulders and/or riding up their thighs, with plenty of breast cleavage (bare breasts, however, no longer were depicted) and bare legs showing. On occasion that was far from rare, the crime stories and illustrations involved heinous offenses perpetrated against white women by Indians, Chinese, and blacks, and the illustrations depicted individuals from these groups in outrageous racist stereotypes. At the same time, however, the *Police Gazette* published photographs of African-American boxers, foot racers, and other athletes in heroic and generally noble poses. Third, the journal consistently presented articles and illustrations of women either engaging in unfeminine athletic events, such as boxing and feats of strength, or wreaking revenge against each other or against miscreant or threatening males. A typical feature of this sort reported on the incident of a woman who used her fists to knock out a masher on a Milwaukee streetcar; another presented a photograph in the gallery of sports celebrities of Belle Gordon, the Police Gazette Champion Lady Bag Puncher.[26]

The portrayal of certain women as capable of physically defending themselves against, attacking, or even besting, men probably represents irony and eclecticism more than it does contradiction or some feminist tendency. Certainly the idea of feminine weakness and dependence on men, which characterized most of the crime and human-interest stories and illustrations, appealed to male readers because it gave men an opportunity to validate their social power. Yet Fox, or one of his editors, undoubtedly recognized the variety of tastes and personalities among *Police Gazette* readers, some of whom might have found sexual attraction in the concept of female power and domination. On the surface, the stories and illustrations of women defending themselves against male aggressors or avenging themselves against male deceivers represent moral lessons and warnings. But the symbolism of these features seems more subtle; it appears to cater to a latent desire by some men to sacrifice their manhood to a dominating woman. Fox was careful not to make this theme too prominent in his publication, but its more than occasional appearance signifies another form of prurience that the *Police Gazette* attempted to satisfy.

On another level, however, the representations of women embodying both masculine and feminine qualities denoted a social message that extended far beyond simple prurience. That is, they conveyed messages of class inversion. In many if not most cases, the vengeance, aggression, and general masculine roles that women in these *Police Gazette* stories and illustrations exhibited were undertaken by working-class females against middle- and upper-class men. Most frequently, the women depicted in these instances were young soubrettes, chorus girls who, like many working-class men and women, lived their lives on the margins of social respectability. As well, the objects of female aggression were often well-dressed "swells" and "mashers," men who, because of their wealth and position, assumed that they could take advantage of the vulnerability of a working girl by jilting her or by physically threatening her. Thus, the depiction of females exerting physical power seems also to have been intended to appeal to working-class male readers, who would have taken vicarious pleasure in the humiliation of men from higher social strata.

This role inversion of aggressor and victim represented variation on a theme commonly portrayed not only in *The National Police Gazette* but also in contemporary burlesque and other forms of cheap theater: the predatory woman or gold-digger, who used her physical wiles to manipulate a man of means for her own material advantage. Usually, the stage served as the arena from which such working-class women plied their trade, as described in *Police Gazette* stories such as "Bewitched by an Actress" and "Dolly of the Casino," in which a performer seduced an "innocent" middle-class theater patron and took all his money. Late-nineteenth-century burlesque dramatizations and, especially, poster advertisements consistently repeated this theme, portraying women in images that ranged from temptresses to dominatrices. Both the gold-digger and the avenging woman exuded a particular kind of allure, what historian Robert Allen has identified as the "power to turn the tables on those men who would attempt to possess her. . . ." But as Allen also has noted, the burlesque patrons and *Police Gazette* readers only were observers of this threat of domination; they were in on the joke and, as spectators, were not victims. Thus both working-class and middle-class men could take pleasure in these displays of sexual power and indulge in masochistic fantasies of female domination while distancing themselves from its threat.[27]

After the turn of the century, Fox took greater note of the male and bachelor retreats that provided greatest access to his publication. Among their many published photographic portraits, weekly editions of *The National Police Gazette* increasingly featured photographs of individual barbers and saloonkeepers, as well as of their establishments. Moreover, on pages 14 and 15 amid the classified ads, feature prose portraits of saloon keepers and barbers (the latter identified as tonsorialists) began to appear. Each of these stories made certain to mention that the *Police Gazette* was available on the premises. By 1903 these articles were regularized in weekly columns titled "Well-Known Bartenders" and "Well-Known Tonsorialists," articles that featured proprietors who were *Police Gazette* subscribers from New York and other major cities. The previous year, as part of its extensive sponsorship of contests of all sorts, the *Police Gazette* offered a championship medal to the champion bartender in a contest that evaluated recipes for unique libations as well as speed and accuracy of performance. In 1903 the newspaper awarded three $150 medals for the most speedy and artistic barbers. Most issues of the early 1900s also included a supplemental page that printed a half-tone photograph of a female stage performer or pugilistic champion. Presumably this photograph could be framed or otherwise posted on the wall of a saloon or barbershop

By 1900 the *Police Gazette* was proclaiming itself The Greatest Sporting Weekly in the World. Fox had stabilized the journal's format, and the *Police Gazette* remained fairly consistent in its content over the next two decades. In the early twentieth century, the paper's crime and gossip news, though far from negligible, took a backseat to sporting news (most crime stories now were relegated to the middle pages), though boxing heavily dominated the athletic segment of the journal's content. Depending on the season, weekly issues also included feature stories on baseball and football plus an occasional peek into less prominent sports such as a 1901 article entitled "Golf and How to Play It" or the $500 prize awarded to *The National Police Gazette* champion bowler in 1902.

But the manly competitions of pugilism, wrestling, and "physical culture" (weightlifting and bodybuilding) attracted the most column space. In addition to its championship belts awarded to boxers, the *Police Gazette* sponsored numerous weightlifting contests, heralding them in ever more excited prose as the date for the competition approached and often making contestants the subjects of feature articles. These competitions appeared to be open to all. In fact the *Police Gazette* explicitly announced, regarding its highly-publicized physical culture contest in 1902, "No Color Line in Contest: All Athletes of Whatever Race or Occupation, Free to Enter the Lists for Diamond Medal."[28]

Throughout Fox's reign, *The National Police Gazette* consistently — even increasingly — presented itself as a bachelor's, as well as a man's, publication. Though its contents obviously were intended to attract a general male readership, certain features seemed especially to target unmarried males. Over time, the products and services listed in the classified section seemed increasingly to cater to the needs and desires of bachelors. The ads for medical cures for venereal disease and male "weakness," for athletic equipment and gambling paraphernalia, for employment agencies, and for semipornographic pictures of females illustrate this appeal. More directly, in the early twentieth century the *Police Gazette* advertised an everlarger number of "marriage agencies," which made claims such as "GET MARRIED. 10,000 LADIES are anxious to marry. Many worth from $10,000–$20,000. . . . List with full descriptions and Post Office addresses mailed FREE."[29] Another ad, posted by the Star Agency of Chicago, proclaimed that subscribers to its "Big list with post office addresses" could "Marry rich!"[30]

These notices notwithstanding, *Police Gazette* content also sometimes expressed an explicitly antimarriage slant. Articles and illustrations often lampooned the henpecked husband and extolled the benefits of an independent, unmarried existence that enabled a man to enjoy *The National Police Gazette* unencumbered by domestic obligations. In 1893, for example, a cover for one issue featured a drawing of a woman lying in bed, smoking a pipe, and reading the *Police Gazette* while a half-empty whiskey bottle sat on the bedstand. The caption announced that "A Young Wife Astonishes Her Erratic Husband by emulating his example and causes him to promptly abandon the vagabond habits of his bachelor days." On the one hand, this representation appears as a satirical attempt to shame husbands into becoming more accommodating to their wives by discarding their objectionable bachelor habits. On the other hand, however, the depiction, especially in the way it was drawn, was clearly antimarriage in intent. Instead of guilt, the artist's objective was to remind a man what he would have to give up — including sacrificing the *Police Gazette* — by succumbing to marital responsibilities.[31] Besides lessons like this one, *Police Gazette* articles de-emphasized marriage by ignoring it. Virtually none of the profiles of male professional and amateur athletes published over Fox's half century of control ever mentioned the featured individual's wife and/or family. In fact, often the biographical accounts strongly implied that the featured men (and most of the women too) were not married. In January of 1903, for example, descriptions of the four prize winners in the *Police Gazette* physical culture contest included references to a broad range of personal information, such as address, occupation, club affiliations, and the like, but there were no allusions to spouse and children, suggesting that these men were not, in all likelihood, married.[32]

STRICTLY FOR BACHELORS

The National Police Gazette, the content of which represented a combination of the modern-day *Playboy*, *National Enquirer*, and *Sports Illustrated* publications, made a generally indirect appeal to bachelors. Around the turn of the century, however, there were a number of journals and advice books that spoke directly to the subculture of single men. Indeed, their existence may well have owed itself to their publishers' recognition that the number and proportion of bachelors in the American population had enlarged so extraordinarily in the preceding decades that unmarried men constituted a potentially lucrative readership and therefore merited such special attention. These magazines and manuals attempted to attract bachelor readers and subscribers not with the vicariousness and fantasy of the *Police Gazette's* manly sports articles and wanton illustrations; instead, they tried more explicitly to discuss and fulfill more basic everyday needs of urban single life.

The Bachelor Book, a short-lived magazine issued in Chicago in 1900, epitomizes this type of specialized periodical. Curiously, *The Bachelor Book* was published and edited by

Marion Thornton Egbert and Page Walter Sampson, two individuals who called themselves "little old-fashioned young women." Little can be found about the background and careers of these women. Egbert appeared in the Chicago City Directory of 1900 as living at the same address as her journal, 1407 Auditorium Tower, suggesting that the small publication might have operated out of Egbert's residence. Sampson, who was listed in the directory as Miss Page Sampson and who worked as a musician and music teacher before her publishing venture, boarded with other single people at the Holland Hotel during her partnership with Egbert. Egbert and Sampson published their magazine monthly, selling it at a subscription price of one dollar per year, one-fourth the cost of the *Police Gazette*, which, by contrast, was a weekly. The owners of *The Bachelor Book* claimed ten thousand subscribers, though exact figures are unavailable. It is possible that, like *The National Police Gazette*, *The Bachelor Book* circulated inside male haunts such as saloons and barbershops and therefore had a readership that exceeded its subscription list, but Egbert and Sampson's journal makes no specific mention of such a possibility.

The two women announced in their first edition that their periodical was "intended for bachelors, but others may read it." "We approve of matrimony," they allowed, but only "for some people." Their mission, as stated in a later edition, was to devote themselves "to the wants, whims, and foibles of the single man," and they promised "to enter upon a diligent search for everything that may concern, either directly or indirectly, the happiness of that . . . much criticized and overworked individual, . . . that lonesome human soul, the unmarried man."[33]

Unlike *The National Police Gazette*, and perhaps in conscious contrast to that periodical, *The Bachelor Book* avoided salaciousness. "We shall endeavor," asserted Egbert and Sampson, "to make the production of each number of this magazine an ethical performance, and beyond a reasonable hope that we shall succeed in doing so, we expect nothing."[34] As if to underscore their respectability, the editors published, as the first feature of their first edition, recipes for rarebit, white wine punch, and a tea-sherry and whiskey punch (advisable repast and libation presumably for a hypothetical social gathering hosted by a estimable middle-class bachelor), along with news about men's fashions. Other editions included food and drink recipes as well, plus articles on traveling and "refined" sports, such as fishing. No prizefighting reports or theater and vaudeville gossip could be found here. In the final four (later, eight) pages of each edition, Egbert and Sampson also included an advertising section, with listings from haberdashers, stationery sellers, financial brokers, a tooth powder manufacturer, printing companies, restaurants, hotels, railroads, and the Berlitz Schools of Language. No reader could confound the products and services of these ads with those more unseemly products and services regularly promoted in the *Police Gazette*.

In addition to its helpful hints on personal decorum and its dignified advertisements, *The Bachelor Book's* main content consisted of articles, poetry, and fiction, all with bachelor themes. These pieces either provided emotional consolation for those in the bachelor state or satire to which bachelors could relate in a sympathetic way. For example, an essay entitled "A Bachelor Type" offered consoling solace to any single man who may have felt rejected by society. Admitting that a bachelor did have his faults, the anonymous author (possibly Egbert and/or Sampson?) suggested that "his failings are more to be admired than some people's virtues." The ordinary bachelor, according to the essayist, found pleasure in frequenting his club, the racetrack, and the cotillion. He was active but responsible: "the young athlete, who after a night spent in revelry, will take his morning tub and begin the day full of energy and hope." More importantly, he was the one "who will share with a friend his last dollar. . . . Deep down within the insouciance which deceives the non-observer, lies a true manliness, a courage, an honor, which, if need be, will lead him to lay down his life for a friend or stem the tide of battle with his body. . . . He makes no claim to being a saint, but is content to be a man in a world of men."[35]

An editorial entitled "A Bachelor's Liberty" provided similar validation to the unmarried state and presented an especially resonant expression of what might be termed a bachelor's complaint. "Liberty?" the author (again, probably Egbert and/or Sampson) asked.

[The bachelor] has no liberty. We say it boldly, with the supreme authority vested in us by 10,000 bachelor subscribers. From cradle to grave, the bachelor of today is the target for all shots, random or otherwise, that humanity is heir to. He walks alone through Life, on the cold and wintry highway of Dry Happiness. Let him deviate a hair's breadth from the straight and narrow into the pleasant byways and hedges of life, and lo! a woman, it seems, is among the flowers waiting to ensnare him and bind him in the enfeebling bonds of matrimony. Let him call his soul his own, and he is sure to get a bill for it. . . .[36]

A typical short fiction story titled "Pawn Ticket 1155" offered bachelors both a satire of infidelity and a lesson in morality. In the story, a bachelor named Haynes fell in love with a Mrs. Buckley at the same time that her husband, Mr. Buckley, began courting his own secretary. To prove his love, Haynes bought a fur coat for Mrs. Buckley, but he had to scheme a way to give it to her without raising her husband's suspicion. He devised a plan in which he pawned the coat for a small amount and gave the ticket to his lover. She, in turn, informed her husband that she found the ticket and asked him to claim the coat for her since it would cost so little. Buckley agreed, but when he reached the pawn shop and redeemed the ticket, he decided instead to give the coat to his secretary and send his wife a cheap fur collar. Mrs. Buckley, upon receiving the collar, concluded that Haynes had pawned it instead of the coat, and she refused to speak to Haynes ever again, vowing eternal loyalty to her husband while never discovering his philandering.

Haynes walked away from his lover's rejection heartbroken, cursing man's deceit and woman's whim. Only the secretary is happy. The lesson to the bachelor is clear: avoid affairs with married women.[37] The larger lesson that Egbert and Sampson were communicating, however, is to avoid women altogether; a socially-adjusted man can find greater pleasures. Thus, as the poem "A Bachelor's Love" concluded:

> When at my lips first touch
> Her eye, my guiding star!
> Burns fiercer, then I know
> How dear is my — cigar.[38]

In addition to periodicals such as *The Bachelor Book*, a thriving genre of turn-of-the-century prescriptive literature also targeted unmarried men. A book titled *The Complete Bachelor: Manners for Men*, published in 1904, typifies this type of subculture literature. The volume, compiled "by the Author of the 'As Seen by His Papers,'" was written, states the unnamed author, because "I have found the bachelor sadly neglected" by other advice manuals.[39] Again, a media entrepreneur was noticing and attempting to mine profits from the enhanced number of bachelor consumers. Obviously intended for members of polite society, the book included chapters on a bachelor's proper behavior when out and about, how bachelors should dress, how to care for clothes, prescriptions for personal hygiene, how to host and behave at social gatherings, how to treat servants, how to dance, advice on travel, and, lastly and ultimately, how to plan a wedding.

In prescribing correct behavior, *The Complete Bachelor* was also obviously reacting against prevailing negative images of bachelors, images that the author believed were all too real. In the very first chapter, "The Bachelor in Public," the book warned that "staring at or ogling women, standing at the entrance of theaters, churches, or other public buildings, stopping still and turning back to look at someone or something in the street, can be classified as offenses of which no gentleman can be guilty."[40] A few pages later, in the chapter titled "How the Bachelor Should Dress," the author warns, "Jewelry is vulgar. The [proper] ring for a man is a seal of either green or red, or of plain burnished gold with a seal or monogram engraved on it. It must be worn on the little finger. Watch chains and watch fobs are not in vogue. . . ."[41]

Not all of the book's contents manifest such elitist prescriptions. The chapter titled "Care of a Bachelor's Clothes" advises that "a man with a modest salary can dress very well on two to three hundred dollars a year, and even less" and proceeds to explain how such a budget can be wisely spent. And the chapter titled "The City Bachelor as Host" explains that "it does not cost a fortune to return in some manner the civilities once received, and every man, even if his income be limited, can once in a while entertain, even if it be on a very small scale and in a very modest way."[42] Nevertheless, instructions on how to treat servants, whether or not to employ a valet, and how to set a proper table appear to have reflected the snobbish quality of the readership.

Like *The Bachelor Book*, *The Complete Bachelor* exhibited some less-than-subtle antifemale, or at least condescending, inferences. The chapter titled "A Bachelor's Letters" advises that "there is one rule a man must observe: never keep a compromising letter . . . especially from a woman. Sometimes women are foolish and careless, and they allow their pens to run away with them. . . . (W)e must be men and reduce to ashes what would hurt in the very least degree or cast reflection upon an innocent if silly woman. Suppose you were to die suddenly, and among your papers those letters were found, with you alone, dumb in death, perhaps, only able to vindicate the unfortunate writer? We must think of those things."[43]

The Bachelor Book, perhaps the *Esquire* or *Gentleman's Quarterly* of its day, and *The Complete Bachelor*, a consummate how-to book, signify the ways in which promulgators of popular culture attempted to cultivate a specialized but significant market among unmarried men. That attempt would not have been made if the publishers, manufacturers, and proprietors had not recognized the extent and demands of the large bachelor population. But by the turn of the century, the numbers of unmarried men were large enough, especially in big cities such as Boston, Chicago, San Francisco, and New York, that they could sustain a product or service designed almost exclusively for their consumption. Richard Kyle Fox and other publishers of crime and sporting journals, plus the manufacturers and providers of myriad products and services for men, capitalized on *male* consumerism that may have reflected, or even emphasized, needs appropriate to the unmarried state. But Marion Egbert and Page Sampson plus D. Appleton and Company, the publisher of *The Complete Bachelor*, explicitly targeted the bachelor subculture. That subculture, nevertheless, was intricately subsumed under a larger male culture; indeed, it helped considerably to define that culture, a definition that the next chapter will explore.

Bachelor Subculture and Male Culture

Social change has been constant throughout modern history, but during certain periods a society can experience "big change," spikes in the continuum that break out from the normal flow of shifting forces and events. The four decades or so beginning around 1880 and ending around the end of World War I encompass such a time of big change in American history. Virtually all people felt the impact of new and major developments in particular ways. For males, a dizzying array of economic, organizational, and social forces combined to challenge traditional prerogatives of power and prestige that men had always safeguarded for themselves. These forces included, among others, mechanization, bureaucratization, urbanization, migration, immigration, and the entry of women into spheres of politics and paid employment. The notion of a virile and virtuous manliness that had been nurtured in a society of small producers and shopkeepers was eroding and, especially among the middle class, suddenly seemed at risk. As cultural historian Gail Bederman has suggested, a true crisis of manhood did not actually exist—most men still believed in and exercised their inherited power and authority. Nevertheless, as Bederman and others have also noted, a number of American males, especially of the middle class, began to search for ways to revive and remake their manhood in order to meet the challenges that the new society seemed to be posing to them.[1]

Bachelors occupied an anomalous position among those embarking on this search. On the one hand, they embodied one of the principal threats to traditional manhood in that their increasing numbers and percentages within the overall population made them "others" in a society that privileged married men. On the other hand, as men, bachelors operated within the male sphere, and at least some parts of their own experiences were inextricably tied to the experiences of all men. Thus bachelors, like married men, also encountered the challenges that the era posed to manhood. Moreover, their particular subculture of autonomy and male-centered sociability offered a model for those wishing to remake manhood. How bachelor subculture meshed with and diverged from general male culture involved complicated patterns of definition and identity, including the ways that men, married or not, related to women and to each other.

Rehearsals in Youth

Both particular bachelor subculture and general male culture originate, of course, in boyhood when all males are unmarried. A large literature exists on the historical and psychological differentiation of gender in childhood, the analyses of which far exceeds the scope of this study. Suffice it to say here that recent studies agree that a new and distinct boy culture emerged in the United States over the course of the nineteenth century. According to E. Anthony Rotundo, the historian whose research has most illuminated this culture, during these years a cluster of social changes, ranging from urbanization to compulsory school attendance, isolated boys both from the female-oriented sphere of the household and from males of older generations. By the mid-nineteenth century, in schools, playgrounds, backyards, vacant lots, and the streets, urban boys cultivated much denser and more time-consuming contact with peers than had their rural counterparts of earlier generations. The outdoor world of the city became the boys' special habitat, and, except for the attic and the cellar—those mysterious regions of the household normally shunned by other family members—the home was not a hospitable place for this new homosocial peer culture. Rather, the open-air retreats where boys could evade adult eyes furnished the milieu for the cultivation of boys' experiences and relationships.[2]

Thus, by the mid-nineteenth century, a sharp cultural contrast marked the division between boys and girls. As Rotundo has observed, "With great clarity a boy saw that female meant fettered and male meant free." Obviously boys did not completely lack restraints nor were girls slaves, but, as Rotundo also notes, "Boys had a freedom to roam that girls lacked."[3] Moreover, an ideology of aggressive competitiveness, based on rivalry rather than cooperation, characterized boys' relationships with each other. Most importantly, boys intentionally evaded contact with and even conflicted with adult male society, while girls frequently shared space with and interacted within the world of adult women. Whereas girl culture was integrated into the household, boy culture was one of independence and undomesticated liberty. Boys had to return home at day's end for shelter and sustenance, but the domestic sphere gave them only a restless respite from their daily life of action, noise, and aggression. Eddie Cantor, the famous vaudevillian, led such a life as a New York City youth in the late nineteenth century. He wrote in his autobiography, "I grew lean, big-eyed, eager, eating from grocery barrels, singing in back yards, playing in gutters and on the roofs of houses, and combining with it all the smatterings of a public school education. I was not introspective — whatever that is. I simply took to life as a darky takes to rhythms, and vibrated with it. In short, I was a typical New York street boy who, by a peculiar and deft twist of fortune, eventually lands either in the Bowery Mission or in a bower of roses."[4]

Unlike the deep, lasting friendships that girls created among themselves, relationships between and among boys tended to be tenuous and episodic, relying on loyalty but not intimacy.[5] Boy culture was a divisive, combative one, centered around dares and physical prowess. A special kind of individual and reckless courage marked the highest value; conversely, to be a crybaby represented the lowest embarrassment. Rivalry, usually expressed in physical terms, created an emphasis on what Rotundo calls mastery, domination over other boys, over material objects and over nature (as exhibited creatively in the building of things and destructively in behaviors such as vandalism and cruelty to animals). Such mastery also included control over one's emotions. In this context, the violence that boys often exhibited toward each other could represent an expression of fondness because more direct forms of emotional display were taboo.

The importance of mastery explains how sports—defined broadly as nonutilitarian physical contests—became so vital to urban boy culture. According to one theorist, boys have engaged and continue to engage in competitive sports because of "insecurity, loneliness, and especially a need to connect with other people."[6] According to this theory, unlike girls, who define themselves primarily through connections with others and who view highly competitive situations as threats to their relationships, boys construct a sense of self as separate from others. Boys fear that intimacy will result in a loss of identity. Yet they still crave some sort of social cohesion, so they use physical competition as a safe place for attachment to others. At the same time, however, sports undermine true expressions of intimacy because, by placing the highest value on success— winning at all costs—sports create an emotional distance between rivals.[7]

Above all else, however, the value that boy culture most cherished was independence. A special autonomy separated boys from younger children and girls on one side of the age and gender spectrums and from adults on the other side. A boy was expected by his peers to learn how to deal with other boys on his own, without help from adults or friends. Again, as Rotundo has concluded, "At the heart of nineteenth-century boy culture, then, lay an imperative to independent action. Each boy sought his own good in a world of shifting alliances and fierce competition. He learned to assert himself and to stand emotionally alone while away from his family. For the part of each day that he lived among peers, he received a strenuous education in autonomy."[8]

FIGURE 7.1. Boy culture was the bud from which bachelor subculture blossomed. Reckless, boisterous, aggressive, and running in packs, boys used outdoor spaces to pursue their independence away from adult supervision. In the process they engaged in a self-apprenticeship for bachelorhood. (George Eastman House)

Conflict between fathers and sons was a fellow traveler as a boy journeyed toward autonomy. Relationships between male generations had been deteriorating since the mid-eighteenth century. According to some scholars, the discord reached its height of intensity around 1900 because fathers, in both working-class and middle-class families, were trying to assert an authority that was slipping from their grasp. Working away from home and unable to supervise their sons with the same power as their forebears had, fathers also could not guarantee their sons the property, skills, and other measures of economic security that formerly had undergirded their patriarchal prerogatives. They became a phantom power rather than a real force in their own household. Moreover, tensions increased when, by the turn of the century, sons possessed better education than their fathers and thus were better prepared to contest the authority over their behavior.[9]

For many boys, especially those of the white middle class, the independence and emotional distances cultivated by boy culture became liabilities once they crossed the threshold into young manhood and encountered new social demands. As they matured sexually and socially into their mid- and late teens, boys reentered a world populated by women, a world in which a boy's sense of mastery confronted impulses he could not control. As Rotundo and others have pointed out, some youths became obsessed over their desire to pursue and understand women, while others panicked over a feared loss of autonomy to a domestic dependence. The lifelong bachelor Henry David Thoreau, though an extreme case, articulated this fear of what would happen to a man when he abandoned his accustomed outdoor domain and succumbed to social pressures for a more domestic life. "His house is a prison," Thoreau wrote in his *Journal*, "in which he finds himself oppressed and confined, not sheltered and protected. He walks as if he sustained the roof; he carries his arms as if the walls would fall in and crush him, and his feet remember the cellar beneath. His muscles are never relaxed. It is rare that he overcomes the house, and learns to sit at home in it."[10]

Several scholars have demonstrated that, contrary to recent anxieties over the presumed prolonged period of dependency in youth, American males of the late twentieth century have experienced a more highly systematic and sequenced entry into adulthood than did their counterparts a century ago.[11] Older boys and young men of the late nineteenth century, however, often floated between the independence to which they had become accustomed as part of their boy culture on the one side and the proto-adult life of responsibility and commitment that they previewed as part of their courtship rituals on the other. These were turbulent times for youths, filled with uncertainty about their relationship to an unfamiliar world where young women outside their own family suddenly intruded into their lives. Prior female-controlled systems of "calling" and chaperonage were disappearing, to be replaced in the early twentieth century by male-controlled dating. And, as historian Kevin White has pointed out, young men were unprepared for the complexities and uncertainties of the choices they had to make. White has written, "An individual man had to choose and to learn the sexual boundaries that worked best for him through trial and error. . . ."[12]

Eddie Cantor reflected on such anxiety when he recalled one of his first romantic episodes: "Tanya was only sixteen but she acted like much older. She urged me to sit beside her and hold hands, but I pleaded with her to let me go because the boys were waiting for me. It was my first rehearsal in life of a scene I have since used on the stage in many diverse forms—the seduction of the bashful boy by the bold, bad lady. . . . I knew that if the fellers on the block found out that I had held a girl's hand, I'd be branded as a 'sissy' for life."[13] As he became a little older, Cantor also felt tension between the tug of a career, which he knew his family expected of him, and the familiarity, thrill, and carefree independence of his youth on the city streets. "I vacillated," he recalled, "drifted between impulses to act and amuse and a desire to slouch around street corners, hang out in pool rooms, join guerrilla gangs, and become a gangster's tool."[14]

There were few, if any, guideposts to help male youths negotiate the winding passage to adulthood. Having distanced
themselves in boyhood from older male generations and having abjured dependence on the female-oriented family for emotional support, boys becoming men lacked the mentoring that
girls received from mothers, aunts, grandmothers, older sisters,
and female teachers. As a result, young men turned to the only
remaining resource they had at hand: other males who, like
themselves, shared the same uncertainties and daily experiences.[15] Carrying their boy culture with them, these individuals
together created the foundation for a bachelor subculture that
existed within, and sometimes coincided with, male culture.

COMPETITION AND MANLINESS

As boys tentatively made their way into the realm of manhood,
they did not easily abandon the aggressive competitiveness that
had defined their childhood, and by the late nineteenth century
this competitiveness was assuming a new prominence in male
culture. Once content to accept a society of separate spheres
and to tolerate women either as keepers of the domestic sphere
or as nuisances to be eluded, men of the late nineteenth century—especially middle-class men—began to view women as
threats. Women were demanding entry into most of the arenas
that men had formerly monopolized, whether those arenas
were workplaces, the professions, institutions such as schools
and organizations, or the law. As well, many men found their
sense of personal autonomy slipping away, to be replaced by
bureaucracies, managers, and salespersons.[16]

To protect their prerogatives and their masculine identities,
men fashioned new values and new concepts of themselves.
The term "manliness," which in the early nineteenth century
had signified the opposite of childishness, now took on the
meaning of the opposite of femininity. In addition, men found
themselves engaged in a balancing act between domestic mas-

culinity—the still-valued responsibilities to home and family—and a preoccupation with virility—the competitive independence of the nondomestic male sphere.[17]

The cultural as well as spatial qualities of the two spheres—domestic/female and public/male—contained critical differences. According to sociologist Leon Ellis, the domestic sphere was and is a place "where order is based on the natural social relationships embedded in reproduction." In the domestic sphere, Ellis explains, a hierarchical, generational, and gendered order of power is the principal norm. In contrast, the basic feature of public space is that it is "created through and organized around culturally produced, universalistic systems of norms, ideals, and standards of evaluation and differential worth that enable men to order relationships among themselves." Thus, in contrast to the rigidly structured household, a more complex, disorderly give-and-take characterizes the public sphere.[18] The give-and-take of male-oriented public life includes such activities as verbal dueling, swearing, abilities in comedy and music, adroitness in eluding police and other symbols of authorities, and prowess in athletics as well as in overt physical combat and violence—all qualities which characterized the bachelor subculture that emerged in the late nineteenth century (see chapter 4).

Historian Kevin White has concluded that as men confronted the new uncertainties in work and ethics and tried to cope with a sense of powerlessness in the family, they "searched for relief in intense experience" that fed the "primitive" component of their masculinity.[19] Thus, in the late nineteenth century and early twentieth, athletics particularly and the strenuous life generally represented specific means by which young adult men channeled their aggressive competitiveness into positive directions and combated female intrusion into their lives. Here is where the sustained values of boy culture merged with the bachelor subculture of the saloons and clubs to create a new concept of manliness.

The closed masculine world of manly self-assertion, found in

FIGURE 7.2. Sports offered bachelors the kind of all-male competitive organized activity that reinforced their subculture. Not only did participation
in sports exclude women, but also, as the all-male audience in photograph
reveals, so too did sports spectatorship. (Library of Congress)

both participant and spectator athletics, gave men a place to
which they could escape the structured life of both work and
family as well as enabling them to erect a barrier between the
sexes. As sports historian Melvin Adelman has noted, sports
provided men with a commonly recognized opportunity to
demonstrate virile achievement, the "arena in which to teach

226

and test manhood" as demonstrated in "all-or-nothing competition."[20] Moreover, the idea that being manly meant not being
womanly as well as being strenuous transferred a craving for
strife beyond the domain of leisure into other venues, such as
politics, business, labor relations, and war. This ideology cap-
tured the interest of men of all classes and ages.[21]

The symbiotic relationship between manliness and competition, especially within sports, carried new risks, however. Before the last decades of the nineteenth century and first decades
of the twentieth, men had more second chances in their en-
deavors than they would later have. In an earlier era more
dominated by fear of sin, a man who fell from grace though
some moral transgression or in his livelihood could ask for-
giveness. In a society of producers that valued sober and purposeful hard work such as that which existed in the early nineteenth century, an artisan, clerk, or merchant who renounced
leisurely diversions as a waste of time would find a community
of support, and a man who failed in a craft or business could
pick up stakes and try his luck somewhere else. By the end of
the century, these options still remained to some extent, but as
consumerism and commercial leisure-time pursuits arose to expand one set of choices, choices of another sort narrowed. A
male who forswore sports or daring behavior risked the stigma
of being considered unmanly, indeed, even of being labeled "effeminate." Previously shunned, the competitive values attached
to sports had achieved a measure of respectability, and victory
at all costs reigned as the supreme value.[22]

Masculine, or manly, victory carried with it a singularly important reward: honor. As historian Elliott Gorn has asserted,
honor in the late nineteenth century was a virtue dependent on
external ratification; that is, it had to be conferred by a group.
In the case of men, the group consisted of one's peers, and the
means to honor was demonstration of prowess within or to the
peer group. One proved one's mettle through acts of valor, but
in a society in which wars were rare, valorous acts had to be
demonstrated on other kinds of battlefields. Brawling, espe-

cially over affronts to personal respect or to the respectability of a woman, provided one opportunity for such demonstration, especially among the working class. But more often the physical contests of athletics provided the safest means of achieving honor. Moreover, as Gorn and others have added, men acknowledged and displayed honor — their own as well as someone else's — by "buying drinks, spending money lavishly, or toasting one another's accomplishments."[23] In this regard too, the cultural components of manly rivalry and victory intertwined with the saloon, pool hall, and other venues of bachelor subculture.

Sports, both participant and spectator, formed a major component of the new male culture, but there were other aspects as well. In the company of other males, men played rough sports and cheered for their favorite athletes, but in private they lived the vicarious life of valor and honor by reading stories, real and fictional, about the daring exploits of great explorers, cowboys, detectives, and hunters as well as of sports heroes. Moreover, a new kind of male mass consumerism that included all the products advertised in *The National Police Gazette* and other men's publications — such items as semipornographic photographs, adventure literature, sex aids, patent medicines for male problems, gambling paraphernalia, and the like — emerged to link males of all social classes through joint consumption.

All of these products and activities furnished what Gorn defines as a "temporary refuge from those forces which challenged . . . manhood, whether routinized work, soulless corporations, aggressive women, smothering mothers, rich new industrialists, radical laborers, or swarthy foreigners." By emphasizing personal appearance and self-control, this consumerism also provided men with an illusion of sexiness and, perhaps more importantly, control over women.[24] In these ways, these products and services served as the foundation for an even more elaborate male (as opposed to female) consumer culture of the latter half of the twentieth century that included

Superman comics, *Playboy* centerfolds, John Wayne movies, and an expert knowledge of fast cars, fine wines, and expensive stereo equipment.[25]

If aggressive activity and vicarious fantasy characterized manly leisure culture, liquor was its solvent. Drinking, according to Rotundo, Ellis, and others, accompanied virtually every male recreational pursuit. The ritual of taking a drink with another man provided a means of demonstrating the tough-guy image that defined manhood. Alcohol played an especially important role in lowering inhibitions about social interaction and easing the bonding function of the unique style of male conversational discourse. As chapter 4 noted, the saloon and pool hall cultivated a distinctive form of male intercourse, one involving the calling of nicknames; sharing of war stories from the playing field, bedroom, or ballpark; teasing; telling of bawdy jokes; complaining about women; and, occasionally, serious debate on public issues or elections. Man talk was a substitute for the intimacy that men suppressed from each other, and it explains why husbands as well as bachelors retreated into the homosocial world of the saloon and other male bastions (see below).[26]

Smoking also became a ritual of the new manhood. Before the early nineteenth century, tobacco use consisted of two forms: snuff and pipe smoking. As the 1800s progressed, however, two new types of tobacco use emerged, both of which were acceptable only for men. First, chewing tobacco replaced snuff, with sales peaking around 1890 and surpassing those sales for smoking tobacco. About this time, cigars became the major form of tobacco use. Then, after World War I, tobacco companies and their allies in the advertising industry made cigarettes (which had been in the marketplace for almost four decades) the new accompaniment to the tough-guy image, especially when they enlisted sports heroes and movie stars to endorse their products.[27]

In some respects, the development of a mass male culture represented a victory of masculine working-class social standards over feminine middle-class morality. The enhanced positive—or at least, less stigmatized—value placed on formerly bad habits of smoking, betting, swearing, drinking, and engaging in casual sex was abetted by advertisers who unwittingly cultivated antibourgeois, antifeminine behavior. Picking up a "chippie" at an amusement park or visiting a prostitute to satisfy a sexual urge, formerly proscribed by middle-class probity, diminished as reasons for reproach, though such behavior was still not widely acceptable. Among middle-class men, an expanding bureaucracy that trapped white-collar workers in sedentary positions that offered them little hope of rising, along with the feminization of the workplace that included the banning of spittoons and the introduction of plants and carpets in offices, undermined male dominance of the work segment of the public sphere. As a result, men rebelled against the "civilizing" effects that they feared were not manly, and many of them reacted by infusing their manhood with a restoration of the once-condemned activities and values of boyhood—troublemaking, boisterousness, ribaldry, and rivalry.[28]

Autobiographies of men who experienced bachelorhood in the late nineteenth century and early twentieth confirm many of these patterns. For example, the tramp-poet Harry Kemp wistfully remembered how his married and unmarried male relatives and friends gathered weekly for distinctly male activities. "Sunday afternoons were the big gambling and card-playing times in our neighborhood," he recalled. "The 'boys' spent the day till dusk in the woods back of Babson's Hill. They drank and played cards. Landon taught me every card game there was."[29] Kemp's theme of finding role models among these men who were escaping female reproach is repeated by con-man and criminal Jack Black, who claimed that his first role model, after his rogue of a father, was a saloon keeper with whom he could easily converse. "Cy was a bachelor," Black wrote, "and lived in a single room in the hotel. He opened and closed his bar, did all the work, was always drinking, but no one ever saw him drunk. . . . I decided to pattern my life after

Cy's. He was a popular successful man. I began swinging my arms about, talking in a loud, hoarse voice, wearing my hat on the back of my head."[30] The saloon, the competition of the card game, the bottle, the talk, and the swaggering, cavalier demeanor—all provided young males with the context of their masculine identity.

Men thus related to each other and defined their manhood in particular ways that emphasized manly action. Those just entering manhood found role models among men who epitomized the explicit values that inhered in the manly action and interaction that existed in the cult of athletics and comradely loyalty to and within a group, whether the group was a team, a club, a work cadre, or just a bunch of "fellers" who regularly gathered at the corner saloon or pool hall. Yet men, especially unmarried men, also related to other males on a more personal, primary level as friends and even lovers. Bachelors played an important role in defining the parameters of these more private types of masculine interaction as well.

INTIMACY AND MANLINESS

Recent studies by psychologists confirm the peculiar nature of male-to-male social interaction that seems to have developed at the end of the nineteenth century and persists to the present. These studies have concluded that men's relationships with each other display a kind of shallowness, compared to the intimate, lasting friendships between and among women, because men have been socially conditioned to act competitive and emotionally inexpressive. For example, Dr. Lillian Rubin, employing a psychoanalytic perspective, has argued that men tend to place high value on spending time with other men, but that their early developmental experiences—basically, the aggressive, boisterous culture of boyhood—have left them with a deep fear of sharing one's inner emotions with another person. As a result, Rubin concludes, men tend to distance themselves

231

from each other by organizing their time together around an activity that is external to themselves. Thus, in pastimes such as sports and drinking, men could and can enjoy the company of other men — even become close — without having to become intimate in ways that might threaten the firm ego boundaries that they have constructed to delimit their individual self-image.[31]

Social historians generally acknowledge that before the mid-to-late nineteenth century, men's social duties and roles defined their identity, and, unlike the modern men Rubin describes, their roles were tightly bound to their communal responsibilities of family, church, and village. But as the century progressed, the individual self, as represented by the achievements and experiences attained through personal effort, assumed heightened prominence in the definition of a man's identity. The individual, rather than the family or the community, became the fundamental unit of society, and intimacy acquired a more important value in the achievement of individual fulfillment. Because the intimacy that existed in male-to-male relationships was tenuous and sporadic, more than ever before marriage completed a man's quest for intimacy. Marriage, previously a communal and religious obligation, by the late nineteenth century provided the chief emotional resource for two people who sought individual satisfaction and well-being in an intimate relationship. Here is where the subculture of single men diverged from that of married men. Matrimony distinguished bachelors from husbands not only in legal status but also in cultural status. For if the activities of bachelor subculture centered around the demonstration of an individualized manliness, the act of marriage brought the male over the threshold into true adult manhood where he entered a world in which mutuality and responsibility to wife and family supposedly took priority over loyalty to peers.[32] And if married men were individuals who had attained a sense of intimacy and the sharing of self, bachelors were men who had attained and retained a strong sense of individualism but had not (yet) achieved — or who were avoiding — the ultimate goal of intimacy.

Yet, unmarried men were not devoid of intimacy. Using personal correspondences, autobiographies, diaries, and other private materials, historians of late-nineteenth-century American society recently have uncovered evidence of strong emotional friendships between males that resembled the intense romantic bonds that existed between women of the same era.[33] While ardent relationships occurred among women of all ages and social classes, however, it appears that such attachments involving males were confined mostly to the middle class and to young, mainly unmarried men. These intimate friendships derived in large part from the comradeship and loyalty that characterized boyhood ties, and their intensity was often not appreciated until after the bonds had dissolved. For example, journalist and novelist Homer Croy expressed both regret and resentment when a formerly close friend abandoned him when he and the friend had moved to New York City. "As so often happens when old friends meet on new soil," he lamented in his autobiography, "he was distant and aloof. But that was all right, for I do believe people farm-born learn to depend only on themselves. However, I did miss someone to go places with and talk to."[34]

Sometimes, however, common predicaments and experiences in young manhood nurtured feelings of affection. Literary critic and editor Ferris Greenslet recalled an intense companionship that he sustained with a fellow bachelor during the stressful time of World War I. "The brightest memory of that dark, cold, ill-fed winter," he wrote in his autobiography, "is of the growth of my friendship with John Buchan. . . . We had, we found, things in common; how many, it took a quarter of a century to discover. We were of precisely the same age. . . . We spoke the same language. . . . My rather Shandean sense of humor was matched by Buchan's mildly Rabelaisian turn."[35]

Though romantic and sexual emotions rarely were manifest in expressions of male-to-male friendship among heterosexuals, they obviously existed in those intense bonds that devel-

oped between homosexual male lovers. The stigma of homosexuality suppressed most explicit evidence of romantic
thoughts and professions of strong affection between men who
lived a century or more ago, but a few pieces of evidence for
such emotions have surfaced in recent years. One example
comes from the private papers of the upstate New York writer
and poet, Frederick Shelley Ryman, whose diaries, private
notes, and scrapbooks, dating from the 1880s to the early
1900s, provide revealing insights into the life of a complex and
often troubled personality. Ryman lived a tortured existence,
torn between social pressures — and, apparently, his own confused proclivities — for heterosexual relationships and marriage
on the one hand and a latent and sometimes overt homosexuality or bisexuality on the other. Ryman was capable of intense love for both men and women, but he also was capable
of inordinate hostility toward women, especially those who
spurned him, and he wrote angry diatribes against marriage.
At the same time, however, his affectionate feelings toward
male friends and lovers never wavered.

In his early twenties, Ryman often struggled with his inner
uncertainties about intimacy with women, vacillating wildly
between attraction and repulsion. In about 1882, at the age of
twenty-four, he fell deeply in love with a woman named Eliza.
Ryman was so enamored that he wrote poetry to Eliza and
even became engaged to marry her. Then, when Eliza apparently broke the engagement, Ryman turned resentful and vin-
dictive, railing against the institution of marriage and all its
conventions. Late in 1883, for example, he wrote in his journal,

> I do honestly and truly feel *glad*! that Eliza treated me in the
> cursed cold contemptible way that she did, and I thank the ever
> blessed muses that I am not married. I am not *"gone"* on any
> other girl and I am certain her treatment of me will make me less
> susceptible to the d — d siren smiles and wiles of the *gentler* gen-
> der and it will also teach me to stand grief and to trust no per-
> son or thing implicitly for *all* my happiness. I know it is un-

gallant to curse a woman but I could curse her from the bitterest bottom of my heart for her damned vile coquettish treachery.[36]

A few weeks later, he sneered, "I despise marriage if possible as much as I do religion and dread it worse than I dread death." And on several occasions throughout his journal Ryman repeated the rhyme,

> No wife to scold me
> No children to squall
> God bless the gay man
> Who keeps bachelor's hall.[37]

Use of the term "bachelor" may well have signified a coded meaning in Frederick Ryman's thoughts, for at the same time that he dithered over his feeling for women, he candidly expressed his emotional and physical attraction to men. Ryman apparently loved and had affairs with several men, even while he was engaged to Eliza. In April of 1883, he entered into his journal a wish that women could more closely resemble one of the men to whom he felt a romantic intimacy. " 'Lucifer' [a code name for an unidentified male lover] was in the post office tonight," Ryman wrote, "and asked if I would be too much occupied to have a game of poker & of course I was only too glad to have him come over. My God how I love him & how I wish I could find some woman who was half as loving . . . and good as he is. . . ."[38] Three years later, Ryman voiced his affection even more explicitly, confessing, " 'Rob' Luke (perhaps this man was Lucifer?) is one G——d D——d good fellow I think. I truly love him. He gave me his picture tonight & as I left him he took my hand in his and quick as thought put it up to his lips & kissed it before I knew it hardly. I am truly proud to be so loved by any one & especially by one whom I can love & respect in return as I certainly do him."[39]

Ryman tried to rationalize his confusion—or, perhaps, his confirmed bisexuality—in two related ways. One tactic involved hiring prostitutes. Early in 1885 he wrote of an experi-

FIGURE 7.3. Early in the twentieth century, the homosexual component of the bachelor population experienced severely negative images and publicity. Sensational tabloid publications such as this one mocked gay men by identifying their rendezvous, such as bathhouses, as places of perversions and using derogatory terms such as "fag" and "joyboy" to describe the men. (The New York Historical Society)

ence with a prostitute as "the first time in my life that I ever took a Vigil of Venus in a regular Villa of Venus and it is the second time I ever gave any woman money as a direct payment for pleasure." Shortly thereafter, he visited a brothel and hired "a lovely little blonde" who "was truly one of the finest little armfuls of feminine voluptuousness I ever yet laid on the top of." He subsequently penned a short poem in her honor, crudely observing:

> My Dear Little Lillie Costello
> I met you and crammed you today
> And I would I might be your best fellow
> So I with you often could play[40]

By describing his experiences with prostitutes so graphically, Ryman seemed to be claiming his manhood as well as his masculinity. He also articulated such an assertion by adamantly stating his preference for bachelorhood. Early in 1882 he wrote in his journal, "Whenever I hear anyone tell how happy their married life is I always secretly feel that they lie like hell as the fox did who got his tail cut off in their trap and tried to make all the other foxes believe that that was the fashion so they would cut theirs off & he would have company. Rochefoucauld was right: 'There may be good but there are no happy marriages.'"[41] The occasion of his twenty-fifth birthday in April of 1883 gave Ryman an opportunity to reflect further on his personal experiences and relationships. An entry marked 11 P.M., April 25, noted, "In one hour more I will be twenty-five years of age and thank the blessed muses free as the air I breathe. . . . I am neither married or to be given in marriage thank God."[42] Two days later, he wrote, "I was 25 yesterday and I never yet lay with a widow whore virgin or bride to have complete copulation with them unless I am most d—dly mistaken on the girls I have been with."[43] And again the next day, "Have just been reading in Byron's letters notes on some of his remarks on matrimony. They are as just as they are comic. G——d d——n imbecile idiot of myself it was when I became engaged to be married. . . ."[44]

True to his character, Ryman remained ever inconsistent in his attitudes about intimacy and relationships, always drawn to and then repelled by women. He even confessed his vacillation, observing late in 1883, "In the main points of life I think I am a unit but in most other things my mind is a regular d——d conglomeration of contradictions."[45] For a while, Ryman reconciled his inner turmoil by advocating free love, a lifestyle that presumably would accommodate his homosexual and bisexual desires. He wrote in a secret part of his journal in 1886, "It makes me just wild to read where some innocent person has been made miserable by the imbecile [illegible] of some artificial system. I have often almost wished that I were in fact an 'illegitimate child' that I might thus have an additional reason for fighting the G——d d——d fools who try to denounce free love."[46] Ryman apparently never resolved his contradictory feelings about women. He actually married in 1893 but ten years later still could subject women to a vitriolic attack, snarling in his journal, "The very existence of such God *damned Bitches*—the simple fact that they are on Earth makes Murder not merely a luxury but a necessity."[47]

Frederick Shelley Ryman's candid thoughts on love and intimacy are indeed rare among men of the late nineteenth century and early twentieth. Most men, especially unmarried men, of that era appear to have manifested what psychologists have called bonding without intimacy. Yet, as sociologist Michael Messner has suggested, scholars who accept such a conclusion may be guilty of mistakenly assessing male intimate relationships according to standards of female interrelationship and, in the process, overlook the depth of affection that may exist and has existed among certain men. Messner cites another sociologist, Scott Swain, who has observed that, in contrast to male interaction, female intimacy depends on a mutual communication of the secrets of their inner lives, conveyed through heart-to-heart talking. Since male bonding occurs through doing things rather than spending time in intimate conversation, men seem to develop an active style of intimacy. Men thus nurture a different kind of friendship, but one that is not necessarily less intense than that of women.[48]

This active style of masculine intimacy, it seems to me, derived largely from the bachelor subculture that emerged in the late nineteenth century. The homosocial interaction that took place in the saloon, the pool hall, the ballfield, the street corner, the hunting lodge, the fishing camp, and the club room fostered a form of masculinity that honored boldness, ambition, and active rather than reflective forms of self-expression. This individual expression, however, could only become manifest within a group—the male peer group—in which men could define themselves only in comparison and contrast to their peers. The separation of gender spheres that reached full extent by the early 1900s made sex more important than marital status in defining individual identity. Both single and married men frequented social institutions of the male sphere outside the home, whether these institutions were clubs, saloons, social clubs, fraternal lodges, or brothels. Nevertheless, since virtually all men lived a bachelor existence for at least a part of their adulthood, the values of individual worth were fixed before a man married.[49]

At the end of the nineteenth century, all men—but especially middle-class men—confronted a threat to their manhood. The alleged debilitating effects of urbanization and industrialization, with their sedentary and routinized work environments, were thought to undermine men's dignity and independence. These processes combined with the male fear of becoming effeminate as a result of the intrusion of women into the public sphere—not only in politics and the workplace but also in the attack on men's habits through efforts such as the Women's Christian Temperance Union and crusades for sexual purity—to impel men to seek new ways to reassure themselves of their manliness and their masculinity. They did so by revolting against the refinements of "civilization"—against, that is, the moral values of female civility. This revolt involved an enhanced validation of bachelor subculture and the boyish behavior that underlay it. In this way, bachelor society and American masculinity became intrinsically linked.[50]

BACHELOR ROLE MODEL AND THE ULTIMATE MAN

Theodore Roosevelt, with his obsession for pursuing the strenuous life, often is identified as the most influential model of American manliness in the closing decades of the nineteenth century. Cowboy, big-game hunter, rough-riding soldier, outdoorsman, vicarious athlete, and proponent of the importance of victory in all walks of life, Roosevelt symbolized the panacea for an emasculated manhood that was presumed to be characterizing the modern American male population.[51] In essays, such as "The American Boy" and "Manhood and Statehood," Roosevelt asserted his belief in the relationship between manly physical vigor and success in business, politics, and war.[52] An active and competitive life, Roosevelt believed, could transform a man's character and condition him to strive to accept only victory in the competition between men and between nations that the modern age required. He once wrote, "I feel we cannot too strongly insist upon the need for the rough, manly virtues. A nation that cannot fight is not worth its salt, no matter how cultivated and refined it may be."[53]

Turn-of-the-century middle-class intellectuals, educators, and reformers of all types undoubtedly found Roosevelt's panegyrics to a new robust manliness appealing. But the men of all classes who tippled a few at the corner saloon, read the sports section of the popular press and perused *The National Police Gazette* and other such publications at the neighborhood barber shop may well have located their symbol of American manhood in another, less respectable individual. They could not have found a more accessible hero in a raucous, brutish, giant whose exploits promised to relieve them of their worries about the influence of coddling females and the dangers of flabby family and work lives. That man was the Strong Boy of Boston, John L. Sullivan, bare-knuckle prizefighting's heavy-weight champion, conqueror of all challengers, a man's man, and the archetypal bachelor. A man who rejected the staid life of regular work and family for the barroom and the prizefight arena, Sullivan consciously chose to live by his fists and his wits. As boxing historian Elliott Gorn has concluded, "If one may think of culture in terms of gender, then John L. Sullivan, the greatest American hero of the late nineteenth century, rep-resented a remasculinization of America. . . . To turn-of-the-century American men, Sullivan symbolized the growing desire to smash through the fluff of bourgeois gentility and the tangle of corporate ensnarements to the throbbing heart of life."[54]

Born in 1858 to Irish immigrant parents who lived in the Boston suburb of Roxbury, Sullivan quickly grew impatient with the mundane working-class life of his father and spent much of his young manhood in the bachelor haunts of the street and the saloon. Here, amid the active expressions of bra-vado and prowess, Sullivan constructed his persona through sporting competition, first as a baseball player and then with mammoth feats of strength. Weighing nearly two hundred pounds as a teenager, Sullivan gained a reputation for his power and his braggadocio—he claimed in his autobiography that he once single-handedly lifted a horse car back onto a track from which it had deviated.[55]

By the time he was twenty, Sullivan had launched his career as a prizefighter, entering theaters and music halls where box-ing "exhibitions" were taking place (prizefighting was illegal in Massachusetts and several other states, but promoters and contestants circumvented the law by staging supposedly light hitting sparring matches as entertainment rather than as com-petition) and challenging all comers to battle. Soon, he was traveling throughout the eastern part of the country, offering fifty dollars to any man who could last four rounds with him—he is reputed to have entered each establishment and exclaimed, "'My name is John L. Sullivan, and I can lick any son of a bitch alive! If any of 'em here doubts it, come on!'" Using devastating punching ability, Sullivan disposed of all opponents, including some of the era's most feared pugilists.[56] Before long, he was competing in more formal matches against professionals. In 1882, largely at the instigation of Richard Kyle Fox and *The National Police Gazette* (see chapter 6), Sullivan dispatched the reigning heavyweight champion, Paddy Ryan, at a celebrated match outside of New Orleans. For the next ten years, this hulking Irish hero completely dominated the American prize ring, and, because of the attention he drew from the popular media, Sullivan's name became one of the most recognized in the country.

Several sports and cultural historians have ably chronicled and analyzed John L. Sullivan's experiences as a boxer. What is more important in this context is his career as a cultural hero and symbol of manliness. Though he married in 1883, Sullivan lived a bachelor's existence for most of his early and middle adulthood. Just a year after his marriage and shortly after the birth of his son, Sullivan and his wife, the former Annie Bates, a tall, hefty woman who weighed almost as much as her husband, rarely saw each other even though they were not divorced until twenty-five years later.[57] John and Annie were probably too much alike. Both had violent tempers, and both were alcoholics. During the brief period that they lived together, Sullivan subjected Annie to considerable physical abuse, allegedly beating his wife severely on several occasions. John L. found the saloon much more gratifying than the hearth, and he left Annie for long periods of time, even when he was not traveling to seek or engage in a professional fight. It did not take long for the abuse, drunkenness, and neglect to take its toll. In the spring of 1884, Annie left John for good, moving from Boston to live with relatives in Rhode Island.[58]

Though Sullivan's marital troubles were widely published—the *Police Gazette* was especially energetic in its coverage—the reports did not diminish his fame. Indeed, they only seemed to

FIGURE 7.4. John L. Sullivan, the Boston Strong Boy and world champion prizefighter, stood as the model of masculine physical prowess. At the same time, his obstreperous lifestyle of drinking, womanizing, and bravado epitomized the most churlish limit of bachelor subculture. (Culver Pictures, Inc.)

243

make John L. more of a celebrity. He was a man whom people constantly talked about and went to see, even if he was only posing on a stage or, as occurred later in his career, acting in some hastily staged melodrama. Sullivan lived his life in public view, and although people did not always adulate him, there can be no doubting his flair and brute charisma. There was something vicariously appealing about his raw, unrestrained, violent masculinity. It validated an antiauthoritarian bent of the working class, especially of the Irish-American working class, and offered a surrogate aggressiveness to the sedentary middle class.

Sullivan avidly cultivated both the bright and inglorious sides of his notoriety. Stories spread of how he would swagger down a street, tossing coins around to the youths who invariably followed him. Boys and men dogged him ceaselessly, eager for a chance to receive his famous bone-crushing handshake. Sullivan's picture hung in countless saloons and pool halls across the country, a wax museum exhibited his likeness, and one enterprising musician composed a song to him titled, "Let Me Shake the Hand That Shook the Hand of Sullivan." Long before Babe Ruth linked his name to, and derived a handsome income from, the advertising of consumer products, Sullivan endorsed numerous goods, and publishers, including his purported enemy Richard K. Fox, sold fawning biographies of him. At the same time, darker tales also spread of his drunken tirades in one or another saloon, where he smashed glassware and furniture, then disdainfully handed over a fistful of dollar bills as recompense to the barkeeper while at the same time buying a drink for everyone in the house — and, of course, later accepting one in return.[59]

Sullivan achieved and displayed his persona in an all-male and largely bachelor environment, the milieux of the saloon and the prize ring, where drink, cigars, violence, money, braggadocio, and comradely generosity all blended together to create and reinforce the male peer group. These settings gave Sullivan innumerable opportunities to throw around both his weight and his money. The ritual of the bottle—toasting and treating—cemented male bonding and created prestige. Sullivan clearly loved this subculture and used it for his own aggrandizement. He once explained to his manager, "I can't help it, Al. Everybody's running after me with, 'John, have a drink' here and 'John, have a drink' there. I don't like to make anybody mad by refusing."[60]

Like many an Irish bachelor—and, as chapter 3 has suggested, many bachelors of all ethnicities—Sullivan lived at home with his parents until he was twenty-four years old. But even then, and especially thereafter, he lived the unfettered bachelor existence that moralists feared and some men secretly craved. He not only hopped from bar to bar; he also bought, lavishly remodeled, and opened his own commercial drinking establishment, the Champion's Saloon, on Washington Street, two blocks from New York's City Hall.[61] Sullivan seemed to be able to do what he wanted, when he wanted, and where he wanted, and he never suffered from the torments and vacillations that plagued someone like Frederick Ryman. He was, as Gorn has remarked, "a creature of impulse." No one tied him down; not his parents, certainly not his wife, no other woman, not his various managers, and not even his profession.

But time and the high life eventually took their toll. Before he was even thirty, John L. Sullivan's body had surrendered to his dissipation. His punch still was powerful, but more than a decade of intense hedonism was beginning to fatten his girth and weaken his legs. After defeating the great Jake Killrain in a seventy-five-round marathon July 8, 1889, the last bare-knuckle championship fight to be held,[62] the Boston Strong Boy abandoned the ring for the stage. He toured North America and Australia, performing in a drama written expressly for him. By 1892, with his stature as a hero fading, Sullivan agreed to a championship fight with an upstart pugilist from San Francisco, the dapper James J. Corbett (Gentleman Jim, as he was known). Unlike Sullivan's previous fights, this one would be fought with the pugilists wearing gloves, and instead of the

Police Gazette promoting the battle, Joseph Pulitzer's *New York World* arranged the contest. In contrast to Sullivan, Corbett was clean-cut, a former college student, and a "scientific" boxer who followed training and dietary rigors. The bout took place on September 7, 1892, in New Orleans. Corbett, eight years younger and twenty pounds lighter, out-boxed his slower, flabbier opponent, finally felling an exhausted Sullivan in the twenty-first round.[63] An era had ended but was not forgotten.

By the time of John L. Sullivan's downfall, American males worshipped an expanded panoply of masculine heroes. But the Boston Strong Boy had served a vital purpose. He had given American men a model of action, whether it be in the role of bon vivant or reckless brute. Even in defeat, Sullivan continued to attract male fascination. Theodore Dreiser ranked Sullivan among those individuals who had impressed him the most as a young man, labeling him "a sort of prize-fighting J. P. Morgan." Dreiser recalled approaching Sullivan for an interview and hearing the great one retort,

> Sit down and have some champagne. Have a cigar. Give 'im some cigars, George. These young newspaper men are all right to me. . . . Write any damned thing yuh please, young fella, and say that John L. Sullivan said so. That's good enough for me. If they don't believe it bring it back here and I'll sign it for yuh. But I know it'll be all right, and I won't stop to read it neither. That suit yuh? Well, all right. Now have some more champagne and don't say I didn't treat yuh right, 'cause I did. I'm ex-champion of the world defeated by that little dude from California, but I'm still John L. Sullivan—ain't that right? Haw! haw! They can't take that away from me, can they? Haw! haw! Have some more champagne, boy.[64]

Sullivan's self-indulgence derived from a bachelor existence, one of individualism and diminished responsibility. He became a hero to those who lived outside of, or who tried to escape from, the patriarchal family and the social expectations for success in business or a profession. He acted as a raucous

246

bachelor who expanded upon the tenets of boy culture and epitomized the subculture of physical prowess and alcoholic gregariousness. He was "a drunken bullyboy with heart of gold," who encapsulated all of the contradictions that a bachelor's life represented: the tension between personal freedom and self-control, the struggle between financial responsibility and the temptations of the flesh, the safety of stability versus the thrill of the impulsive.[65] Sullivan left a problematic legacy in an era of both the refashioned manhood and the increasingly conspicuous bachelorhood that characterized the period between his rise to prominence in the early 1880s and his death in 1918.

THE LEGACY OF BACHELOR SUBCULTURE

By the end of the 1920s, the heyday of bachelorhood among the American population had passed. Proportionately, bachelors as a segment of the total male population were on the decline. The percentage of unmarried males aged fifteen and older had dropped to 34.1 in 1930, after peaking at 41.7 in 1890 and remaining relatively high at 38.7 in 1910.[66] Marriage, it appeared, was coming back in style. Whereas just fifty-nine out of every one thousand American men of marrying age in 1890 had tied the knot during the year, the annual ratio rose to the mid-seventies during the 1920s, falling back during the deep depression years of 1930–1933, but only temporarily so. Average age at marriage, which for men stood at 26.1 years in 1890, also declined, reaching 24.3 in 1930.[67]

More importantly, however, even as marriage rates increased and marriage ages declined, American society continued to feel the impact of the large numbers of bachelors who had lived in its midst, particularly in its cities, during the late nineteenth century and early twentieth. As American males strived to refashion their masculinity, they frequently had looked to the bachelor model of self-expression and its revolt against civilized society. The search for male essence had led to figures like John L. Sullivan, whose bachelor lifestyle rebelled against feminized civilization by unleashing the rough, animal passions of the inner man. The quest for greater freedom to play and compete — among friends, in the outdoors, or on the ballfield — and the boldness and risktaking that accompanied such actions became acceptable and desirable. The means to this end involved infusing manhood with more behaviors that had been common to boyhood and to bachelorhood, those qualities of exuberance and spontaneity that once had been condemned by moralists and reformers intent upon creating a civilized society.[68]

The spreading consumer culture adopted and enhanced this theme. Advertisements in mass circulation magazines provide one example of such adoption. The discussion of *The National Police Gazette* in chapter 6 presented illustrations of how advertisements in a widely-circulated men's publication reinforced certain images of manhood, but also advertisers in more generally circulated journals such as *Collier's*, *Century*, *Harper's*, and *Life* followed similar directions in presenting their products for male consumption. Though the ads for men's products in these magazines did not necessarily target bachelors directly, they accentuated masculine attributes that derived more from the values of autonomy and action inherent in bachelor subculture than they adopted from the settled domestic responsibility of married life.[69]

Particularly relevant in these advertisements was the depiction of camaraderie, especially the friendship and respect that males cultivated in the all-male environment of the tavern, the pool hall, and the outdoors. Obviously, ads for beer and spirits, which became highly prevalent in these magazines around the turn of the century, emphasized images of drinking as a social activity — but invariably situated that activity as occurring within the sole company of men. A common image involved two men raising their glasses in a toast to each other, while the text of the ad proclaimed, "When you do drink, Drink Trimble (Whiskey Green Label). May we always mingle in the friendly bowl/The feast of reason and the flow of soul."[70] Women almost never appeared in such illustrated ads. As well, advertisements for cigarettes reflected similar male-oriented images and locations. Bonds of male friendship could also be sealed in the great outdoors, and Swift's Premium Bacon, according to another ad, was just the medium for securing those bonds. Picturing three men relaxing in their campsite at a riverbank, the advertisement advised, "For it's always fair weather—when good fellows get together on the banks of a rushing trout stream and Swift's Premium Bacon starts to sizzle on the frying pan."[71] The blend of good fellows with the outdoors made all the difference. Companionship free of female intrusion pervaded these and countless other appeals to the consuming male public.

To a considerable extent, the development of mass culture around the turn of the century signaled a victory of sorts for bachelor standards of autonomy over middle-class, largely feminine, morality. This victory was reflected in the way advertisers and the media attempted to induce and reinforce habits of smoking, drinking, betting, escape from domestic confines, and other antifeminine (and anti-bourgeois) habits that long had been identified with bachelor subculture. In spite of attempts to prohibit or provide substitutes for them, these "bad habits" nonetheless became immovably entrenched in American culture because the combination of high proportions of unmarried, unfettered male consumers with the felt need to remake manhood so as to restore a lost essence of self-expression resulted in the acceptance of norms, habits and commodities that derived from bachelor life.[72] In this way, bachelors during their peak years of visibility between 1880 and 1930 existed as an active social group that reoriented consumer culture and provided it with incentive to value the qualities of the bachelor subculture.

Moreover, by the 1920s, the presence and pastimes of large numbers of unmarried men had made bachelorhood fashionable, if not acceptable. As historian Kevin White has pointed out, magazine articles of the 1920s joyfully heralded the "joys of single blessedness" and the rejection of marriage. A bachelor, proclaimed one article, could dance "on a table . . . [and] . . . vamp three other women" simultaneously, while another article related that a man could easily find relief from loneliness by getting himself "a female Mexican jumping bean" (a pejorative term for a flapper).[73] Perhaps the best expression of this attitude came from playwright Avery Hopwood, who observed,

> Living conditions today are entirely favorable for the bachelor. He can be quite comfortable. If he possesses enough of the world's goods he can be just as comfortable as if he were married. The idea that a bachelor cannot get food and service is a myth. I have seen several friends whose houses were run much better before they were married than they have been since.[74]

Such expressions marked a triumph, of sorts, for the subculture of bachelorhood.

★ CHAPTER EIGHT ★

The Decline and Resurgence
of Bachelorhood, 1930–1995

In a feature article entitled "Games Singles Play," *Newsweek* magazine boldly announced on July 16, 1973, "Within just eight years, singlehood has emerged as an intensely ritualized — and newly respectable — style of American life." Noting that a "profound shift in mating patterns" had overtaken the country, the article focused on what its authors labeled as the new "singles-oriented society." "Until recently," the writers observed,

> the term 'single' usually connoted a lonely heart, a temporary loser whose solitary status was simply a way station on the passage to matrimony. The lonely hearts may still bleed, but for millions of other under-35, middle-class folk, singlehood has become a glittering end in itself — or at least a newly prolonged phase of post adolescence. And while much of the younger singles' fun and gamesmanship is also tinged with frustration, loneliness, and quiet desperation, many of the players contend that they have found the Good Life.[1]

Bachelorhood — as well as its female counterpart — had, it seemed, suddenly re-emerged into the public limelight.

By the 1990s, two decades later, those who were unmarried had gained even more public acceptance and prominence. With marriage age at an all-time high, men were tying the knot an average of almost six years later than had their fathers, an extraordinary rise in such a short time. Single people in general enjoyed new-found status. Hit television programs such as "Seinfeld" and "Friends" glorified the companionship of single life while scoffing at marriage. And according to University of

251

Chicago sociologist Linda Waite, "What has changed is the tolerance for not getting married. People are far-more neutral on what other people do than ever before, so there isn't the social pressure that there once was."[2]

This new outburst of marital avoidance would never have received such accolade a generation or two earlier. In the glow of postwar optimism that illuminated the familism of the late 1940s and 1950s, journalists and social scientists alike rekindled the disdain for the unmarried person that had always smoldered beneath the surface of American culture. Writing in an aptly titled volume of essays, *Why Are You Single?*, published in 1949, psychiatrist Bernard Glueck implied that marriage and emotional maturity were equivalent and that people — he mostly meant men — who did not marry suffered from some kind of psychological defect. Glueck identified three basic types of bachelors. One, he observed, was the "sexually incompletely differentiated person," that is, a man who remained single because he lacked the ability to achieve emotional independence from his mother or sister. The second category was the "excessively narcissistic type"; a man in this class, Dr. Glueck noted, not only thought only of himself but often exhibited sadistic tendencies and therefore was not marriageable. Third was the "impulse-ridden" personality, an individual who was so poorly adjusted socially that he could not complete any responsible task and therefore could never attract a marriage partner. The dysfunctional and threatening possibilities of all of these types, in Glueck's expert eye, made it imperative that Americans stress marital responsibilities in educating their youth. To Glueck, bachelorhood represented "primitive and infantile modes of thinking," whereas human progress depended on healthy married life. "The permanent union between the sexes, which marriage sanctions, offers . . . the most dependable opportunity for the fostering of the culturally indispensable enterprise for transmitting physiological hunger and biological pursuit into human values and human ideals," he wrote.[3]

As American society struggled to emerge from the hard times of the 1930s, the bachelor life that had been so prominent in the previous half century faded beneath emphases on family solidarity and the communal effort to battle economic and foreign demons. By the beginning of the Second World War, marriage rates began to rise rapidly, and during the so-called marriage boom that followed the war, social commentators, such as Bernard Glueck, had no tolerance for individuals who they believed shirked the responsibilities of family and parenthood. But slowly and somewhat furtively during the late 1950s, the bachelor subculture regrouped, aided in part by a new outburst of affluence and consumerism that created diversions in the same way that consumer culture had distracted men from marriage in the late nineteenth century. As well, new cultural values, expressed in sports, the movies, and especially men's publications such as *Playboy* magazine, in many ways *The National Police Gazette* of the late twentieth century, worked to make bachelorhood respectable as well as appealing.

By 1970 the marriage rate was plunging as it had a century earlier, and single men (and women) multiplied in new urban singles communities to the point that the *Newsweek* article of 1973 quoted Columbia University anthropologist Herbert Passin's expert opinion: "For the first time in human history, the single condition is being recognized as an acceptable adult life style for anyone."[4] Just a few years later, in a study on "The Way 'Singles' Are Changing the U.S.," *U.S. News and World Report* listed three highly beneficial ways that unmarried people were affecting contemporary society. First, by establishing upscale residential communities in the cores of the nation's cities, they were revitalizing slums. Second, their numbers and spendable incomes were creating demands for specialized products and services that were boosting the national economy. Third, their new political awareness was prompting them to demand and win modification of policies that unfairly favored married people with regard to issues such as taxes, insurance, banking and lending policies, and airline fares.[5]

What had happened to bring about both a demographic and a cultural shift that enabled bachelors to become objects of this new appreciation? Did the subculture of bachelorhood of the late twentieth century basically replicate that of the late nineteenth century? Or did new conditions and relationships distinguish it from its predecessor? Has the unmarried state actually elicited respectability? Or are bachelors still considered to be less than true men, "rogue elephants" who threaten the stability and morality of modern society? The answers to these and similar questions, including predictions about the future, are not simple; as in the past, they derive from American society's views of both family and manhood.

MARRIAGE IN FAVOR

After peaking in 1890, the median age at marriage for men and the proportion of all adult males who were unmarried slowly declined, then leveled off between the crash of 1929 and the end of the Second World War. In 1930, the median marriage age of American men stood at 24.3, and 34.1 percent of all males aged fifteen and older were unmarried; four decades earlier, median marriage age had peaked at 26.1 and 41.7 percent of adult men were single. During the depression years of the 1930s, when the national economic malaise discouraged marital commitments, the median marriage ages and the percentages of men who were remaining bachelors hovered at about the same levels they had been at the end of the 1920s.

But as the country pulled itself out of the depression, demobilized from a world war, and entered a period of postwar prosperity, these statistics plunged as marriage and family life became ever-more-valued statuses in American culture. In 1949, the year that Bernard Glueck offered his critical explanation for why bachelors were single, the median marriage age among men dipped below 23.0 for the first time since the Census Bureau began keeping detailed marriage statistics. That median stabilized between 22.5 and 23.0 until 1975, when it suddenly climbed to 23.5. During the middle of the twentieth century, the proportions of adult males who were single also reached a nadir, falling from 33.2 percent in 1940 and bottoming out at 23.2 percent in 1960 — close to half of what the percentage had been in 1890.[6]

The retreat in the incidences of bachelorhood, of course, derived from a postwar marriage boom. Early in the 1940s, as increasing multitudes of bachelors faced the prospect of overseas military combat, the country experienced a brief outburst of "good-bye marriages," men who wed their sweethearts and then left for the war. Then, immediately after demobilization brought hundreds of thousands if not millions of still unmarried men back home, marriage rates soared, chiefly as a result of two developments. First, economic expansion, which seemed to be providing good jobs and incomes that had not been available for almost a generation (between 1940 and 1955, personal income rose almost 300 percent), buoyed young people's outlook on their future. Second, veterans' benefits, especially those government-subsidized provisions facilitating the financing of home ownership, brightened young people's prospects of settling down and raising a family. In 1946 alone, some 2.2 million couples rushed into wedlock, twice the number who had married in any single year before the Second World War.[7]

Men and women sped to the altar not just because they could afford to do so but because their society encouraged, indeed pressured, them to do so. The 1949 volume *Why Are You Single?*, mentioned above, typified the prevailing attitude among medical experts, social scientists, and the clergy: the unmarried state was unnatural and socially dysfunctional. Consisting of fourteen essays written by psychologists, psychiatrists, and academics, the book consistently pounded home the point that in the United States being single was a problem. As objects of derision and humor, according to the book's editor, journalist Hilda Holland, single people suffered from anxiety, lack of self-assurance, and other psychological maladjustments. Accordingly, Holland stated that she intended her book to help the unmarried cope with their problem by enabling them to understand why they had reached their present state and by guiding them to the inner change that would enable them to attain a healthier family relationship.[8] Covering topics with titles such as "Are Parents to Blame?", "Are You an Oedipus?", and "Are You Emotionally Mature?" (the last was Glueck's essay mentioned above), the book's chapters starkly illustrate the authors' as well as their society's norms and cast a very dim light on bachelors.

Ironically—though perhaps appropriately—one essay in Holland's collection repeated the notion that bachelor subculture represented the ultimate expression of male culture. This piece, titled "The Marriage-Shyness of the Male," was authored by the noted psychoanalyst and Freudian, Theodore Reik. In the piece, Reik articulated his basic assumptions that "the truth is that marriage is originally contrary to the instincts of men," and that men "have to conquer certain tendencies within themselves, fierce and independent traits of their nature, to accept [the role of husband]." Reik believed that men's innate biological impulses militated against marriage. Young men, he contended, want to be footloose and free; the boy in the man wants to play and to elude any tinge of obligation and responsibility. Because of this conditioning, a man's sense of honor is so strong that he fears being unable to live up to society's expectations in marriage, and thus his superego, even more than society's pressures, inhibits him from marrying. To counteract this tendency, according to Reik, women need to try better to understand the bachelor's proclivity to avoid marriage, rather than chastise him for shirking his responsibilities. "No man *is* the 'marrying kind,' but most men *become* the marrying kind," Reik concluded.[9] Thus the assertive, competitive independence that had been celebrated in the new male at the turn of the century had been transformed into a semi-neurotic state of all males—but especially of bachelors—a half century later.

The final essay in Holland's book, a piece titled "Why Be Single?", summarizes the social attitudes of the baby boom era that was just getting underway. The author, Clifford R. Adams, director of the Marriage Counseling Clinic at Pennsylvania State College and author of the "Marriage Clinic" series of articles for *Woman's Home Companion* magazine, flatly stated — in contradiction of Reik — that "nearly everyone, male or female, wants to be happily married." To support his contention, Adams listed the major reasons why someone should marry: to escape loneliness, to achieve sexual satisfaction, to have children, and to attain emotional and financial security. He then detailed a prescription for how men and women could prepare themselves for marriage, a formula that included fourteen hints for finding a mate and a twenty-five-item set of questions requiring yes or no responses concerning the personal and physical qualities suitable for marriage. Adams concluded, "If you answered twenty or more of these questions *yes*, your chances of getting married are excellent. Get busy if your "yes" score was less than half." Adams did recognize that the freedom that men developed as boys enabled them to live without marriage more easily than women could, but he accused men who did not marry of being fearful and selfish. He did not prescribe how to "get busy," however.[10] Holland's book and others like it floated on the waxing tide of marriage but also rode the wave of the "procreation ethic" that washed over American society from the late 1940s through the 1950s. In an era that still placed high value on premarital chastity, marriage legitimated sexual intercourse; it provided a means for young adults to endorse the social prescriptions of fertility while at the same time escaping the sexual constraints placed on the unmarried.

From such a cultural pool the baby boom was born. Indeed, during the outburst of fertility that lasted from 1947 until 1964, a set of family-centered values, which emphasized self-sufficient, child-centered suburban domesticity, became a powerful ideal even though the ideal was unattainable for large numbers of people, especially racial minorities and the poor. The family model emphasized strong emotional and sexual bonds between husband and wife, and in the process it made the term "bachelor" — and its female counterpart, "spinster" — dirty words. Moreover, as economist Richard Easterlin pointed out, young men born during the deprivation years of the depression found that by the 1950s, a more favorable employment situation could enable them to improve upon the material situation of their youth. As a result, noted Easterlin, these men, unlike their fathers, could marry and still have available income to use for a modest enjoyment of consumer goods. Thus they had fewer impediments and more incentives to marry.[11] Among the middle class and even among the working class of the postwar generation, then, being a husband was "in"; being a bachelor was "out" — but only temporarily.

MARRIAGE IN DISFAVOR

During the social and political upheavals of the 1960s, an unheralded but momentous demographic shift began: the long linear decline in the proportions of men who were postponing or avoiding marriage reversed. In 1970, 28.1 percent of males aged fourteen and over were single, marking the first rise in this category in eighty years, and by 1977, 30.2 percent of marriageable males were single. Also, in the important category of males between ages twenty and twenty-four, the proportion of men remaining bachelors increased from 53 to 64 percent between 1960 and 1977, an impressive rise of over 20 percent.[12]

From the late 1960s through the early 1970s, an even more noteworthy trend accompanied the new increase in proportions of people remaining single. Between 1970 and 1977, the number of "primary individuals" — persons who maintained their own households while living alone or living with people unrelated to them — expanded from 11.9 million to 17.7 million, an increase of over 50 percent in just seven years and double what the number had been in 1960. (In comparison, during the years between 1970 and 1977, the total number of households in the United States grew by only 10 percent.) Most of the increase in nonfamily households involved young men and women in their twenties and early thirties who had postponed marriage. In just one generation, the proportion of all Americans between ages twenty-five and thirty-four who lived alone rose by almost 500 percent, from 5.1 percent in 1950 to 29.1 percent in 1976. The major experience of these so-called primary individuals was that of living alone away from kin, and the proportions of those coresiding with family members significantly declined. Thus between 1960 and 1970, the proportion of single men aged twenty-five to thirty-four who lived with a parent or other relative declined from 57.7 percent to 50.9 percent.

In 1977, nine out of ten "primary individual households" consisted of just one person; the other 10 percent consisted of two-person households, with 43.3 percent of these two-person domiciles consisting of living quarters shared by persons of the opposite sex (Demographers labeled these people as POSSLQ's: "persons of the opposite sex sharing living quarters."). To be sure, many of the primary individuals were elderly persons, especially widowed women; almost half of females in the category of all solitary individuals (people who lived alone) were sixty-five years of age and older. But nearly 60 percent of male primary individuals were younger than forty-five, and almost one-fifth were under twenty-five. As well, only about one in five relatively young (under forty-five) male primary individuals shared living quarters with a woman.[13] Thus, unlike two decades later, not many men were cohabiting with women in surrogate marriages.

Rising incomes accounted for most of the increase in the propensity to live alone. Demographers Robert Michael, Victor Fuchs, and Sharon Scott, using 1970 census data across a number of states, attributed about three-fourths of the increase in solitary living to economic improvement (pensions and social security for the widowed, better jobs for the young). Michael, Fuchs, and Scott also found that geographical mobility, more advanced education, and, especially for young people, a factor that they labeled "social climate" — meaning the desire for unsupervised sociability — also accounted for the rising numbers of primary individuals.[14] Thus, the major characteristic of the new population of bachelors was domestic isolation — that is, men living by themselves.

This isolation prompted some experts to build on earlier conclusions about the dysfunctional social and psychological status of bachelors in American society. For example, psychiatrists Genevieve Knupfer, Walter Clark, and Robin Room published a study in 1966 confirming the conclusion that a higher proportion of single men than either of single women or of married men showed obvious indications of maladjustment. Knupfer, Clark, and Room defined the concept of maladjustment in terms of selective factors and reactive factors. Men have greater selective freedom in the marriage market than women do, Knupfer, Clark, and Room asserted, and thus when they do not marry, the cause must be that they were psychologically impaired to begin with. Data from the Knupfer, Clark, and Room study suggested that this impairment mostly resulted from a higher incidence of childhood stress among single men than among any other group. Reactive factors, the researchers suggested, meant that men who lacked the satisfactory qualities that marriage required had a greater tendency than women to become socially isolated and antisocial.[15]

Knupfer, Clark, and Room maintained that their study overturned the popular assumption that because men long for freedom and view marriage as a defeat, their evasion of marriage would make them better adjusted than women who failed to marry. But in many ways, the male-oriented popular culture arising at the very time in which Knupfer *et al.* were writing was celebrating men's longing for freedom in ways that revived and embellished the bachelor subculture that had prevailed at

FIGURE 8.1. Hugh Hefner, publisher and editor of *Playboy Magazine*, is shown here with "bunnies," who were employees of one of his Playboy Clubs Hefner and his publication gave bachelorhood a heightened respectability, even desirability, by linking male social and sex lives with "sophisticated" consumerism. (Corbis-Bettmann)

the beginning of the century. That is, from the late 1950s through the 1970s, a newer, more assertive image of bachelor-hood came to dominate American styles, and that image emerged from the pages of *Playboy* magazine. *Playboy* was more than just another men's magazine, and it devoted itself to more than just describing and promoting the leisure pursuits of the single man. In the mid-twentieth century, most other men's maga-zines, such as *Field and Stream*, *The American Outdoorsman*, and *Sports Illustrated*, were designed to satisfy the desires of men seeking temporary diversions from their work and family responsibilities. *Playboy*, however, consciously fashioned its appeal to the man who, by condition or by desire, was a *full-time bachelor.*

Unlike the role models of other men's publications, the *Playboy* bachelor did not have to display his manhood by conquering the wilderness or by scoring the winning touchdown. Nor did he need such products as hernia trusses, muscle-building devices, or cures for shyness or venereal disease that previous men's periodicals had advertised. Rather, as publisher — and unmistakable bachelor — Hugh Hefner declared in the magazine's first issue in the fall of 1953, *Playboy* men liked to spend most of their time indoors, in their own apartment, "mixing up cocktails and an hors d'oeuvre or two, putting a little mood music on the phonograph, and inviting a female acquaintance for a quiet discussion on Picasso, Nietsche, jazz, sex." In other words, Hefner's model was what sociologist Michael Kimmel has called a "domesticated bachelor."[16] The presentations of bare-breasted, artfully photographed female "playmates" who, to be sure, were the magazine's main attraction, nevertheless supposedly were merely a component of a "philosophy" in which seductive and available young women constituted the reward for sophisticated consumerism. In his monthly feature, "What Sort of Man Reads Playboy?", Hefner repeatedly emphasized that the *Playboy* man was a modern man: a world traveler, wine connoisseur, suave dresser, one who lives the good life, and seeker of culture and cool. This man and fellow *Playboy* readers were card-carrying members of the "Upbeat Generation."[17] And whatever the commodities, whether they be stereos, wine, or women, *Playboy* men liked them in the same way: sleek, full-bodied, and pleasurable.

Playboy was not the first mass-market men's magazine to purvey the image of the successful, urbane, unfettered, and sexually conquering male; *Esquire* had been doing so since 1933. But Hefner's publication, with its circulation of nearly 7 million in the 1970s — far more than *Esquire* could ever boast — reached out in more directions by appealing to the college-educated but not-yet-affluent bachelor as well as to the sophisticated elite bachelor. In adopting this approach, *Playboy* both reflected and altered the times in which it existed.

Even before the sexual revolution of the late 1960s, *Playboy* was heralding a new hedonism, one that challenged puritan values and urged men to press beyond outmoded social conventions to experience all the pleasures of mind and body. It promoted a combination of the old bachelor independence with new, civilized libertinism. This lifestyle even had its own clubhouse: not the disreputable saloon or pool hall of the previous century but, beginning in 1960, the Playboy Club. Opened in several big cities, these establishments affected an impression of exclusivity by requiring potential patrons to apply for membership and giving them door keys once they had been accepted, mimicking old-fashioned elite men's clubs. Inside the Playboy clubs, women specially trained and specially selected for their beauty (bunnies) would serve members and their guests. Though hired for their physical attributes, the bunnies (almost like taxi-dancers of the early twentieth century) maintained an air of sexuality that was just out of reach, never allowing any hint of prostitution yet at the same time providing the pampering that a sophisticated man supposedly craved. The effect was to make club members — and those who aspired to be members by reading about club activities in the magazine — feel that their bachelorhood had a special and valued status.[18]

Most importantly, even without the clubs (most of which folded in the 1980s), *Playboy* elevated the bachelor life to a desirability, perhaps even a respectability, it had never before experienced. It also reinforced a common bachelor attitude that divided women into three categories: nuisances to be avoided, namely wives and women in search of marriage; objects of sentiment, mostly mothers and sisters; and sexual playthings — all the rest. As social critic Barbara Ehrenreich observed, the *Playboy* man "loved women" but "hated wives."[19] And as one of the magazine's early reader surveys revealed, "Approximately half of *Playboy's* readers (46.8%) are free men and the other half are free in spirit only."[20] According to the *Playboy* code, then, to achieve freedom a man had to remain, or to affect the appearance of being, unmarried. In this regard, rather than the harbinger of the sexual revolution, *Playboy* heralded what Ehrenreich called the male rebellion. "The real message," she wrote, "was not eroticism, but escape . . . [and that] a playboy didn't have to be a husband to be a man."[21] Moreover, according to Michael Kimmel, "As the magazine's title intimated, American men experienced their manhood most profoundly when they were boys at play, not men at work."[22] Here was the ultimate expression of modern bachelorhood.

The New Bachelors of the 1970s

The new bachelors of the 1970s were children of the baby boom, having been born in the 1950s, the boom's peak years. Just why they seemingly avoided marriage when their parents had subscribed so diligently to familism and all its ideals remains a complex and somewhat mysterious question. To a certain extent, the baby boomers' fathers, who had been born in the 1920s and 1930s, constituted the aberrant group; they were the ones who deviated the most from the normal historical pattern in that their marriage rates and median marriage ages dipped so exceptionally far below the figures for previous generations. The statistical behavior of their sons, the baby boomers, more closely resembled that of generations born before the 1920s.[23]

Nevertheless, certain socioeconomic characteristics and historical experiences distinguished the bachelors of the 1970s from their forebears of the turn of the century. First, as noted above, prosperity and the rising standard of living that characterized the Vietnam War era enabled many young, unmarried men to live independently in their own households rather than occupying boardinghouses or living with families who took in

FIGURE 8.2. As marriage age and proportions of people who were unmarried rose in the 1960s and 1970s, reversing a long-term trend, apartment complexes for "swinging singles" spread across the country's metropolitan areas. This advertisement for Seagrams beverages celebrates young bachelors and their female counterparts enjoying the good life around the pool of such a residence and represents the new positive image of the unmarried state. (*Life*, June 9, 1972)

boarders and lodgers. Many of these bachelors were college-educated, middle-class, and upper-working-class men who had avoided or evaded the military draft or who were returning Vietnam veterans seeking a new, independent life.

Moreover, for the first time in American history, the housing market could both satisfy the demand for and create a supply of low-cost housing that could accommodate individuals who needed only space for a bed, a small kitchen, and enough living area for a sofa, a chair or two, and, of course, a TV and a stereo. As well, the men who occupied such dwelling units were individuals, who did not want to, or could afford not to, share these amenities with a roommate. Unlike the boarding and lodging bachelors of the late nineteenth century and early twentieth, whose incomes could usually manage only at best a single room in some kind of aggregate living arrangement, the modern bachelors had the means and the opportunities to inhabit apartments in buildings designed explicitly for swinging singles. Starting in California in the early 1970s and spreading eastward to big cities such as Houston, Detroit, Chicago, and Atlanta, developers constructed singles-only apartment complexes, replete with swimming pools, tennis courts, party houses, restaurants, and organized activities designed to cater to the singles' needs. Many occupants of this type of housing had participated in the explosion in college attendance that began during the 1960s when the first of the baby boomers had begun to graduate from high school. Having obtained jobs that enhanced their spendable income, the new singles simply transferred their accustomed social life from campus to complex. As one resident of Atlanta's Riverbend Apartments crowed, "It's just like being in college again. Every apartment building is like a coed dormitory. And instead of going to the student center, you go to the Riverbend's clubhouse."[24]

At the same time, the quest for individual self-fulfillment, which in the 1950s and early 1960s had brought young adults back to the gratification of intimate ties to spouse and family, took on a more individualistic tone in the late 1960s and 1970s. A person's emotional and material satisfaction, rooted perhaps in the fear and uncertainty that seemed rife in politics, international affairs, the economy, and personal safety amid a society beset by the dual threat of nuclear holocaust and urban disorder, replaced the rewards of community, family, and even spousal commitment.[25] As a result, the new bachelor subculture contained an even greater element of self-gratification than had been prevalent in the bachelor subculture at the turn of the century, including full subscription to the sexual revolution that the allegedly new permissive society had fostered. As one presumably self-deluded "swinging" bachelor proudly overstated to a *Newsweek* reporter, "There are so many sexual options to being single in the city that you have to cut down the numbers to keep your sanity."[26]

An ethic of consumerism drove the new singles, and a variety of businesses arose to serve them. Just as cafés, pool parlors, and taxi-dance halls had sprung up to satisfy the needs of turn-of-the-century bachelors, organized parties, dating services, and singles bars proliferated across the urban landscape in the 1970s. The new singles-oriented commercial institutions differed from their antecedents of an earlier era in that they aimed to satisfy a more heterosocial clientele while their previous counterparts had served a more homosocial population. Moreover, though from one perspective, bachelors and their female equivalents could utilize the singles bars and other social establishments to search for a potential spouse, these places more frequently functioned as sexual rather than marriage markets, intended to pair off people in temporary rather than permanent liaisons. As historians John D'Emilio and Estelle Freedman have pointed out, the singles nightlife in the dance halls and amusement parks at the turn of the century, particularly among the working class, also contained a strong component of sexual pursuit. But, note D'Emilio and Freedman, the sexual quality of these establishments elicited fear and disdain from middle-class moralists who linked it to prostitution and other forms of presumed degeneration. By contrast, the middle-class singles of the 1960s and 1970s, having marched in the vanguard of the sexual revolution, not only subscribed to but also glamorized the new singles diversions.[27]

CHANGING CONDITIONS: THE 1980s AND 1990s

At first glance, the resurgence of bachelorhood that began in the 1970s seemed to continue into the 1990s, only at an accelerated pace. Whereas in 1977, 33.2 percent of men aged fourteen and older were single, by 1990, 36.2 percent were unmarried. More dramatic changes occurred among men in the most marriageable age groups: in 1994 some 81 percent of males aged twenty to twenty-four were single, compared to just 63.7 percent in 1977; among men aged twenty-five to twenty-nine, the proportions who were single almost doubled in just seventeen years, 50 percent in 1994 and only 26 percent in 1977. A remarkable rise in median marriage age accompanied — indeed accounted for — these contrasting figures. In 1977, the median age at first marriage for men stood at 24.0, still well below the historic high of 26.1 in 1890 but notably higher than the record low median of 22.5 in 1960. But over the next decade, the median marriage age soared, reaching 26.2 years in 1989 and rising to a new historic apex of 26.7 in 1994. (Similar trends occurred among women; in 1994, two-thirds of women aged twenty to twenty-four were unmarried compared to 45.3 percent in 1970, and median age at first marriage climbed to 24.5 in 1994, compared to 21.6 in 1980.)[28] The new prominence of bachelor society seemed to be stronger than ever. Or was it?

The bachelors of the 1980s and early 1990s diverged from their counterparts of the previous decade and a half in one very important regard. While in the late 1960s and early 1970s, bachelors — indeed, young single people of both sexes — took advantage of their own affluence and a congenial housing market to live alone in singles apartments, many of their younger brothers and those of the next generation subscribed to cohabitation, especially with members of the opposite sex. Still others rediscovered the haven of the parental household. Between 1970 and 1994 in the United States, the total number of unmarried couples — defined by the Bureau of the Census as two co-habiting unrelated adults of the opposite sex — increased by an astounding 600 percent, from 523,000 to 3.7 million. The federal census of 1970 counted one unmarried couple for every one hundred married couples; by 1994, the ratio had climbed to seven unmarried couples for every one hundred married couples. In 1990, the booming incidence of nonmarital cohabitation induced the Census Bureau to define a

new category for household members called "unmarried partner," and in that year it counted over three million such individuals.[29] The definition of an unmarried partner, however,
only pertained to someone of the opposite sex with whom the
householder was personally involved; the notable, and perhaps
increasing, incidence of personally-involved partners of the
same sex would have increased the figure significantly.

At the same time, the decade and a half between the late
1970s and early 1990s witnessed a marked increase in the proportions of young adults—especially men—who continued to
live, or returned to live, in the parental household. Between
1980 and 1994, the proportion of males aged eighteen to
twenty-four who coresided with one or more parents increased
from 54.3 percent to 59.5 percent, and the proportion aged
twenty-five to twenty-nine in this category rose by almost half,
from 10.5 percent to 15.6 percent. (Contrary to widespread
assumptions about the declining ability of women to live independently amid a tightening job market, the increases in the
proportions of young adults returning to the parental household were smaller among women than they were among men.)
In addition, the proportions of young unmarried men who
lived alone declined slightly between 1980 and 1994.[30]

During this most recent period, economic stringency, especially those pressures related to high rates of inflation and unemployment, along with a slight expansion in the proportions
of young men remaining in school (both college and graduate
education), accounted for most of this change. In addition,
housing prices rose more rapidly than did wages or the prices
for other goods and services.[31] The young bachelors of this
later period had been born after the baby boom had ended,
and though they might still have considered themselves to be
swinging singles, the arc of their undulation had noticeably
shortened.

The economic stagnation of the 1970s and 1980s had a profound effect on attitudes within and toward marriage that carried over into the late 1980s and 1990s. According to studies

of income trends, for the first time since the Second World War, young men emerging into adulthood faced the prospect of failing to exceed their fathers' standard of living. On the one hand, this expectation influenced a change in attitudes about women's roles, making married women's labor-force participation and careers for all women more acceptable and prompting many married couples to cope with economic pressures by depending on the incomes of two employed spouses. On the other hand, the discouraging economic circumstances also acted as a disincentive to marriage, inducing both men and women to wait longer before making marital commitments. The effects of the sexual and contraceptive revolutions still prevailed, so that young men and women sought out each other for cohabitation. Now, however, fears surrounding AIDS and other sexually transmitted diseases pushed people into more quasi-monogamous relationships in which they presumably could better minimize the risk of infection than they could in the multiple sexual relationships that had been more common in the 1960s and 1970s. But even though they mimicked a marital relationship in their sexual, employment, and consumption habits, the need for independence amid anxiety over the future restrained these young adults from tying the knot.

While *Playboy*, now joined by a host of more explicit sexually oriented imitators such as *Penthouse* and *Hustler*, continued to celebrate the bachelor life into the 1980s and 1990s, women's magazines recruited self-deprecating testimony from men who were willing to rebuke all bachelors as well as themselves. Expressing what the unmarried and married female readers of these magazines apparently wanted to read, these male writers focused on the inflexibility and juvenile indulgence that they and their fellow bachelors displayed. Writing in *Mademoiselle* in 1985, for example, one "lonely guy" confessed that most unmarried men wanted only to stay loyal to their sports interests rather than try to accommodate a woman. He concluded that too many single men subscribed to the "Ralph

Cramden philosophy of our fathers," which is "A man's gotta do what a man's gotta do."[32] A few years earlier in the same magazine, an unmarried man opened his essay with the boast "We [bachelors] go where we want, when we please, down the fast lane in little red convertibles that shine in the sun, on roads leading to adventure, . . . that's where we feel at home." But he then described an anxious date in which his female dinner guest refused his overtures for sex, causing him to ponder his loneliness and inability to commit. His experience forced him to admit, "I feel weary of the single life. I'm sick of repeating myself . . . I want someone to say, 'Stop it, relax, I'll love you forever anyway.'"[33] Another writer summed up his and, by extension, every bachelor's reputed lifestyle by quoting a psychologist who had concluded, "The one thing about not having a partner is that you can be a perennial adolescent. You can deny that you're getting older."[34] The new contingent of bachelors still attracted the disdain they always had attracted, only now bachelors themselves were being induced into admitting their own qualms.

In addition to the continuing rise in the number and proportion of never-married men in the final decades of the twentieth century, an accelerating divorce rate created a new contingent of bachelors—those who formerly had been married. Though the country's divorce rate has been increasing almost consistently since 1860, the rate of increase accelerated after 1960, especially among young adults (under the age of thirty-five). In 1977, for example, one-fourth of all couples who had married in 1970—just seven years previously—had divorced. The overall divorce rate leveled off in the 1980s, yet demographers still predict that if the current trend is sustained, over half of all marriages from the late 1970s onward will end or already have ended in divorce.[35] Throughout American history, most men and women whose marriages have been disrupted by divorce or death have remarried, and that pattern has continued to hold down to the present. But since the 1980s, the trend toward remarriage has declined somewhat while at the same time the number of divorced people who cohabit with a new partner but do not remarry has increased. Figures cited by demographer Andrew Cherlin in a Census Bureau publication, *National Survey of Families and Households*, revealed that the number of separated and divorced adults who remarried within five years of marital disruption dropped by 16 percent between 1970 and 1984, but also that the number who cohabited with an unmarried partner increased and that cohabitation before remarriage was more frequent than cohabitation before first marriage. One study, for example, found that one-fifth of all American men had lived with a woman other than their spouse at some time or other and that the majority of these men had been previously married.[36]

It was no surprise, then, that during the 1980s and into the 1990s mass-market publications addressed both seriously and satirically the issue of how previously married men could negotiate their new bachelor status. There was a proliferation of singles clubs and personal advertisements in newspapers and magazines explicitly directed toward individuals who were sailing the rough seas of postdivorce life. Dances for older singles, special singles outings at resorts, plus meetings and lectures for Parents Without Partners and other such groups arose alongside the bars, weekends, trips, and other entertainments that still attracted the not-yet-married. As well, singles clubs explicitly for people in their thirties, forties, and fifties formed across the country.

The previously married bachelor seemed to take a somewhat apprehensive, if not jaded, view of his condition, which probably accounted for his willingness to seek cohabitation before committing to remarriage. For example, as one man in his late forties observed, "After twenty-five years in two successive long-term relationships, I know that achieving real intimacy is a slow, arduous process that has nothing to do with bed hopping or sexual conquest or deception. I am cautious; I go slow."[37] Bachelorhood thus developed a new dimension.

THE GAY BACHELOR

Perhaps more than ever before the cohorts of bachelors in the last quarter of the twentieth century were pervaded and augmented by homosexual men. Though in certain social circles the term "bachelor" has long been a code word for a homosexual man, the term "gay bachelor" has taken on a new meaning in recent years. Statistics on the numbers of unmarried and married men who can be identified as gay have been and continue to be impossible to determine, but as coming out has acquired greater legitimacy, the social and political visibility of gay men has increased markedly over what had prevailed in any previous era. Gay liberation, inspired by the Stonewall riots of 1969 in which gay men actively resisted a police raid on a bar in New York's Greenwich Village, has challenged the notion that a gay male is somehow not a man and has contested homophobia in general. As result, gay subcultures and gay enclaves have sprouted and expanded in virtually every city in every region of the country.

Gay communities have had a rich history in the second half of the twentieth century. Among its other disruptions, the Second World War uprooted millions of young men from their families and communities and thrust them into environments that provided new opportunities for intimate personal relationships. For some individuals, especially those serving in the armed forces, these conditions provided outlets for same-sex desires and liaisons. In the civilian world as well, young men migrating to the city and servicemen on leave gravitated to settings like the YMCA, which, according to some accounts, long had had a reputation for tolerating homosexual connections (see chapter 5). After the war, gay men continued to pursue their "different" sexuality by remaining in urban communities that supported their way of life. These communities were common in metropolises such as New York, Chicago, and San Francisco but also existed in smaller cities such as Kansas City,

Denver, and San Jose. As historians John D'Emilio and Estelle Freedman have pointed out, gay bars particularly served as important centers of the postwar homosexual subculture; over two dozen such places existed in Boston alone during the 1950s. But also, gay "cruising" became common in certain parks, bus stations, bathhouses, and street corners of most cities.[38]

Since the 1960s, taboos against public discussion of homosexuality have eased, at least to some extent, and popular magazines, movies, and television programs tentatively have begun to depict the gay subculture in more accepting ways than previously had been common. At the same time, gay activists, represented by so-called homophile organizations, have rallied on college campuses and in urban enclaves and have sponsored gay-pride parades and campaigns for equal rights. Elevating unconventional roles, gay men especially assumed an active role in encouraging others to come out and to take pride in their homosexuality. One survey counted almost eight hundred gay and lesbian organizations in 1973; a few years later, the number reached well into the thousands. By the late 1970s, a thriving commercial culture that included health clubs, travel agencies, newspapers and magazines, and law offices had arisen to service gay consumer needs. In 1980, the national platform of the Democratic Party included a gay rights plank, and across the country, police harassment of gay people lessened, though it would be impossible to presume that equality had been achieved and that discrimination had disappeared. Physical assaults on gay people have continued and perhaps increased, and the AIDS epidemic has spread fear within and against gay male communities everywhere.[39]

Gay men's — and even to some extent gay women's — awareness and liberation altered society's assumptions about sex and indirectly affected all bachelors, regardless of their sexual orientation. As several commentators have observed, coming out of the closet made sexuality and sexual expression emblematic of self-affirmation. According to these observers, the gay per-

274

FIGURE 8.3. Mostly hidden from public view from the late nineteenth through the mid-twentieth century, gay males emerged as a visible, active, and significant segment of the bachelor population in the late twentieth century. In parades and other demonstrations, gay men expressed their pride and solidarity in a quest for justice and rights. (AP Photo/Eric Miller)

son's relationship to sex, increasingly a matter open to public discussion and even display, has forced other people more self-consciously to stake out their own alternative identity, whether it be straight, bisexual, or some other labeled status.[40] This process, more than ever before, provoked discussions in various publications that prompted unmarried men especially to examine what the concept of manhood meant to them and whether or not they had achieved it.

BACHELORS AND THE NEW MASCULINITY

In June 1985, the usually staid *U.S. News and World Report* ran a somewhat uncharacteristic feature article titled "The American Male." Responding to factors such as the social and economic changes brought about by the women's movement, the political reconfigurations accompanying the presidency of Ronald Reagan, and the maturing adulthood of the baby boom, the article's authors examined the complexities that constituted what they believed to be a new form of masculinity in the United States. The theme of the article was that macho was no longer enough. Uncertainty seemed to characterize the outlook of American men, the authors concluded, and a definition of masculinity less rigid than that which had previously prevailed was taking shape. To be sure, to some observers the persona of Ronald Reagan, with his image as a cowboy and stubborn individualist, embodied the same kind of manly hero that Theodore Roosevelt had represented nearly a century earlier. Reagan thus seemed to inspire a new macho ideal among American men. Nevertheless, most experts identified previously non-masculine values of emotional support and sharing as characterizing the new masculinity. "Where once independence and aloofness were desirable, now openness, sensitivity, and intimacy are prized," the article noted. "The shift in society's icons tell the story. John Wayne and Humphrey Bogart have been replaced by Dustin Hoffman and Robert Redford."[41]

Several other writers in the 1980s heralded the formation of men's liberation, whose subscribers believed that the patriarchal attitudes of past eras had oppressed both women and men, and that truly modern men could lead a more productive existence by rejecting the old images of valiant warrior and win-at-all-costs sports hero.[42] Men, according to the liberationists, had too long suppressed their emotions and spontaneity; they needed to get in touch with their feminine sides and break free from artificial sex-role stereotypes. Some writers even suggested that homosexual manhood, which seemed more accommodating to intimacy and emotion, could provide a viable model for heterosexual males.[43]

It did not take long, however, for the old bachelor/male mentality of aggressive competitiveness and physical exploit to reassert itself. Reacting against militant women's rights advocates ("feminazis," in the mind and terminology of one commentator), affirmative action, and even men's liberationists (who came to be identified as quiche-eaters and wimps), a number of men protested that all the self-criticism and self-reexamination had made them victims and that they needed to recover their rights as men. No less a medium than *Playboy* itself whipped up the backlash with its monthly column, "Men," authored by Asa Baber. Asserting that American manhood was under attack, Baber and other men's rights advocates believed that the legal system (including especially the divorce courts) and government laws and bureaucracies were discriminating against men in matters such as alimony and child custody (though ironically, issues of breach of marriage promise that had dogged bachelors a century earlier rarely arose) and that sensationalized publicity of sexual assault and harassment of women created an image of all men as beasts when in fact men were recipients of such abuse as much as women were.[44] The new male assertiveness gave enhanced attraction to — and demand for — cinematic displays of testosterone power in the movies of macho male stars such as Arnold Schwarzenegger, Sylvester Stallone, Steven Segal, and Bruce Willis. Usually, though not always, unmarried, the characters played by these actors exhibited many of the manly traits rooted in bachelor subculture: reckless bravery, obstinate confidence, and all-conquering physical forcefulness. The women in these films, when present at all and even when they displayed pluck and wit, served almost always as helpmate or sex object in need of rescue.

Poet and author Robert Bly carried the discourse on manhood to a further, though not unrelated, level with his exceptionally successful best-seller, *Iron John: A Book About Men* (1990). Bly's book, an eclectic blend of myth, poetry, and psychology, centered around a parable adapted from a Grimm fairy tale. The story follows the life of a young prince who becomes attached to a hairy forest-dwelling wildman named Iron John. As they wander through the forest, Iron John initiates the prince into manhood through a series of trials and tasks. Once he successfully completes these rites, the prince marries a beautiful princess and discovers that Iron John is really a majestic king, released from an enchantment by the prince's emergence into manhood.

Bly's book emphasized the virtue of male initiation and the necessity of a father figure to guide every young man into manhood. Arguing that the modern world has left boys bereft of a father's mentoring influence, Bly contended that society's and, especially, men's problems could be attributed to fatherless boys who had become confused and impotent as adults because they had only their mothers to guide them. In essence, they had become wimps. As a remedy, Bly constructed an eight-step plan—imitating the step process developed by Alcoholics Anonymous and other self-actualization programs—to enable men to recapture their true manhood. As a means to implement these steps, Bly, his associates, and scores of disciples established multiday workshops in the woods of California, New Mexico, and other rugged locations. Here, in the primeval forests of their symbolic heroic ancestors, the all-male participants in these workshops could find their spiritual manhood by shedding their confining suits and ties, donning masks and warpaint, acting as Indians and other warriors, and by talking about their common masculine bonds.[45] Such separation from women and bonding with other men constituted the theme of another best-seller as well, Sam Keens's 1991 book, *Fire in the Belly*.[46]

Bly did not necessarily reject feminism, but he did charge that in filling the void left by missing fathers (who either were completely absent from boys' lives or too consumed by the marketplace to pay their sons much attention), women had made men soft. To a considerable extent, Keen agreed, saying that men had become too bound to women and needed to find happiness in self-help activities. Unlike Bly, however, Keen suggested that men exhibit their manhood through participating in humanitarian social action and becoming "husbands to the earth."

In a curious way, the ideas of Bly and Keen seemed to revive a fundamental aspect of nineteenth-century bachelor manhood and thereby reinforce the subculture of the new multitude of unmarried males in late-twentieth-century American society. That is, by concluding that a fatherless boy would naturally—and detrimentally—bond with his mother and thereby develop a female mode of thinking, Bly and Keen found their solution in urging males on the threshold of manhood to reverse the process and recover the autonomy from female influence that bachelors had always sought. No less a commentator than polemicist Camille Paglia seemed to agree when she wrote that teenage boys—and, by extension, young unmarried men—represented "the masculine principle struggling to free itself from woman's cosmic dominance." She continued, "Teenage boys, goaded by their surging hormones . . . , run in packs like the primal horde. They have only a brief season of exhilarating liberty between control by their mothers and control by their wives."[47]

On the other hand, in focusing on refashioning a relationship between sons and fathers, these writers moved in exactly the opposite direction from the late-nineteenth and early-twentieth-century patterns in which boys and, by extension, unmarried young men strove to break free of *all* adult supervision (see chapter 7). Such autonomy stood at the center of bachelor subculture and enabled men, rightly or wrongly, to experience initiation into the adult male world with the guidance of their peers.

Whatever their relationship to their own manhood or to women, American bachelors are entering the twenty-first century more numerous and as a segment of the male population proportionately more prevalent than at any time in the country's history. Yet, in spite of their numbers, their existence as an autonomous social group may be less secure than it has ever been. Indeed, as a result of high incidences of cohabitation with a female or with a male lover, many bachelors are acting more like a spouse than did their counterparts of previous generations. Moralists may decry the demeaning of marriage that these actions portend, but such quasi-marital arrangements have nonetheless diluted the image of bachelors as rogue elephants.

As well, the new social situation in which many unmarried men find themselves may reflect a certain kind of institutional and associational loss. The old bachelor hangouts such as saloons, pool halls, and clubhouses that fostered communal, if not intimate, relationships between men have declined relative to more private and self-indulgent activities such as watching televised sports and consuming products such as clothes, cars, and electronic equipment. The result has been that today single men, compared to their counterparts a century ago, lack what Leon Ellis has called "an everyday life that includes all-male relationships that are both public in structure and primary in substance."[48] That is, the principal activities of contemporary bachelors seem to revolve more around both anonymous market negotiations and one-on-one relationships than had been the case for bachelors in an earlier era. The large-group social interaction and camaraderie that once characterized public and semi-public places have faded in comparison to the more private leisure-time pursuits to which single people now devote themselves. These changes have affected all of American society, but they may have left a special mark on bachelors, whose access to a sustained sense of community has always been limited.

Regardless of these constraints, the impact of unmarried men on American culture remains strong. Over the decades that accompanied and followed their rise to significant minority numbers in the population, bachelors' "bad habits" attracted entrepreneurs who legitimized their behavior and, in a maturing consumer society, at times even made it desirable. The various institutions that surrounded the bachelor subculture and the multifarious associations that bachelors developed became important components of a reorganized urban society. Moreover, the bachelor existence influenced conceptions of manhood and masculinity in ways that still pervade modern-day society. Not as threatening to society as moralists feared nor as lonely or maladjusted as social analysts predicted, bachelors have for the most part adapted to social change while at the same time creating their own subculture, which helped to generate that change.

* *Appendix* *

More Information on Race and Nativity

The discussion in chapter 2 of the proportions of males who were single noted that data published in the censuses of 1890 and 1920, years during which the bachelor subculture thrived, showed some particular contrasts between racial and nativity categories and general similarities among different cities. The following tables depict specific percentages of unmarried men in these categories for the twelve cities discussed in that chapter. The various lines for each table are labeled "T" for the total of all males in the category, "NW–NP" for native-whites of native parents, "NW–FP" for native-whites of foreign parents, "FB" for foreign-born, and "Black" for African Americans. As noted in the chapter, compared to the rates of nonmarriage among native-white men of native-born parents, the rates of nonmarriage were consistently lower among the foreign-born in most age cohorts in every city and consistently higher among native-white men of foreign parents. Also, in those cities inhabited by a substantial number of African American males, the rates of nonmarriage among those black males were generally lower than those among white men, but mostly in the younger age cohorts. (Certain race and nativity categories have been omitted from those cities where the numbers in these categories were too small to facilitate comparative analysis.)

How the Census Samples Were Selected and Elaborated

Not many ordinary men who were bachelors left written records of themselves. Letters, journals, autobiographies, and other materials which might yield insights into their habits and lifestyles are scarce. Yet, I believed it important to examine the inarticulate as well as the articulate among unmarried men in order to try to understand how the entire group organized their lives. Consequently, I turned to the manuscript census as a source because here I could find information on large numbers of individuals and I could utilize this information to construct some empirical snapshots of their characteristics and

TABLE A-1
Percentages of Men Aged Fifteen and Older Who Were Single
Selected Cities by Ethnicity and Race, 1890

	Total 15 +	20–24	25–29	30–34	35–44
Boston					
T	46.3	87.5	59.1	37.9	22.5
NW-NP	42.1	86.3	60.0	39.3	24.7
NW-FP	70.0	91.9	66.5	45.3	29.5
FB	35.5	84.2	53.6	32.1	17.8
Baltimore					
T	41.2	82.4	45.4	27.6	16.6
NW-NP	35.6	83.6	47.1	29.3	18.8
BLACK	38.7	75.1	40.4	28.1	16.3
Chicago					
T	44.0	85.1	51.0	29.3	17.5
NW-NP	46.1	83.0	57.0	36.2	23.2
NW-FP	76.7	89.1	55.8	32.4	21.2
FB	33.1	83.1	46.3	25.0	14.4
Cincinnati					
T	44.0	85.6	49.7	29.4	18.4
NW-NP	47.6	82.5	50.0	31.8	21.6
NW-FP	61.6	87.9	52.0	31.3	13.2
FB	21.2	87.5	43.8	23.3	7.3
Denver					
T	56.4	89.7	70.2	49.7	31.3
NW-NP	55.1	89.5	70.4	49.8	30.0
NW-FP	64.8	91.8	69.6	45.6	32.9
FB	49.3	89.4	70.2	48.9	29.7
Detroit					
T	38.8	83.8	43.4	20.8	11.1
NW-NP	39.0	81.9	45.0	25.0	12.8
NW-FP	64.7	88.7	53.2	27.4	17.9
FB	26.4	80.0	36.9	15.6	8.3
Louisville					
T	45.4	83.7	50.2	30.8	17.9
NW-NP	50.1	83.1	53.4	31.8	18.9

TABLE A-1 (*cont.*)

	Total 15 +	20–24	25–29	30–34	35–44
NW-FP	62.6	87.7	51.6	31.9	19.6
BLACK	44.0	77.3	44.1	30.6	20.7
Minneapolis					
T	49.5	90.1	62.7	36.8	22.1
NW-NP	44.2	88.4	59.0	34.3	18.6
NW-FP	63.4	91.1	59.0	33.4	20.1
FB	47.3	90.8	65.7	38.9	24.4
New Orleans					
T	43.8	81.7	47.8	30.3	19.4
WHITE	46.4	86.4	52.0	32.3	21.2
BLACK	36.1	66.9	34.2	22.3	14.9
New York					
T	44.9	84.2	51.8	32.5	20.6
NW-NP	48.2	84.7	57.3	39.5	28.1
NW-FP	68.6	89.9	60.6	39.7	27.0
FB	31.7	78.1	44.7	26.3	16.5
St. Louis					
T	46.5	86.6	52.6	31.8	18.8
NW-NP	50.6	86.1	55.9	35.0	24.5
NW-FP	65.4	88.8	53.2	32.4	20.5
FB	27.6	78.8	51.4	29.3	28.9
BLACK	42.2	75.3	41.7	30.9	20.0
San Francisco					
T	56.8	90.1	70.8	56.0	25.3
NW-NP	51.2	88.5	64.0	48.8	32.4
NW-FP	74.8	92.7	68.6	48.4	47.7
FB	42.3	89.9	69.2	50.2	34.9

Source: U.S. Bureau of the Census, *Eleventh Census of the United States, 1890, Volume 1: Population* (Washington, D.C.: Government Printing Office, 1892), pp. 883–908.

TABLE A-2
Percentage of Men Aged Fifteen and Older Who Were Single
Selected Cities by Ethnicity and Race, 1920

	Total 15 +	*20–24*	*25–34*	*35–44*
Boston				
T	41.3	83.2	44.1	24.3
NW-NP	43.0	81.3	44.3	27.4
NW-FP	58.6	86.3	52.4	33.5
FB	27.6	79.8	38.1	18.5
Baltimore				
T	35.6	68.9	32.0	18.3
NW-NP	37.7	67.8	30.6	17.8
BLACK	34.7	50.2	32.7	22.2
Chicago				
T	36.5	78.2	36.3	18.8
NW-NP	40.6	76.4	36.0	20.5
NW-FP	51.0	82.4	41.1	22.4
FB	23.7	74.3	32.3	15.8
Cincinnati				
T	36.1	74.6	38.1	20.8
NW-NP	41.5	73.9	34.2	18.7
NW-FP	36.4	82.0	43.7	25.1
FB	19.6	73.3	29.6	16.2
Denver				
T	35.8	75.4	39.9	22.8
NW-NP	35.2	74.1	38.2	21.7
NW-FP	42.7	77.7	40.1	21.7
FB	29.0	77.4	45.0	26.0
Detroit				
T	39.1	75.2	38.7	19.1
NW-NP	41.9	73.0	36.0	18.8
NW-FP	47.6	78.7	39.5	21.0
FB	31.8	76.7	40.8	17.9
Louisville				
T	34.3	67.1	32.7	19.0
NW-NP	37.4	66.4	30.8	15.9

TABLE A-2 (*cont.*)

	Total 15 +	*20–24*	*25–34*	*35–44*
NW-FP	33.5	78.1	39.8	24.6
BLACK	33.3	58.9	33.2	21.8
Minneapolis				
T	37.7	78.7	39.1	20.6
NW-NP	37.9	75.6	33.6	15.8
NW-FP	47.6	81.1	42.6	21.3
FB	27.2	79.3	39.9	22.8
New Orleans				
T	40.1	72.2	37.1	20.7
NW-NP	47.4	75.3	37.6	21.3
NW-FP	34.1	75.8	37.6	21.3
BLACK	33.3	57.3	28.8	16.3
New York				
T	38.1	80.8	36.9	17.5
NW-NP	45.7	79.9	40.4	22.4
NW-FP	54.7	84.4	44.9	25.2
FB	25.3	78.0	30.9	13.0
St. Louis				
T	36.5	71.9	35.3	20.4
NW-NP	42.1	70.5	33.0	19.6
NW-FP	37.7	78.1	39.7	22.5
FB	23.6	73.3	33.5	17.0
BLACK	34.7	60.5	36.0	23.1
San Francisco				
T	43.8	79.1	47.4	31.2
NW-NP	45.9	75.8	41.9	27.2
NW-FP	48.6	83.6	48.8	31.8
FB	38.5	78.1	51.3	33.9

Source: U. S. Bureau of the Census, *Fourteenth Census of the United States, 1920, Volume 2: Population* (Washington, D.C.: Government Printing Office, 1922), pp. 466–523.

their environments. The results of this analysis have been integrated into chapter 3 and used to a lesser extent in chapter 2.

For each of three years — 1880, 1900, and 1920 — I sampled individual bachelors from censuses for three cities — Boston, Chicago, and San Francisco — a total of nine samples. It was important in each instance to construct a sample that was large enough to analyze in some detail, but also to ensure that each sample represented the general population of unmarried men inhabiting each particular city in each particular census year. I determined a target sample size of 900 individuals from each of the nine samples. The sampling method did not always render results that exactly matched this numerical goal, but the results were remarkably close, given the difficulty of the process.

The actual process of selecting these samples was time-consuming and laborious, but worthwhile. To make each sample representative, I either estimated or determined the approximate total of unmarried (never-married, divorced, and widowed) men aged sixteen and older in each city in each census year. (That is, in 1880, estimates were necessary because the published census volumes did not present specific counts of how many unmarried men there were aged sixteen and over. In later years, such data did exist.) I then, with aid from research assistant Todd Nelson, recorded every "nth" unmarried male in the desired age category from each census so as to produce a sample of 900. Thus, in 1900, Boston had 89,901 unmarried males aged sixteen and over, so we selected every 100th unmarried man; we recorded every 275th man from the 249,158 unmarried males in the Chicago population; and we sampled every 80th man from San Francisco's 72,621 unmarried males in the desired age category.

For each sampled individual, we recorded personal information presented in the census, information such as relation to head of household (i.e., whether the individual was head, son of head, sibling of head, boarder, etc.), age, place of birth, parents' places of birth, and occupation. But also, I believed it important to include information about the household in which the sampled individual was living. Therefore, we tabulated and added to each individual record details about the number of household heads, the presence and number of the sampled individual's parents, the number of siblings and other kin living with the sampled individual, the number of boarders living with the sampled individual, the size (number) of the head's family, the size of the sampled individual's family, the total in the entire household, the head's age, birthplace, and occupation, and the dwelling type (family residence, boarding-house, or other). This information then was coded and aggregated into data files that were processed by SPSS programs to produce a variety of tables, some of which are presented in chapter 3.

Notes

INTRODUCTION
THE AGE OF THE BACHELOR

1. "The Way 'Singles' Are Changing U.S.," *U.S. News and World Report* (January 31, 1977), pp. 59–60.

2. Quoted in Wolfgang Mieder, ed., *The Prentice-Hall Encyclopedia of World Proverbs* (Englewood Cliffs, N.J.: Prentice-Hall, 1996), p. 17.

3. Mary Beard, "Economics," in Ira S. Wile, ed., *The Sex Life of the Unmarried Adult* (New York: Pantheon Books, 1934), pp. 158–61.

4. See Peter J. Stein, *Single* (Englewood Cliffs, N.J.: Prentice-Hall, 1976), p. 4.

5. George Chauncey, *Gay New York: Gender, Urban Culture, and the Making of the Gay Male World, 1890–1940* (New York: Basic Books, 1994), pp. 76–77, 132–33, 166.

6. Ibid.

7. Margaret Mead, "The Sex Life of the Unmarried Adult in Primitive Society," in Wile, ed., *Sex Life of the Unmarried Adult*, p. 53.

8. Ernest W. Burgess, "Sociological Aspects of the Sex Life of the Unmarried Adult," in Wile, ed., *Sex Life of the Unmarried Adult* pp. 116–54; Leonard Cargan and Matthew Melko, *Singles: Myths and Realities* (Beverly Hills, Calif.: Sage Publications, 1982), pp. 17–18; and Alan G. Davis and Philip M. Strong, "Working without a Net: The Bachelor as a Social Problem," *Sociological Review*, n.s., 25 (February 1977): 112–13.

9. Burgess, "Sociological Aspects," p. 118; Cargan and Melko, *Singles*, p. 17; and Elmer Spreitzer and Lawrence E. Riley, "Factors Associated with Singlehood," *Journal of Marriage and the Family* 36 (August 1974): 533.

10. Davis and Strong, "Working without a Net," pp. 113–14.

11. Ibid., pp. 116–17.

12. Ibid., p. 120; Cargan and Melko, *Singles*, pp. 81–82; Leonard Ellis, "Men among Men: An Exploration of All-Male Relationships in Victorian America" (Ph.D. diss., Columbia University, 1982), p.

425; and Milton C. Regan, *Family Law and the Pursuit of Intimacy* (New York: New York University Press, 1993), p. 23.

13. Cargan and Melko, *Singles*, pp. 17–18.

14. James F. Short, Jr., "Subculture," in Adam Kuper and Jessica Kuper, eds., *The Social Science Encyclopedia* (London: Routledge and Kegan Paul, 1985), p. 839.

15. J. Milton Yinger, "Contraculture and Subculture," *American Sociological Review* 25 (October 1960): 627.

16. Ibid.

17. J. Milton Yinger, *Countercultures: The Promise and the Peril of a World Turned Upside Down* (New York: The Free Press, 1982), p. 23.

18. William W. Zellner, *Counterculture: A Sociological Analysis* (New York: St. Martin's Press, 1995), p. vii.

19. Yinger, "Contraculture and Subculture," p. 629.

20. See, for example, Davis and Strong, "Working without at Net," pp. 109–29; Ellis, "Men among Men," pp. 629–30; Elizabeth H. Pleck and Joseph H. Pleck, "Introduction," in Elizabeth H. Pleck and Joseph H. Pleck, eds., *The American Man* (Englewood Cliffs, N.J.: Prentice-Hall, 1980), p. 19; Christine Stansell, *City of Women: Sex and Class in New York, 1789–1860* (Urbana and Chicago: University of Illinois Press, 1987), pp. 100–101; Kathy Peiss, *Cheap Amusements: Working Women and Leisure in Turn-of-the-Century New York* (Philadelphia: Temple University Press, 1986), pp. 16–21.

21. See Michael A. Messner, *Power at Play: Sports and the Problem of Masculinity* (Boston: Beacon Press, 1992), p. 8.

22. Nancy Cott, "On Men's and Women's History," in Mark C. Carnes and Clyde Griffen, eds., *Meanings for Manhood: Constructions of Masculinity in Victorian America* (Chicago: University of Chicago Press, 1990), pp. 206–10.

23. Clyde Griffen intimated such an approach in his essay, "Reconstructing Manhood," in Carnes and Griffen, eds., *Meanings for Manhood*, p. 184.

24. See, for example, Michael Kimmel, *Manhood in America: A Cultural History* (New York: The Free Press, 1996), p. 32. I am indebted to Gail Bederman for insights on the particular issue of interaction between male culture and bachelor subculture.

25. This point has been ably made by Clyde Griffen in "Reconstructing Masculinity from the Evangelical Revival to the Waning of

Progressivism: A Speculative Synthesis," in Carnes and Griffen, eds., *Meanings for Manhood*, pp. 183–204.

26. I have adapted these ideas from Eric Silla, " 'People Are Not the Same': Leprosy, Identity, and Community in Colonial and Post-Colonial Mali" (Ph.D. diss., Northwestern University, 1995), pp. 51 and 182, and from Barry Adam, *The Survival of Domination: Inferiorization and Everyday Life* (New York: Elsevier, 1978), pp. 12, 115.

27. Adam, *The Survival of Domination*, p. 12; James C. Scott, *Weapons of the Weak: Everyday Forms of Peasant Resistance* (New Haven: Yale University Press, 1985), p. 338.

CHAPTER ONE
BACHELORHOOD IN EARLY AMERICAN HISTORY

1. Anne Macvicar Grant, *Memoirs of an American Lady* (London: Longman, Hurst, Rees, and Orme, 1808), quoted in Arthur Wallace Calhoun, *The Social History of the American Family from Colonial Times to the Present* (1917; reprint, New York: Barnes and Noble, 1945), 1:165.

2. I refer here explicitly to whites because racial minorities experienced even more circumscribed situations.

3. Milton C. Regan, *Family Law and the Pursuit of Intimacy* (New York: New York University Press, 1993), p. 17; and Mary P. Ryan, *Cradle of the Middle Class: The Family in Oneida County, New York, 1790–1865* (Cambridge: Cambridge University Press, 1981), pp. 167–68.

4. Data taken from Robert V. Wells, *Revolutions in American Lives: A Demographic Perspective on the History of Americans, Their Families, and Their Society* (Westport, Conn.: Greenwood Press, 1982), pp. 21–25 and 80–82. Wells notes that by the time of the Revolution, sex ratios in some colonies, notably Massachusetts and Rhode Island, showed female majorities, mostly resulting from the out-migration of males; nevertheless, migration patterns continued to create large imbalances in favor of males in most western and southern communities. See also, Darret B. Rutman and Anita H. Rutman, *A Place in Time: Middlesex County, Virginia, 1650–1750* (New York: Norton, 1984), p. 77.

5. See John D'Emilio and Estelle B. Freedman, *Intimate Matters: A*

History of Sexuality in America (New York: Harper and Row, 1988), chap. 2.

6. Steven Mintz and Susan Kellogg, *Domestic Revolutions: A Social History of American Family Life* (New York: The Free Press, 1988), pp. 36–37.

7. On European marriage ages for men, see John Gillis, *Youth and History: Tradition and Change in European Age Relations, 1790– Present* (New York: Academic Press, 1981), p. 46. Most accounts of American Indians place marriage at a very early age, around twelve for females and fifteen for males. Such young ages meant that almost all native men married without ever experiencing a time of adult bachelorhood. Also, since it is very difficult to determine age at marriage for African and Indian slaves, it is also difficult to identify how many and how long such slaves were bachelors. Though many slave children were born out of wedlock in Anglo terms, their fathers had entered long-lasting relationships with a "wife" while in their twenties. See Mintz and Kellogg, *Domestic Revolutions*, pp. 30 and 35.

8. Wells, *Revolutions in American Lives*, p. 42; Philip J. Greven, Jr., *Four Generations: Population, Land, and Family in Colonial Andover, Massachusetts* (Ithaca, N.Y.: Cornell University Press, 1970), pp. 31–37 and passim; Kenneth A. Lockridge, *A New England Town: The First Hundred Years* (New York: W. W. Norton, 1970), p. 66; John T. Gillis, *Youth and History: Tradition and Change in European Age Relations* (New York: Academic Press, 1974), p. 14.

9. Thomas P. Monahan, *The Pattern of Age at Marriage in the United States* (Philadelphia: The Stephenson Brothers, 1951), pp. 82–83.

10. Calhoun, *Social History of the American Family*, 1:202, 246.

11. See Mintz and Kellogg, *Domestic Revolutions*, pp. 56–57.

12. Quoted in Beatrice M. Hinkle, "Spinsters and Bachelors," in Hilda Holland, ed., *Why Are You Single?* (New York: Farrar Straus, 1949), p. 158.

13. Calhoun, *Social History of the American Family*, 1:202, 241– 42; Steven Mintz, "Regulating the American Family," *Journal of Family History* 14 (1989): 389.

14. Willystine Goodsell, *A History of Marriage and the Family* (New York: Macmillan Co., 1934), p. 368.

15. Ibid.

16. E. Anthony Rotundo, *American Manhood: Transformations in*

Masculinity from the Revolution to the Modern Era (New York: Basic Books, 1993), pp. 279–80.

17. Quoted in Richard Stott, *Workers in the Metropolis: Class, Ethnicity, and Youth in Antebellum New York City* (Ithaca, N.Y.: Cornell University Press, 1990), p. 121.

18. Ibid.

19. See, for example, David T. Courtwright, *Violent Land: Single Men and Social Disorder from the Frontier to the Inner City* (Cambridge: Harvard University Press, 1996), pp. 47–50.

20. Wells, *Revolutions in American Lives*, pp. 94–95.

21. Merle Curti, *The Making of an American Community: A Case Study of Democracy in a Frontier County* (Stanford, Calif.: Stanford University Press, 1959), pp. 56, 67–68. Curti's figures, however, show considerable mobility among married men as well as unmarried men; between 1860 and 1870 and between 1870 and 1880, only 13 percent fewer married men stayed in the county as unmarried men. See table in Curti, p. 68.

22. See, for example, Timothy R. Mahoney, "'A Common Bank of Brotherhood': The Booster Ethos, Male Subculture, and the Origins of Urban Social Order in the Midwest of the 1840s," unpublished paper; and Courtwright, *Violent Land*, pp. 56–59.

23. Courtwright, *Violent Land*, pp. 70–75; Michael Kimmel, *Manhood in America: A Cultural History* (New York: The Free Press, 1996), pp. 61–62.

24. Elliott Gorn, *The Manly Art: Bare Knuckle Prize Fighting in America* (Ithaca, N.Y.: Cornell University Press, 1986), p. 141; John C. Schneider, "The Bachelor Subculture and Spatial Change in Mid-Nineteenth-Century Detroit," *Detroit in Perspective* 3 (1978): 24. Courtwright, p. 52, claims that cities in the mid-nineteenth century harbored excesses of women, but such does not appear to have been the case among young adults. The relatively low sex ratios of men to women that Courtwright identified may have resulted mainly from surpluses of females among the very young and the elderly.

25. Stott, *Workers in the Metropolis*, pp. 215–16, 255–56.

26. Schneider, "The Bachelor Subculture," pp. 25–26.

27. St. George Tucker, *Blackstone's Commentaries: with Notes of Reference to the Constitution and Laws of the Federal Government of the United States and of the Commonwealth of Virginia*, 5 vols. (1803; reprint, New York: Augustus M. Kelley, 1969), 4:169.

28. Stott, *Workers in the Metropolis*, pp. 215–16, 255–56.

29. D'Emilio and Freedman, *Intimate Matters*, p. 123.

30. Michael Lynch, "New York City Sodomy, 1796–1873," (paper presented at the Institute for the Humanities, New York University, Feb. 1, 1985), pp. 1–2, cited in D'Emilio and Freedman, *Intimate Matters*, p. 123.

31. Stuart M. Blumin, *The Emergence of the Middle Class: Social Experience in the American City, 1760–1900* (Cambridge: Cambridge University Press, 1989), p. 217; Mary P. Ryan, *Cradle of the Middle Class: The Family in Oneida County, New York, 1790–1865* (Cambridge: Cambridge University Press, 1981), pp. 167–68; Clyde Griffen, "Reconstructing Masculinity from the Evangelical Revival to the Waning of Progressivism: A Speculative Synthesis," in Mark C. Carnes and Clyde Griffen, eds., *Meanings for Manhood: Constructions of Masculinity in Victorian America* (Chicago: University of Chicago Press, 1990), p. 190; Michael B. Katz, *The People of Hamilton, Canada West: Family and Class in a Mid-Nineteenth-Century City* (Cambridge: Harvard University Press, 1975), pp. 261 and passim.

32. Blumin, *The Emergence of the Middle Class*, pp. 212–13.

33. Timothy J. Gilfoyle, *City of Eros: New York City, Prostitution, and the Commercialization of Sex, 1790–1920* (New York: W. W. Norton Company, 1992), pp. 99–106; Elliott Gorn, *The Manly Art* pp. 141–42; Benjamin Rader, *American Sports: From the Age of Folk Games to the Age of Televised Sports*, 2d ed. (Englewood Cliffs, N.J.: Prentice-Hall, 1990), pp. 31–33; Steven Riess, *City Games: The Evolution of American Urban Society and the Rise of Sports* (Urbana: University of Illinois Press, 1989), pp. 15–21.

34. Gilfoyle, *City of Eros*, pp. 112–14.

35. Courtwright, *Violent Land*, pp. 9–21.

36. Ibid., p. 106.

37. Tony Pastor, *Tony Pastor's Complete Budget of Comic Songs* (New York: Dick and Fitzgerald, Publishers, 1864).

38. Ibid.

39. Gilfoyle, *City of Eros*, pp. 102, 115.

40. Patricia Cline Cohen, "The Helen Jewett Murder: Violence, Gender, and Sexual Licentiousness in Antebellum America," *National Women's Studies Association Journal* 2 (1990): 374–89; John D. Stevens, *Sensationalism and the New York Press* (New York: Co-

lumbia University Press, 1991), pp. 34–53; Gilfoyle, *City of Eros*, pp. 92–99.

41. *New York Herald*, April 13, 1836, quoted in Gilfoyle, *City of Eros*, p. 95.

42. Quoted in Gilfoyle, *City of Eros*, pp. 96, 98.

43. Richard Robinson, *A Letter from Richard P. Robinson . . . to His Friend, Thomas Armstrong* (New York, 1837) quoted in Gilfoyle, *City of Eros*, p. 97. Recent historians have raised serious doubt that Robinson actually wrote this letter, but, as Gilfoyle points out, it nevertheless represents a prevailing sentiment about the moral dangers confronting young men in the city. See Gilfoyle, *City of Eros*, n. 8, p. 359. For a full analysis of the Robinson-Jewett affair, see Patricia Cline Cohen, *The Murder of Helen Jewett: The Life and Death of a Prostitute in Nineteenth-Century New York* (New York: Alfred A. Knopf, 1998).

44. Quoted in Gilfoyle, *City of Eros*, p. 98.

45. Cited in Milton C. Regan, *Family Law and the Pursuit of Intimacy* (New York: New York University Press, 1993), p. 27.

46. Quoted in ibid.

47. Leonard Ellis, "Men among Men: An Exploration of All-Male Relationships in Victorian America" (Ph.D. diss., Department of Sociology, Columbia University), 1982, p. 348.

48. The Olympic Club of San Francisco, *Centennial, 1860–1960* (privately printed, n.d.).

49. Kimmel, *Manhood in America*, p. 175.

50. Junius Henri Browne, *The Great Metropolis: A Mirror of New York* (San Francisco: H. H. Bancroft and Company, 1869), p. 453.

51. J. Bixby, "Why Is the Single Life Becoming More General?" *Nation* 6 (March 5, 1868).

52. Francis Gerry Fairfield, *The Clubs of New York* (New York: Henry L. Hinton, Publisher, 1873), p. 74.

53. Ibid., pp. 11–12.

54. Ibid., p. 12.

55. Ellis, "Men among Men," p. 351.

56. Ibid., pp. 364–65.

57. Ibid., p. 370.

58. Fairfield, *The Clubs of New York*, p. 27.

59. Quoted in Calhoun, *Social History of the American Family*, 3:200.

CHAPTER TWO
WHY SO MANY BACHELORS?

1. Ernest R. Groves, *Marriage*, rev. ed. (New York: Henry Holt & Co., 1941), pp. 17–20.

2. Nancy Cott, "Giving Character To Our Whole Civil Polity: Marriage and the Public Order in the Late Nineteenth Century," in Linda Kerber, Alice Kessler-Harris, and Katherine Kish Sklar, eds., *U.S. History as Women's History* (Chapel Hill: University of North Carolina Press, 1993), pp. 107–9. See also Thomas J. Espenshade, "Marriage Trends in America: Estimates, Implications, and Underlying Causes," *Population and Development Review* 11 (June 1985): 193.

3. Groves, *Marriage*, p. 614.

4. Ernest W. Burgess, "Sociological Aspects of the Sex Life of the Unmarried Adult," in Ira S. Wile, ed., *The Sex Life of the Unmarried Adult* (New York: Pantheon Books, 1934), p. 118.

5. As Peter Stein has pointed out, these terms apply to a divergent group of people who have one common characteristic: they are not married. Moreover, their status implies the opposite to a positive choice, a "bad choice" in which they "lack" a partner, are not "complete," and are "alone." See Peter J. Stein, *Single* (Englewood Cliffs, N.J.: Prentice-Hall, 1976), p. 9.

6. Stein, *Single*, p. 4.

7. U. S. Bureau of the Census, *Eleventh Census of the United States: Volume 1: Population* (Washington, D.C.: Government Printing Office, 1890), p. 387. Demographer Paul Harold Jacobson estimated the proportion of males who were single to be even higher, at 45.9 percent. See Paul Harold Jacobson, *American Marriage and Divorce* (New York: Rinehart, 1959), p. 34. The census did not begin tabulating marriage data until 1890, but most sources suggest that rates of single males in the population, though rising, were somewhat lower in the country as a whole before the tabulation of 1890. Of course, proportions of males who were single in individual communities exceeded those of the nation before 1890, as chapter 2 has demonstrated.

8. Louis Dublin, "These Are the Single," in Hilda Holland, ed., *Why Are You Single?* (New York: Farrar, Straus, 1949), p. 69.

9. Kingsley Davis, "The American Family in Relation to Demo-

graphic Change," in Charles F. Westoff and Robert Parke, Jr., eds., *Report of Commission of Population Growth and the American Future, Volume 1: Demographic and Social Aspects of Population Growth* (Washington, D.C.: Government Printing Office, 1972), table 2, p. 243.

10. Paul H. Jacobson, *American Marriage and Divorce* (New York: Rinehard and Company, 1959), p. 35.

11. U. S. Bureau of the Census, *Special Reports: Marriage and Divorce, 1867–1906* (Washington, D.C.: Government Printing Office, 1909), part 1, p. 8.

12. Ibid., p. 11.

13. Figures adapted from Davis, "The American Family in Relation to Demographic Change," table 1, p. 243.

14. U. S. Bureau of the Census, *Eleventh Census of the United States, 1890; Volume 1: Population* (Washington, D.C.: Government Printing Office, 1895), pp. lxvii, 888–90.

15. U. S. Bureau of the Census, *Fourteenth Census of the United States, 1920; Volume 2: Population* (Washington, D.C.: Government Printing Office, 1922), pp. 57, 60, 65, 468, 473, 523.

16. This category includes both those born of foreign parents and those born of one foreign and one native parent, but for purposes of simplification in reference, I use the term "foreign parents" for both subcategories.

17. There could, of course, have been important variations among individual foreign nationalities. The data available do not permit comparison and contrast between, for example, Irish, German, Russian, Italian, and other ethnic groups. Nevertheless, the general contrast between foreign-born and native-born men seems significant.

18. Isaac Metzker, ed., *A Bintel Brief* (New York: Ballantine Books, 1972), pp. 50, 68.

19. Some people may wish to marry but are constrained from doing so. Those institutionally confined, such as prisoners, come to mind. There also can be legal restrictions and discouragements, such as prohibitions against bigamy, against marriage between relatives, against marriage between different racial groups, and against persons below certain ages. Others may be resolute in their desire to remain single; individuals such as members of religious orders and confirmed bachelors and spinsters fall into this category. See Thomas P. Mon-

ahan, *Patterns of Age at Marriage in the United States* (Philadelphia: Stephenson Brothers, 1951), pp. 32–33.

20. Ruth B. Dixon, "Late Marriage and Non-Marriage as Demographic Responses: Are They Similar," *Population Studies* 32 (November 1978): 449–50.

21. This observation contradicts the assertion by David Courtwright that differential migration rates gave cities higher proportions of women than men because men tended to move to the frontier while women moved to cities. Courtwright, however, presents no figures to support his claim. See Courtwright, *Violent Land: Single Men and Social Disorder from the Frontier to the Inner City* (Cambridge: Harvard University Press, 1996), pp. 50–53.

22. Neil Larry Shumsky and Larry M. Springer, "San Francisco's Zone of Prostitution, 1880–1934," *Journal of Historical Geography* 7 (1981): 73.

23. The figures for these cities and those in the following paragraphs were derived from marital status breakdowns in the published tables for the 1890 and 1920 federal censuses.

24. The figures for Cincinnati, Louisville, New Orleans, and Denver were as follows:

	Single women 20–29 to single men 25–34	Proportion of males 25–34 who were single	Proportion of males 20–34 who were single
Cincinnati	1.52	40.0	64.6
Louisville	1.50	41.4	61.6
New Orleans	1.70	39.5	61.3
Denver	0.49	60.0	69.5

25. Whereas the 1890 census aggregated people in the five-year age groups of twenty-five to twenty-nine, and thirty to thirty-four, the 1920 census combined all those aged twenty-five to thirty-four into one category.

26. Demographer Clifford Adams found that as late as 1940 all but four of the country's largest 106 cities showed excesses of males over females aged thirty to thirty-five relative to females aged twenty-five to thirty. Clifford R. Adams, "The Geography of Mating," in

Hilda Holland, ed., *Why Are You Single* (New York: Farrar Straus, 1949), pp. 50–66.

27. U.S. Bureau of the Census, *Fourteenth Census of the United States, Volume 2: Population, 1920* (Washington, D.C.: Government Printing Office, 1922), p. 387.

28. Adna Weber, *The Growth of Cities in the Nineteenth Century* (New York: Macmillan Company, 1899), pp. 289–98.

29. Demographer Thomas Espenshade has hypothesized an alternate theory, using what is called "exchange theory." Espenshade suggests that late marriage age and relatively high rates of bachelorhood would tend to occur in communities where there is a *shortage* of men because men would have a "favorable balance of exchange." That is, in societies in which men are in short supply, marriageable males have more bargaining power than in societies with excesses of men. Where men are in short supply, Espenshade theorizes, heterosexual relationships tend to be transient and, because single men have so many options, they place lower value on marriage and family. They therefore would marry at later ages and there would be an increase in the proportion of men who remain single. See Espenshade, "Marriage Trends in America: Estimates, Implications, and Underlying Causes," *Population and Development Review* 11 (June 1985): pp. 231–32. Espenshade's theory may well apply to places like Boston, where there were shortages of men in the late nineteenth century, but other explanations must be applied to American cities where men were the majority.

30. Stanley H. Brandes, in "*La Soltriea* or Why People Remain Single in Rural Spain," *Journal of Anthropological Research* 32 (Fall 1976): 205–33, makes this point convincingly for rural Spanish society, but it applies to North American urban society just as, if not more, appropriately.

31. Ibid., p. 208.

32. Dixon, "Late Marriage and Non-Marriage," p. 466.

33. Weber notes that in many cities the marriage rate — the annual number of marriages per thousand population — was higher than in the surrounding countryside, but he adds that such figures are misleading. Because cities contained higher proportions of people of marriageable age and lower proportions of children and older people than rural areas, the real comparisons should be made between marriage rates among people of marriageable age. These comparisons, he

pointed out, show that the marriage rate of urban populations was invariably lower than that of rural populations. See Weber, *The Growth of Cities*, pp. 319–21.

34. Timothy J. Gilfoyle, *City of Eros: New York City, Prostitution, and the Commercialization of Sex, 1790–1920* (New York: Norton, 1992), p. 239; Courtwright, *Violent Land*, pp. 47–50.

35. Kingsley Davis, "The American Family in Relation to Demographic Change" in Charles F. Westoff and Robert Parke, Jr., eds., *Demographic and Social Aspects of Population Growth: The Commission on Population Growth and the American Future Research Reports, Volume 1* (Washington, D.C.: Government Printing Office, 1972), pp. 244–45; Dixon, "Late Marriage and Non-Marriage," pp. 499–500; and Herman Hausheer and Jessie O. Mosely, "A Study of the Unmarried," *Social Forces* 10 (March 1932): 394–404.

36. Easterlin's theory is explained in Espenshade, "Marriage Trends in America," pp. 229–30.

37. Ibid., p. 326.

38. This phenomenon was clearly identified by Philip J. Greven, Jr., in *Four Generations: Population, Land, and Family in Colonial Andover, Massachusetts* (Ithaca, N.Y.: Cornell University Press, 1970).

39. See, for example, Michael B. Katz, *The People of Hamilton, Canada West: Family and Class in a Mid-Nineteenth-Century City* (Cambridge: Harvard University Press, 1975), p. 264.

40. See, for example, Brandes, *"La Soltriea,"* pp. 210–22.

41. These data were collected for a study of marriage patterns in Providence I undertook a number of years ago. Providence in the late nineteenth century was a fast-growing secondary city in many ways similar to other American industrial centers. See Howard P. Chudacoff, "Newlyweds and Family Extension in Providence, Rhode Island, 1864–1880," in Tamara K. Hareven and Maris A. Vinovskis, eds., *Demographic Processes and Family Organization in Nineteenth-Century America* (Princeton, N.J.: Princeton University Press, 1978).

42. Robert V. Wells, *Revolutions in American Lives: A Demographic Perspective on the History of Americans, Their Families, and Their Society* (Westport, Conn.: Greenwood Press, 1982), pp. 161, 190,

43. Dixon, "Late Marriage and Non-Marriage," pp. 449–50.

44. J. Bixby, "Why Is the Single Life Becoming More General?" *The Nation* 6 (March 5, 1868).

45. Quoted in Arthur W. Calhoun, *A Social History of the American Family, Volume 4: From 1865 to 1919* (New York: Barnes and Noble, 1919), pp. 210–11.

46. Kathy Peiss, *Cheap Amusements: Working Women and Leisure in Turn-of-the-Century New York* (Philadelphia: Temple University Press, 1986); Lewis A. Erenberg, *Steppin' Out: New York Nightlife and the Transformation of American Culture, 1890–1930* (Chicago: University of Chicago Press, 1981); David Nasaw, *Going Out: The Rise and Fall of Public Amusements* (New York: Basic Books, 1993); Paula Fass, *The Damned and the Beautiful: American Youth in the 1920s* (New York: Oxford University Press, 1977).

47. Ellen K. Rothman, *Hands and Hearts: A History of Courtship in America* (Cambridge: Harvard University Press, 1987), pp. 203–4; Nasaw, *Going Out*, p. 2.

48. Nasaw, *Going Out*, p. 2.

49. Henry Canby, *The Age of Confidence: Life in the Nineties* (New York: Farrar and Reinhart, Inc., 1934), p. 52.

50. Burgess, "Sociological Aspects," p. 120.

51. Frank Lillie to Frances Crane, September 24, 1894, quoted in Rothman, *Hands and Hearts*, p. 188.

52. See, for example, Erenberg, *Steppin' Out*, pp. 155–56; and George Chauncey, *Gay New York: Gender, Urban Culture, and the Making of the Gay Male World, 1890–1940* (New York: Basic Books, 1994), chaps. 5–7.

53. Rothman, *Hands and Hearts*, pp. 223–24. The trend of privacy and even anonymity continues to the present, with personal communication being exchanged via E-mail and "chat rooms" on the Internet.

54. Ibid., pp. 207–10; 289–90.

55. Ernest W. Burgess, "Sociological Aspects of the Sex Life of the Unmarried Adult" in Ira S. Wile, ed., *The Sex Life of the Unmarried Adult* (New York: Pantheon Books, 1934), pp. 116–54.

56. Ibid., pp. 214–15; 222–23.

57. M. E. Ravage, *An American in the Making: The Life Story of an Immigrant* (New York: Harper and Brothers, 1917), p. 80.

58. Steven Mintz and Susan Kellogg, *Domestic Revolutions: A So-*

cial History of American Family Life (New York: The Free Press, 1988), pp. 114–16.

59. Burgess, "Sociological Aspects," p. 119.

60. Elizabeth Lynn Linton, "The Revolt against Matrimony," *Forum* 10 (January 1891): 585–95.

61. Quotation from Brown is presented in Rothman, *Hands and Hearts*, pp. 195, 197, and 201.

62. Abe Hollandersky, *The Life Story of Abe the Newsboy: Hero of a Thousand Fights* (Los Angeles: Abe the Newsboy Press, 1930), p. 326.

63. Bixby, "Why Is the Single Life."

64. Ibid.

CHAPTER THREE
THE DOMESTIC LIVES OF BACHELORS

1. Milton C. Regan, in *Family Law and the Pursuit of Intimacy* (New York: New York University Press, 1993), makes the point that Americans in the late nineteenth century upheld the family as the essential means of constructing an ethic of personal responsibility and self-control, qualities that were vital in the modern rational and competitive economy. This ethic included a sense of duty, a communal obligation, that checked individual egoism. Only through family roles and family cohesion, thought the Victorians, could an individual cultivate these values, and thus bachelors, who seemingly paid no attention to communal obligations and detracted from family cohesion, could be vilified. See, Regan, *Family Law*, pp. 23–24.

2. Quoted in Lewis Erenberg, *Steppin' Out: New York Nightlife and the Transformation of American Culture* (Westport, Conn.: Greenwood Press, 1981), pp. 62–64.

3. U.S. Bureau of Labor, *Report on Conditions of Women and Child Wage Earners in the United States*, Senate Document 645, 61st Congress, Second Session, 5:62.

4. Elizabeth Y. Rutan, "Before the Invasion," in Robert A. Woods, ed., *Americans in Process* (Boston: Houghton Mifflin, 1902), pp. 38, 50. See also Mark Peel, "On the Margins: Lodgers and Boarders in Boston, 1860–1900," *Journal of American History* 72 (March 1986): 813; and Joanne Meyerowitz, *Women Adrift: Independent*

Wage Earners in Chicago, 1880–1930 (Chicago: University of Chicago Press, 1988), p. 111.

5. Harvey W. Zorbaugh, *The Gold Coast and the Slum: A Sociological Study of Chicago's Near North Side* (Chicago: University of Chicago Press, 1929), p. 86.

6. See, for example, Lawrence Veiller, "Room Overcrowding the Lodger Evil," *Housing Problems in America* in *Proceedings of the Second National Conference on Housing* (Philadelphia, 1912).

7. Alfred Benedict Wolfe, *The Lodging-House Problem in Boston* (Boston: Houghton Mifflin, 1906), p. 6.

8. John Modell and Tamara K. Hareven, "Urbanization and the Malleable Household: An Examination of Boarding and Lodging in American Families," *Journal of Marriage and the Family* 35 (August 1973), 467–79; Peel, "On the Margins," pp. 818–19; Wolfe, *The Lodging-House Problem*, pp. 40, 50; Frederick Bushee, "Ethnic Factors of the Population of Boston," *Publications of the American Economic Association*, 3d ser., 4 (May 1903): 34; U.S. Department of Labor, *18th Annual Report of the Commissioner of Labor, 1903: Cost of Living and Retail Price of Food* (Washington, D.C.: Government Printing Office, 1904).

9. Normally, a distinction is made between boarders, who usually received one or more meals along with their room, and lodgers and roomers, who only received lodging but no meals. For purposes of the analysis in this chapter, I do not distinguish between the two.

10. Historian Tamara K. Hareven has found this pattern to have been quite common among working-class families in New England. See Hareven, *Family Time and Industrial Time: The Relationship Between the Family and Work in a New England Industrial Community* (New York: Cambridge University Press, 1982).

11. Peel, "On the Margins," pp. 824–28.

12. In a precise sense, the term "boarding" usually refers to the experience of taking, and usually paying for, meals as well as lodging in someone else's household; "lodging" refers to taking residential, usually sleeping, space only. For simplicity's sake, however, I use the term "boarding" to cover both types of experience.

13. Historians John Modell and Tamara K. Hareven have estimated that as many as half of all urban dwellers in the late nineteenth century had lived as boarders and/or lived with boarders at

some time in their lives. See Modell and Hareven, "Urbanization and the Malleable Household," p. 469.

14. Robert A. Woods, ed., *The City Wilderness: A Settlement Study* (Boston: Houghton Mifflin, 1898), p. 82; Wolfe, *The Lodging-House Problem*, pp. 23–24; Perry Duis, *The Saloon: Public Drinking in Chicago and Boston, 1880–1920* (Urbana: University of Illinois Press, 1983), pp. 193–94; Milton B. Hunt, "The Housing of Non-Family Groups of Men in Chicago," *American Journal of Sociology* 16 (September 1910): 159; William Issel and Robert W. Cherny, *San Francisco, 1865–1932: Politics, Power, and Urban Development* (Berkeley: University of California Press, 1986), pp. 58–60; Peel, "On the Margins," p. 816.

15. Duis, *The Saloon*, p. 193.

16. Ibid.; Robert A. Slayton, "Flophouse: Housing and Public Policy for the Single Poor," *Journal of Policy History* 1 (Fall 1989): 376.

17. Duis, *The Saloon*, pp. 205–6; George Chauncey, *Gay New York: Gender, Urban Culture, and the Making of the Gay Male World, 1890–1940* (New York: Basic Books, 1994), pp. 182–83. On entertaining in a bachelor apartment, see "Bachelor Hosts," *Chicago Inter Ocean* (November 13, 1892), p. 24. This article presented discrete advice on entertaining guests in a bachelor flat, including what to serve and how to serve it, how to send invitations, and how to borrow china and silver from friends.

18. Wolfe, *The Lodging-House Problem*, p. 34; Bushee, "Ethnic Factors," pp. 35–36.

19. Ray Stannard Baker, *Native American: The Book of My Youth* (New York: Charles Scribner's Sons, 1941), p. 260.

20. John T. McCutcheon, *Drawn from Memory* (Indianapolis: Bobbs-Merrill, 1950), p. 80.

21. Will Irwin, *The Making of a Reporter* (New York: G. P. Putnam's Sons, 1942), p. 45.

22. M. E. Ravage, *An American in the Making* (New York: Harper and Brothers, 1917), pp. 72–73.

23. Issel and Cherny, *San Francisco*, p. 125; J. W. Buel, *Metropolitan Life Unveiled: Mysteries and Miseries of Great American Cities* (St. Louis, Mo.: Anchor Publishing Company, 1882), pp. 279–80.

24. Quoted in Slayton, "Flophouse," p. 376. See also, Alice Wil-

lard Solenberger, *One Thousand Homeless Men: A Study of Original Records* (New York: Charities Publications Committee, 1911), pp. 314–21; and Jacob Riis, *How the Other Half Lives: Studies Among the Tenements of New York* (New York: Hill and Wang, 1957), pp. 59–67.

25. Wolfe, *The Lodging-House Problem*, pp. 52–54.

26. Ibid., pp. 58–59.

27. Tekla Grenfell, "Renting Rooms to Young Men: How I Have Successfully Done It for Years," *Ladies Home Journal* 25 (September 1908): 24.

28. McCutcheon, *Drawn from Memory*, p. 80.

29. Ibid.

30. Joanne Meyerowitz, *Women Adrift: Independent Wage-Earners in Chicago, 1880–1930* (Chicago: University of Chicago Press, 1988), p. 25.

31. Bushee, "Ethnic Factors," p. 35.

32. Chauncey, *Gay New York*, pp. 152–53, 184.

33. Duis, *The Saloon*, pp. 194–95; Bushee, Ethnic Factors," p. 35; Peel, "On the Margins," p. 814; Meyerowitz, *Women Adrift*, p. 73.

34. *Eighteenth Annual Report of the Commissioner of Labor, 1903: Cost of Living and Retail Price of Food* (Washington, D.C.: Government Printing Office, 1903), p. 260.

35. Cited in Harvey Green, *The Uncertainty of Everyday Life, 1915–1945* (New York: Harper Collins Publishers, 1992), p. 97.

36. The figures I derived from my San Francisco samples deviate from those derived by Julius Tygiel in his study of working class males in that city at the end of the nineteenth century. Tygiel identified a decline from 1880 to 1900 in the proportion of male boarders (of every marital status) who boarded in a private home and a rise in the proportion who resided in a boardinghouse. He attributes this change to housing construction on the city's outskirts, which relieved housing shortages and created a kind of housing stock not conducive to taking in boarders. Instead, he asserts, boarders were forced to cluster inside boardinghouses located in isolated boardinghouse districts in older downtown areas. Tygiel also contends that by 1900, moralistic reformers were advising families against taking in outsiders who, they claimed, posed threats to the nuclear unit. My data, on the other hand, show continued, indeed, increasing tendencies of

boarders to live in family households, even though I recognize the persistence of the Barbary Coast and other major boardinghouse districts in the inner city. My only explanation for the discrepancy between Tygiel's data and my own is that Tygiel sampled only male members of the working class—chiefly carpenters, teamsters, and laborers—who resided in five different zones of the city while my samples include all occupational categories. See Tygiel, *Workingmen of San Francisco* (New York: Garland Publishing Company, 1992), pp. 199 and 268.

37. Wolfe, *The Lodging-House Problem*, p. 109.

38. Peel, "On the Margins," p. 816.

39. Harry Webb Farmington, *Kilts to Togs, Orphan Adventures* (New York: Macmillan, 1930), p. 294.

40. McCutcheon, *Drawn from Memory*, pp. 68–69.

41. Farrington, *Kilts to Togs*, p. 315.

42. Victor Elting, *Recollections of a Grandfather* (Chicago: A. Kroch, 1940), pp. 65, 78. See also Duis, *The Saloon*, p. 192.

43. Douglas Shand-Tucci, *Boston Bohemia, 1881–1900* (Amherst, University of Massachusetts Press, 1995), pp. 26–27.

44. See Ellen K. Rothman, *Hands and Hearts: A History of Courtship in America* (Cambridge: Harvard University Press, 1984), p. 193; and E. Anthony Rotundo, *American Manhood: Transformations in Masculinity from the Revolution to the Modern Era* (New York: Basic Books, 1993), pp. 83–84; and George Chauncey, Jr., "Christian Brotherhood or Sexual Perversion? Homosexual Identities and the Construction of Sexual Boundaries in the World War I Era," in Martin Dauml Duberman, Martha Vicinus, and George Chauncey, Jr., eds., *Hidden from History: Reclaiming the Gay and Lesbian Past* (New York: NAL Books, 1989), pp. 307–12, 316–17 .

45. See, for example, John Bodnar, *The Transplanted: A History of Immigrants in Urban America* (Bloomington: Indiana University Press, 1985), p. 73; Tamara K. Hareven, *Family Time and Industrial Time: The Relationship between Family and Work in a New England Industrial Community* (New York: Academic Press, (1981), p. 172; Michael B. Katz, *The People of Hamilton West: Family and Class in a Mid-Nineteenth-Century City* (Cambridge: Harvard University Press, 1975), pp. 258–60; and Carole Haber and Brian Gratton, *Old Age and the Search for Security* (Bloomington: Indiana University Press, 1994), pp. 74–75.

46. Peter Stearns, *Be a Man! Males in Modern Society* (New York: Homes and Meier, 1979), p. 62. The delay by working-class men in leaving their parental home does not necessarily contradict the assertion in the previous chapter that working-class men were marrying at earlier ages than those higher on the occupational scale. Rather, the point of the observation in the previous chapter was that among those who did marry, working-class men were marrying at earlier ages than nonmanual workers.

47. Richard J. Butler and Joe Driscoll, *Dock Walloper: The Story of "Big Dick" Butler* (New York: G. P. Putnam's Sons, 1933), p. 26. See Joseph Kett, *Rites of Passage: Adolescence in America from 1790 to the Present* (New York: Basic Books, 1977), and Rotundo, *American Manhood*, pp. 52–53.

48. Al Smith, *Up to Now: An Autobiography* (New York: Viking Press, 1929), p. 61.

49. Eddie Cantor, *My Life Is in Your Hands* (New York: Harper and Brothers, 1928), pp. 63–66.

50. Again, my sample figures for San Francisco differ from those derived by Tygiel, but in this case, the trends we both identify move in the same direction. Tygiel found that between 1880 and 1900 the proportion of adult sons still living with their parents doubled, from 8.3 percent in 1880 to 17 percent in 1900. These figures are about half of those I derived, but they increase in the same direction and magnitude as mine. Tygiel, however, does not say whether or not his figures include sons living with one parent; my figures include sons living either with both parents or with one. See Tygiel, "Workingmen of San Francisco," p. 216.

51. See, for example, Howard P. Chudacoff and Tamara K. Hareven, "Family Transitions into Old Age," in Tamara K. Hareven, ed., *Transitions: The Family and Life Course in Historical Perspective* (New York: Academic Press, 1978).

52. Rotundo, *American Manhood*, p. 61. See also, Meyerowitz, *Women Adrift*, p. 111.

53. Rotundo, *American Manhood*, pp. 62–64.

54. Ibid., pp. 282–83.

55. Regan, *Family Law and the Pursuit of Intimacy*, pp. 1–3.

56. Tygiel, "Workingmen of San Francisco," p. 204.

CHAPTER FOUR
INSTITUTIONAL LIFE

1. George Esdras Bevans, "How Workingmen Spend Their Spare Time" (Ph.D. diss., Department of Political Science, Columbia University, 1913), p. 27.

2. Bevans, "How Workingmen Spend Their Spare Time," pp. 27–32, 77. Percentages calculated from tables on pp. 27 and 31.

3. See, for example, Daniel T. Rodgers, *The Work Ethic in Industrial America, 1850–1920* (Chicago: University of Chicago Press, 1978); Roy Rosenzweig, *Eight Hours for What We Will: Workers and Leisure in an Industrial City, 1870–1920* (Cambridge: Cambridge University Press, 1983); and David Nasaw, *Going Out: The Rise and Fall of Public Amusements* (New York: Basic Books, 1993).

4. Jon M. Kingsdale, "The 'Poor-Man's Club': Social Functions of the Urban Working-Class Saloon," *American Quarterly* 25 (October 1973): 472.

5. Perry Duis, *The Saloon: Public Drinking in Chicago and Boston, 1880–1920* (Urbana and Chicago: University of Illinois Press, 1983), p. 195; Thomas J. Noel, *The City and the Saloon: Denver, 1858–1916* (Lincoln: University of Nebraska Press, 1982), p. 75.

6. John Bodnar, ed., *Workers' World: Kinship, Community, and Protest in an Industrial Society, 1900–1940* (Baltimore, Md.: Johns Hopkins University Press, 1982), pp. 105–6.

7. Figures cited in Leonard Ellis, "Men among Men: An Exploration of All-Male Relationships in Victorian America" (Ph.D. diss., Columbia University, 1982), pp. 126–27; Noel, *The City and the Saloon*, p. 75.

8. Kingsdale, "The 'Poor Man's Club,'" pp. 475–77.

9. Jack Black, *You Can't Win* (New York: Macmillan, 1927), p. 153.

10. Ibid., pp. 140–41; Duis, *The Saloon*, pp. 234–40; Kingsdale, "The 'Poor Man's Club,'" p. 481.

11. Raymond Calkins, *Substitutes for the Saloon* (Boston: Houghton Mifflin, 1901), p. 18.

12. Royal Melendy, "The Saloon in Chicago, I," *American Journal of Sociology* 6 (November 1900): 296, quoted in Duis, *The Saloon*, p. 55.

13. Oscar Ameringer, *If You Don't Weaken* (Norman: University of Oklahoma Press, 1983), p. 71.

14. Black, *You Can't Win*, p. 153.

15. Elliott Gorn, *The Manly Art: Bare-Knuckle Prize Fighting in America* (Ithaca, N.Y.: Cornell University Press, 1986), p. 183.

16. Duis, *The Saloon*, p. 253; Kingsdale, "The 'Poor Man's Club,'" p. 480; Calkins, *Substitutes for the Saloon*, pp. 8–13.

17. Kingsdale, "The 'Poor Man's Club,'" p. 480; Ellis, "Men among Men," pp. 189–90.

18. Ellis, "Men among Men," p. 161.

19. Ibid., p. 167.

20. Ibid., pp. 161, 167.

21. Quoted in George Chauncey, *Gay New York: Gender, Urban Culture, and the Making of the Gay Male World, 1890–1940* (New York: Basic Books, 1994), p. 42.

22. Ibid., pp. 37, 42–43.

23. M. E. Ravage, *An American in the Making: The Life Story of an Immigrant* (New York: Harper and Brothers, 1917), p. 130.

24. Calkins, *Substitutes for the Saloon*, p. 156.

25. The vernacular of the period made an important distinction between the terms "billiard room" and "pool hall" on the one hand and "pool room" on the other. The first two terms were used to refer to establishments that contained tables for the game that used balls and sticks (cues). The third term, "pool room," referred to an establishment in which betting, usually on horse races, took place—hence betting "pools"—and it was distinct from the other two terms. See Anthony Comstock, "Pool Rooms and Pool Selling," *North American Review* 157 (November 1893): 601–10.

26. Calkins, *Substitutes for the Saloon*, p. 157.

27. Ibid.

28. Alfred Benedict Wolfe, *The Lodging-House Problem in Boston* (Boston: Houghton Mifflin, 1906), p. 29.

29. Willie Hoppe, *Thirty Years of Billiards* (New York: G.P. Putnam's Sons, 1925), pp. 178–79.

30. Ellis, "Men among Men," p. 62.

31. Steven A. Riess, *City Games: The Evolution of American Urban Society and the Rise of Sports* (Urbana: University of Illinois Press, 1989), pp. 74–75; Ellis, "Men among Men," pp. 64–65.

32. Riess, *City Games*, pp. 74–75; Ellis, "Men among Men," p. 66.

33. Ellis, "Men Among Men," p. 73.

34. Ibid., pp. 75–79; Melvin L. Adelman, *A Sporting Time: New York City and the Rise of Modern Athletics, 1820–1870* (Urbana: University of Illinois Press, 1986), p. 224; Ned Polsky, "Of Pool Playing and Pool Rooms," in Gregory P. Stone, ed., *Games, Sport, and Power* (New Brunswick, N.J.: Dutton, 1972), pp. 25–26.

35. *Sports Illustrated*, October 16, 1948, quoted in Ellis, "Men among Men," p. 74. Italics are Lassiter's.

36. Eddie Cantor, *My Life Is in Your Hands* (New York: Harper and Brothers, 1928), p. 72.

37. Henry C. Alley, "Moral Problems of the Modern Pool Halls," (M.A. thesis, University of Chicago, 1913), p. 17.

38. Ellis, "Men among Men," p. 109.

39. Ibid., pp. 111–12.

40. Polsky, "Of Pool Playing," pp. 32–34, 43.

41. City Club of Chicago, "A Community Survey in the Twenty-First Ward," *The City Club Bulletin* 6 (March 13, 1913): 96–97.

42. Quoted in Michael Kimmel, *Manhood in American: A Cultural History* (New York: The Free Press, 1996), p. 125.

43. Eugene O'Neill, *The Iceman Cometh* (New York: Random House, 1946), p. 232.

44. These figures all have been derived from listings in the business directories of the city directories for the three cities for the years specified.

45. Harvey W. Zorbaugh, *The Gold Coast and the Slum: A Sociological Study of Chicago's Near North Side* (Chicago: University of Chicago Press, 1929), p. 107.

46. Allan H. Spear, *Black Chicago: The Making of a Negro Ghetto, 1890–1920* (Chicago: University of Chicago Press, 1967), pp. 111–12.

47. Thomas W. Chinn, *Bridging the Pacific: San Francisco's Chinatown and Its People* (San Francisco: Chinese Historical Society of America, 1989), p. 17.

48. John M. Todd, *A Sketch of the Life of John M. Todd: Sixty-Two Years in a Barber Shop and Reminiscences of His Customers* (Portland, Me.: William W. Roberts Co., 1906), pp. 302–4.

49. Charles DeZemler, *Once over Lightly: The Story of Man and His Hair* (New York: privately printed, 1939), p. 153.

50. See, for example, *The National Police Gazette*, January 18, 1902.

51. Chinn, *Bridging the Pacific*, p. 17.

52. University Settlement, *Report of 1899*, cited in Irving Howe and Kenneth Libo, eds., *How We Lived, 1880–1940* (New York: Richard Mark Publishers, 1979), p. 52.

53. John C. Burnham, *Bad Habits: Drinking, Smoking, Taking Drugs, Gambling, Sexual Misbehavior, and Swearing in American History* (New York: New York University Press, 1992), p. 92; John D'Emilio and Estelle B. Freedman, *Intimate Matters: A History of Sexuality in America* (New York: Harper & Row, 1988), pp. 130–31.

54. See, for example, George Bellamy, "Recreation and Social Progress: The Settlement," *Proceedings of the National Conference of Charities and Corrections* (1914), pp. 375–82, cited in Don S. Kirschner, "The Perils of Pleasure: Commercial Recreation, Social Disorder, and Moral Reform in the Progressive Era," *American Studies* 21 (Fall 1980): 28.

55. Duis, *The Saloon*, pp. 194–95; City Club of Chicago, "Community Survey," p. 94.

56. Lewis Francis Byington, *The History of San Francisco* (Chicago: The S. J. Clarke Publishing Company, 1931), 1:356.

57. Bismark Café (San Francisco), "Bill of Fare" (1906).

58. Untitled pamphlet, Normann's Café and Oyster House (San Francisco, n.d.).

59. Albert Payson Terhune, *To the Best of My Memory* (New York: Harper and Brothers, 1930), pp. 114–15.

60. H. L. Mencken, *Newspaper Days, 1899–1906* (New York: Alfred A. Knopf, 1941), p. 188.

61. Calkins, *Substitutes for the Saloon*, p. 232.

62. Ray Stannard Baker, *Native American: The Book of My Youth* (New York: Charles Scribner's Sons, 1941), p. 276.

63. Nels Anderson, *The Hobo: The Sociology of the Homeless Man* (Chicago: University of Chicago Press, 1923), pp. 33–34.

64. Ibid., pp. 183–84; *Charities* 6 (January 5, 1901): 7.

65. Calkins, *Substitutes for the Saloon*, pp. 233–34.

66. Ravage, *An American in the Making*, p. 100.

67. Chauncey, *Gay New York*, p. 185.

68. Nasaw, *Going Out*, p. 154.

69. Sherman C. Kingsley, "The Penny Arcade and the Cheap Theater," *Charities and the Commons* (June 8, 1907): 295.

70. Calkins, *Substitutes for the Saloon*, p. 163.

71. Ibid.; and Fred E. Haynes, "Amusements," in Robert A. Woods, ed., *The City Wilderness: A Settlement Study, by Residents and Associates of the South End House* (Boston: Houghton Mifflin, 1898), pp. 176–80.

72. Haynes, "Amusements," pp. 179–80.

73. Kingsley, "The Penny Arcade," p. 296.

74. Timothy J. Gilfoyle, *City of Eros: New York City, Prostitution and the Commercialization of Sex, 1790–1920* (New York: Norton, 1992), p. 129; Calkins, *Substitutes for the Saloon*, p. 164; Anderson, *The Hobo*, p. 37.

75. Reproduced in Calkins, *Substitutes for the Saloon*, pp. 166–67.

76. Ibid., p. 164.

77. Nasaw, *Going Out*, p. 132.

78. Bevans, *How Workingmen Spend Their Spare Time*, pp. 73–77; Kathy Peiss, *Cheap Amusements: Working Women and Leisure in Turn-of-the-Century New York* (Philadelphia: Temple University Press, 1985), pp. 148–53.

79. Walker Prichard Eaton, "The Latest Menace of the Movies," *North American Review* 212 (July 1920): 84.

80. See, for example, Peiss, *Cheap Amusements*, pp. 88–114; Nasaw, *Going Out*, pp. 104–19; and Lewis Erenberg, *Steppin' Out: New York Night Life and the Transformation of American Culture, 1890–1930* (Westport, Conn.: Greenwood Press, 1981), pp. 20–21.

81. Nasaw, *Going Out*, p. 110.

82. Peiss, *Cheap Amusements*, pp. 98–108; Nasaw, *Going Out*, p. 111.

83. Paul G. Cressey, *The Taxi-Dance Hall: A Sociological Study in Commercialized Recreation and City Life* (Chicago: University of Chicago Press, 1932), p. xvii. See also Zorbaugh, *The Gold Coast and the Slum*, p. 3; Kevin White, *The First Sexual Revolution: The Emergence of Male Heterosexuality in Modern America* (New York: New York University Press, 1993), p. 83.

84. Cressey, *The Taxi-Dance Hall*, pp. 177–95.

85. Ibid., pp. 9, 109–28.

86. Ibid., p. 10.

87. Bruno Lasker, *Filipino Immigration* (Chicago: University of Chicago Press, 1931), pp. 23–25; Cressey, *The Taxi-Dance Hall*, pp. 145–76.

88. Cressey, *The Taxi-Dance Hall*, pp. 224–27.

89. Ibid., pp. 260, 273–74.

90. White, *The First Sexual Revolution*, p. 101.

91. Ibid., pp. 283–85.

92. Ibid., pp. 281–88.

93. Calkins, *Substitutes for the Saloon*, pp. 209–14.

94. Chauncey, *Gay New York*, p. 209. A third type of bathhouse consisted of religious establishments, mostly constructed by Jewish authorities for ritual cleansing, but these facilities mostly serviced women.

95. Calkins, *Substitutes for the Saloon*, pp. 209–14.

96. Homer Croy, *Country Cured* (New York: Harper and Brothers, 1943), pp. 98–99.

97. Joseph Lee, "Preventive Work," *Charities* 6 (April 6, 1901): 303.

98. Wolfe, *The Lodging-House Problem*, p. 31.

99. Zorbaugh, *The Gold Coast and the Slum*, p. 125.

100. Wolfe, *The Lodging-House Problem*, pp. 31–32.

CHAPTER FIVE
ASSOCIATIONS: FORMAL AND INTERPERSONAL

1. E. A. Seligman, ed., *The Social Evil: With Special Reference to Conditions Existing in the City of New York* (New York: Putnam's Sons, 1912), p. 8.

2. Frederic M. Thrasher, *The Gang: A Study of 1,313 Gangs in Chicago* (Chicago: University of Chicago Press, 1927), p. 36.

3. Leonard Ellis, "Men among Men: An Exploration of All-Male Relationships in Victorian American," (Ph.D. diss., Columbia University, 1982), pp. 1–2, 49.

4. Ellis, "Men among Men," p. 47; E. Anthony Rotundo, *American Manhood: Transformations in American Masculinity from the Revolution to the Modern Era* (New York: Basic Books, 1993), pp.

62–67; Howard P. Chudacoff, *How Old Are You? Age Consciousness in American Culture* (Princeton, N.J.: Princeton University Press, 1989), pp. 102–3; David R. Johnson, *American Law Enforcement: A History* (St. Louis, Mo.: Forum Press, 1981), pp. 40, 123; Thrasher, *The Gang*, p. 36. As Ellis points out, the path into public space was completely blocked to girls.

5. Ellis, "Men among Men," pp. 7–8.

6. Ibid., pp. 9–11, 24, 55 (quotation); Michael Kimmel, *Manhood in America: A Cultural History* (New York: The Free Press, 1996), pp. 163–64.

7. Thrasher, *The Gang*, pp. 36, 46, 50.

8. Ellis, "Men among Men," pp. 194–95.

9. Charles J. Cohen, *History of the Penn Club* (Philadelphia: privately printed by John C. Winston Company [1924?], pp. 37–38.

10. Francis Gerry Fairfield, *The Clubs of New York* (New York: Henry L. Hinton, Publisher, 1873), p. 70.

11. Ellis, "Men among Men," pp. 254–63.

12. Kimmel, *Manhood in America*, pp. 171–72.

13. Ibid., pp. 172–75.

14. Ibid.

15. George Chauncey, *Gay New York: Gender, Urban Culture and the Making of the Gay Male World, 1890–1049* (New York: Basic Books, 1994), p. 38.

16. Edward E. Grusd, *B'nai B'rith: The Story of a Covenant* (New York: Appleton-Century, 1966), pp. 105–12.

17. Elliott Gorn, *The Manly Art: Bare Knuckle Prize Fighting in America* (Ithaca, N.Y.: Cornell University Press, 1986), p. 142; Rotundo, *American Manhood*, pp. 200–205, 227–46; Gail Bederman, *Manliness and Civilization: A Cultural History of Gender and Race in the United States, 1880–1917* (Chicago: University of Chicago Press, 1995), pp. 16–20.

18. Benjamin Rader, *American Sports: From the Age of Folk Games to the Age of Spectators* (Englewood Cliffs, N.J.: Prentice-Hall, 1983), pp. 97–98; Steven A. Riess, *City Games: The Evolution of American Urban Society and the Rise of Sports* (Urbana: University of Illinois Press, 1989), p. 16.

19. Riess, *City Games*, pp. 76–81.

20. Alfred E. Smith, *Up to Now: An Autobiography* (New York: Viking Press, 1929), pp. 36–37.

21. Ellis, "Men among Men," pp. 603–4. See also, Gunther Barth, *City People: The Rise of Modern City Culture in Nineteenth-Century America* (New York: Oxford University Press, 1980), pp. 148–91.

22. Ellis, "Men among Men," p. 440; Gorn, *The Manly Art*, p. 142.

23. Richard C. Morse, *History of the North American Young Men's Christian Association* (New York: Association Press, 1913), pp. 1–72; Sherwood Eddy, *A Century With Youth: A History of the Y.M.C.A., 1844–1944* (New York: Association Press, 1944), pp. 1–35; C. Howard Hopkins, *History of the Y.M.C.A. in North America* (New York: Association Press, 1951), pp. 4–53; David I. Macleod, *Building Character in the American Boy: The Boy Scouts, YMCA, and Their Forerunners, 1870–1920* (Madison: University of Wisconsin Press, 1983), pp. 72–74.

24. Hopkins, *History of the Y.M.C.A.*, pp. 256–57; Macleod, *Building Character*, pp. 73–74.

25. Emmet Dedmon, *Great Enterprises: 100 Years of the YMCA of Metropolitan Chicago* (New York: Rand McNally, 1957), p. 210.

26. Bascom Johnson, "Moral Conditions in San Francisco and At the Panama-Pacific Exposition," (New York: Social Hygiene Association, Inc., 1915), p. 20.

27. Homer Croy, *Country Cured* (New York: Harper and Brothers, 1943), p. 110. See also Ludwig Bemelmans, *Life Class* (New York: Viking Press, 1938), p. 103, for a more jaded view of YMCA facilities.

28. Clifford M. Drury, *The San Francisco YMCA: 100 Years by the Golden Gate, 1853–1953* (Glendale, Calif.: Arthur H. Clarke Co., 1963), p. 136.

29. Young Men's Christian Association of Chicago, *Official Bulletin* (1903, 1904, 1905).

30. Ibid.

31. Ibid.; Drury, *The San Francisco YMCA*, p. 141.

32. Drury, *The San Francisco YMCA*, p. 139.

33. Ibid., p. 142.

34. Harry J. Dunbaugh, *The YMCA Hotel of Chicago: History and Financial Policies, 1916–1939* (Chicago: Gunthorpp-Warren Printing Company, 1940), p. 8.

35. Ibid., pp. 7–11.

36. Ibid., pp. 24–33.

37. Chauncey, *Gay New York*, pp. 155–57, 180; Chauncey, "Christian Brotherhood or Sexual Perversion? Homosexual Identities and the Construction of Sexual Boundaries in the World War I Era," *Journal of Social History* 19 (Winter 1985): 189–212; John D. Wrathall, "Taking the Young Stranger by the Hand: Homosexual Cruising at the YMCA, 1890–1980," in Nina Mjagkij and Margaret Spratt, eds., *Men and Women Adrift: The YMCA and YWCA in the City* (New York: New York University Press, 1997).

38. Drury, *The San Francisco YMCA*, p. 142.

39. Nina Mjagkij, "True Manhood: The YMCA and Racial Advancement, 1890–1930," in Mjagkij and Spratt, eds., *Men and Women Adrift*, pp. 138–59; Dedmon, *Great Enterprises*, pp. 169–89.

40. Thomas W. Chinn, *Bridging the Pacific: San Francisco Chinatown and Its People* (San Francisco: Chinese Historical Society of America, 1989), pp. 116–17.

41. Benjamin Rabinowitz, *The Young Men's Hebrew Association, 1854–1913* (New York: National Jewish Welfare Board, 1948), pp. 18–28.

42. *Newark Daily Advertiser*, December 30, 1877, quoted in Amy Lowenstein, *One Hundred Years of the "Y", 1877–1977* (West Orange, N.J.: YM-YWHA of Metropolitan New Jersey, 1977), p. 4.

43. William R. Langfeld, *The Young Men's Hebrew Association of Philadelphia: A Fifty-Year Chronicle* (Philadelphia: YW-YMHA of Philadelphia, 1928), p. 41.

44. Rabinowitz, *The Young Men's Hebrew Association*, p. 87.

45. Ward Adair, *The Road to New York* (New York: Association Press, 1936), p. 121.

46. Ibid., p. 124.

47. Joanne J. Meyerowitz, *Women Adrift: Independent Wage-Earners in Chicago, 1880–1930* (Chicago: University of Chicago Press, 1988), p. 53.

48. "How Cincinnati Catholics Solved the Young Man Problem," *The National Catholic Welfare Council Bulletin* (February 1922), p. 8.

49. Ibid., pp. 8–12.

50. Raymond B. Calkins, *Substitutes for the Saloon* (Boston: Houghton Mifflin, 1901), pp. 142, 145. See also Francis H. M'Lean, "Review," in *Charities* 8 (February 1, 1902): 119.

51. David Nasaw, *Going Out: The Rise and Fall of Public Amusements* (New York: Basic Books, 1993), p. 113; Ellen Rothman, *Hands and Hearts: A History of Courtship in America* (New York: Basic Books, 1984), pp. 289–92; Beth L. Bailey, *From Front Porch to Back Seat: Courtship in Twentieth-Century America* (Baltimore, Md.: The Johns Hopkins University Press, 1988), pp. 13–14, 22–24; Kathy Lee Peiss, *Cheap Amusements: Working Women and Leisure in Turn-of-the-Century New York* (Philadelphia: Temple University Press, 1986), p. 105.

52. Calkins, *Substitutes for the Saloon*, p. 96.

53. Albert Payson Terhune, *To the Best of My Memory* (New York: Harper and Brothers, 1930), p. 122.

54. Article cited in Meyerowitz, *Women Adrift*, pp. 102–3.

55. Roger W. Babson, *Actions and Reactions* (New York: Harper and Brothers, 1935), pp. 97–98.

56. Terhune, *To the Best of My Memory*, p. 122.

57. Peiss, *Cheap Amusements*, pp. 110–13; Lewis Erenberg, *Steppin' Out: New York Night Life and the Transformation of American Culture, 1890–1930* (Chicago: University of Chicago Press, 1981), pp. 82–87; Timothy J. Gilfoyle, *City of Eros: New York City, Prostitution, and the Commercialization of Sex, 1790–1920* (New York: W. W. Norton, 1992), p. 311.

58. Abe Hollandersky, *The Life Story of Abe the Newsboy: Hero of a Thousand Fights* (Los Angeles: Abe the Newsboy Publishing Company, 1930), pp. 248–49, 282.

59. George Jessel, *So Help Me: The Autobiography of George Jessel* (Los Angeles: Friars Publishing Corp., 1943), p. 29.

60. John D'Emilio and Estelle Freedman, *Intimate Matters: A History of Sexuality in America* (New York: Harper and Row, 1988), p. 130. See also Perry Duis, *The Saloon: Public Drinking in Chicago and Boston, 1880–1920* (Urbana: University of Illinois Press, 1983), pp. 235–36; Gilfoyle, *City of Eros*, pp. 197–250; John Burnham, *Bad Habits: Drinking, Smoking, Taking Drugs, Gambling, Social Misbehavior, and Swearing in American History* (New York: New York University Press, 1993), pp. 170–207.

61. Burnham, *Bad Habits*, pp. 176–77.

62. See, for example, Maude E. Miner, *Slavery of Prostitution: A Plea for Emancipation* (New York: The Macmillan Company, 1913); William W. Sanger, *The History of Prostitution: Its Extent, Causes,*

and Effects throughout the World (New York: Eugenics Publishing Company, 1937).

63. Though the number of prostitutes grew substantially over the closing decades of the nineteenth century and opening years of the twentieth, there is some plausibility to the idea that the *ratio* of prostitutes to adult men stayed the same. Thus prostitutes were more numerous, but the institution itself may not have grown relative to the urban male population.

64. Sanger, *The History of Prostitution*, p. 497; D'Emilio and Freedman, *Intimate Matters*, pp. 137–38.

65. Croy, *Country Cured*, pp. 111–12.

66. Quoted in Arthur C. Calhoun, *A Social History of the American Family* (New York: Barnes and Noble reprint, 1960), 3:210.

67. Jessel, *So Help Me*, p. 26.

68. Neil Larry Shumsky and Larry M. Springer, "San Francisco's Zone of Prostitution, 1880–1937," *Journal of Historical Geography* 7 (1981): 81.

69. Ibid., pp. 81–82; Herbert Asbury, *The Barbary Coast* (Garden City, N.Y.: Garden City Publishing Company, 1933), pp. 275–76.

70. Shumsky and Springer, "San Francisco's Zone of Prostitution," pp. 83–85; Asbury, *The Barbary Coast*, pp. 276, 299–314.

71. Gilfoyle, *City of Eros*, p. 177.

72. Albert Benedict Wolfe, *The Lodging-House Problem in Boston* (Boston: Houghton Mifflin, 1906), p. 139.

73. Ibid., pp. 140–41.

74. Gilfoyle, *City of Eros*, p. 309.

75. *Massachusetts Public Documents: Report of the Board of Police of the City of Boston, 1890* (Boston: Wright and Potter Printers, 1891), p. 51. The ratio of arrests per population was published in San Francisco Board of Supervisors, *Municipal Reports, 1890–91: Chief of Police* (W. M. Hinton, 1891), p. 211. Of the nation's ten largest cities, Boston's ratio of arrests-to-population ranked second highest, behind New York, which had a ratio of one arrest per 373 persons. By contrast, Chicago had one arrest per 594 inhabitants in 1890, and San Francisco, with the lowest ratio (presumably the reason that the San Francisco Chief of Police published the study), had one arrest per 734 inhabitants.

76. *Massachusetts Public Documents: Report of the Board of Police of the City of Boston, 1900* (Boston: Wright and Potter Printing

Company, 1901), p. 58; *Massachusetts Public Documents: Report of the Board of Police of the City of Boston* (Boston: Wright and Potter Printing Company, 1911), pp. 104–15. See also, Sam Bass Warner, *Crime and Criminal Statistics in Boston* (Cambridge: Harvard University Press, 1934), table 4, appendix, pp. 140–41.

77. O'Meara in *Massachusetts Public Documents: Report of the Board of Police of the City of Boston, 1910*, p. 31.

78. *San Francisco Board of Supervisors, Municipal Reports: Chief of Police*, 1891 and 1911.

79. *Massachusetts Public Documents: Report of the Board of Police of the City of Boston*, 1891 and 1911.

80. Joel P. Bishop, *Commentaries on the Law of Marriage and Divorce*, 1st edition (London: W. Maxwell, 1852).

81. *Greenup v. Stoker*, 8 Ill 202, 211 (1846) cited in Michael Grossberg, *Governing the Hearth: Law and the Family in Nineteenth-Century America* (Chapel Hill: University of North Carolina Press, 1985), p. 40.

82. Grossberg, *Governing the Hearth*, p. 48.

83. *Bennett v. Beam*, 42 Mich. 346, 351 (1880), cited in Grossberg, *Governing the Hearth*, p. 48.

84. Grossberg, *Governing the Hearth*, p. 40.

85. *Wightman v. Coates*, 15 Mass 2, 2–4, (1818).

86. *The People v. Leslie Kehoe*, 133 Cal. 224 (1898).

87. *The People v. Brewer* 27 Mich. 134 (1873).

88. *Commonwealth v. Morris Rosenthal*, 211 Mass. 50 (1911).

89. *Flick v. Commonwealth of Virginia*, 97 Va. 766, 34 S.E. 39 (1899); see also *Keller v. State of Georgia*, 102 Ga. 506, 31 S.E. 92 (1897).

90. George Lawyer, "Are Actions for Breach of Marriage Contract Immoral?" *Connecticut Law Journal* 38, 272 (1894).

91. Grossberg cities as an example a "Recent Cases" article in *Harvard Law Review* 7, 372 (1894). See Grossberg, *Governing the Hearth*, p. 59.

92. *Walmsey v. Robinson*, 63 Ill. 41, 42–43 (1872); Grossberg, *Governing the Hearth*, p. 57.

93. *McPherson v. Ryan*, 59 Mich. 33,39 (1886); Grossberg, *Governing the Hearth*, p. 57.

94. Grossberg, *Governing the Hearth*, p. 58.

95. See, for example, *Sheehan v. Barry*, 27 Mich. 217 (1873).

96. Grossberg, *Governing the Hearth*, p. 55.

97. Milton Regan, Jr., *Family Law and the Pursuit of Intimacy* (New York: New York University Press, 1993), pp. 3–4.

98. *Maynard v. Hill,* 125 U.S. 190, 211 (1888).

99. Joel Bishop, *New Commentaries on Marriage, Divorce, and Separation* (7th ed., 1891), 1:510.

100. Sherwood J. Norris, *Marriage and Divorce under California Law* (Los Angeles: Gem Publishing Company, 1925), p. 31.

101. Grossberg, *Governing the Hearth*, p. 63.

CHAPTER SIX
THE POPULAR CULTURE OF BACHELORHOOD

1. Jack Black, *You Can't Win* (New York: Macmillan, 1927), p. 12.

2. George Ade, "The Joys of Single Blessedness," in Ade, *Single Blessedness and Other Observations* (Garden City, N.Y.: Doubleday, Page and Company, 1922), pp. 15–16.

3. Frank Luther Mott, *A History of American Magazines: Volume III, 1850–1865* (Cambridge: Harvard University Press, 1938), pp. 331–32; Edward Van Every, *Sins of New York as "Exposed" by the Police Gazette* (New York: Frederick A. Stokes, 1931), pp. vi–vii; John Rickard Betts, "Sporting Journalism in Nineteenth-Century America," *American Quarterly* 5 (Spring 1953): 50; Steven A. Riess, *City Games: The Evolution of American Urban Society and the Rise of Sports* (Urbana: University of Illinois Press, 1989), p. 72.

4. See Kevin White, *The First Sexual Revolution: The Emergence of Male Heterosexuality in Modern America* (New York: New York University Press, 1993), p. 8.

5. Frank Luther Mott, *A History of American Magazines: Volume II, 1741–1850* (Cambridge: Harvard University Press, 1930), pp. 479–80; Timothy J. Gilfoyle, *City of Eros: New York City, Prostitution, and the Commercialization of Sex, 1820–1920* (New York: W. W. Norton, 1992), p. 133.

6. Gilfoyle, *City of Eros*, p. 134.

7. Alan Nourie and Barbara Nourie, eds., *American Mass-Market Magazines* (Westport, Conn.: Greenwood Press, 1990), pp. 284–86; Mott, *A History of American Magazines*, 2:481.

8. Betts, "Sporting Journalism," p. 42; Mott, *A History of American Magazines*, 2:327–28.

9. Nourie and Nourie, *American Mass Market Magazines*, pp. 287–88; Mott, *A History of American Magazines*, 3:329; Riess, *City Games*, p. 72; Van Every, *Sins of New York*, p. xvi; Betts, "Sporting Journalism," p. 50.

10. Mott, *A History of American Magazines*, 3:43–45; Betts, "Sporting Journalism," p. 50.

11. Introduction to Van Every, *Sins of New York*, pp. v-vi; Riess, *City Games*, p. 72.

12. Mott, *A History of American Magazines*, 2:309.

13. Mott, *A History of American Magazines*, 2:335–37; Elliott Gorn, *The Manly Art: Bare-Knuckle Prize Fighting in America* (Ithaca, N.Y.: Cornell University Press, 1986), p. 181; White, *The First Sexual Revolution*, p. 61; Mark Gabor, *An Illustrated History of Girlie Magazines* (New York: Harmony, 1984), p. 3.

14. Mott, *A History of American Magazines*, 2:335–37; Betts, "Sporting Journalism," p. 56; Nourier and Nourier, *American Mass-Market Magazines*, pp. 288–89; Gorn, *The Manly Art*, p. 181, 239.

15. *National Police Gazette* (hereafter *NPG*), May 11, 1878.

16. *NPG*, April 27, 1878.

17. *NPG*, May 1, 1880.

18. Michael T. Isenberg, in *John L. Sullivan and His America*, cites Sullivan's friend and trainer, Billy Madden, as recalling that Sullivan and Fox first met each other in the offices of *The National Police Gazette* in the spring of 1881 and "disliked each other immediately." See pp. 96–97.

19. *NPG*, February 18, 1881.

20. *NPG*, July 22, 1882.

21. *NPG*, August 6, 1883.

22. *NPG*, October 20, 1883.

23. *NPG*, May 28, 1887.

24. *NPG*, January 1, 1887; February 19, 1887.

25. *NPG*, January 19, 1889.

26. *NPG*, February 17, 1900.

27. Robert C. Allen, *Horrible Prettiness: Burlesque and American Culture* (Chapel Hill: University of North Carolina Press, 1991), pp. 198–221, especially p. 219.

28. *NPG*, May 24, 1902.

29. *NPG*, May 16, 1903.

30. *NPG*, February 3, 1904.

31. *NPG*, March 17, 1893.

32. *NPG*, January 3, 1903.

33. *The Bachelor Book* I (March 1900), 1, 22; and *The Bachelor Book* I (May 1900), 23–24. Henceforth referred to as *BB*.

34. *BB*, I (March 1900), 1.

35. Ibid., p. 20.

36. *BB*, (May 1900), 23–24.

37. "Pawn Ticket 1155," *BB*, I (March 1900), 10–12.

38. "A Bachelor's Love," *BB*, I (May 1900), 8.

39. *The Complete Bachelor: Manners for Men* (New York: D. Appleton and Company, 1904), p. v.

40. Ibid., p. 8.

41. Ibid., p. 16.

42. Ibid., pp. 32, 74.

43. Ibid., pp. 119–20.

CHAPTER SEVEN
BACHELOR SUBCULTURE AND MALE CULTURE

1. Gail Bederman, *Manliness and Civilization: A Cultural History of Gender and Race in the Unites States, 1880–1917* (Chicago: University of Chicago Press, 1995), pp. 12–20; E. Anthony Rotundo, *American Manhood: Transformations in Masculinity from the Revolution to the Modern Era* (New York: Basic Books, 1993), pp. 247–55; Michael Kimmel, *Manhood in America: A Cultural History* (New York: The Free Press, 1996), pp. 81–89; Clyde Griffen, "Reconstituting Masculinity from the Evangelical Revival to the Waning of Progressivism: A Speculative Synthesis," in Clyde Griffen and Mark C. Carnes, eds., *Meanings for Manhood: Constructions of Masculinity in Victorian America* (Chicago: University of Chicago Press, 1990), pp. 183–92. Bederman has articulated an important difference between the terms "manhood," "manliness" and "masculinity" that I have tried to adopt. Manhood, Bederman asserts, is "a cultural process whereby concrete individuals are constituted as members of a preexisting social category—as men. Manliness in the Victorian era connoted moral virtues that were expected of a middle-

class man of character. Masculinity was a relatively new term in the late nineteenth century; it referred to those masculine qualities that distinguished men from the feminine qualities of women. The term "masculinity" became important to the attempts by men to refashion their manliness in the late nineteenth century and early twentieth, as it increasingly included ideals of aggressiveness, force, and male sexuality. See Bederman, pp. 5–10, 17–19.

2. Rotundo, *American Manhood*, pp. 32–33. See also, Howard P. Chudacoff, *How Old Are You? Age Consciousness in American Culture* (Princeton, N.J.: Princeton University Press, 1989), pp. 102–5.

3. Rotundo, *American Manhood*, p. 33.

4. Ibid., pp. 37–38; Eddie Cantor, *My Life Is in Your Hands* (New York: Harper and Brothers, 1928), p. 23.

5. Carroll Smith-Rosenberg, "The Female World of Love and Ritual: Relations between Women in Nineteenth-Century America," *Signs: Journal of Women in Culture and Society* 1 (1975): 1–30.

6. Michael A. Messner, *Power at Play: Sport and the Problem of Masculinity* (Boston: The Beacon Press, 1992), p. 31.

7. Messner, *Power at Play*, pp. 32–34; Carol Gilligan, *In a Different Voice: Psychological Theory and Women's Development* (Cambridge: Harvard University Press, 1982), as cited in Messner, *Power at Play*, p. 34.

8. Rotundo, *American Manhood*, p. 46.

9. On male generational conflict, see, for example, Peter Stearns, *Be a Man! Males in Modern Society* (New York: Holmes and Meier, 1979), p. 49.

10. Henry David Thoreau, *The Journal of Henry David Thoreau*, eds. Bradford Torrey and Francis H. Allen (New York: Dover Publications, 1962), 1:253, quoted in Rotundo, *American Manhood*, p. 104.

11. See, for example, John Modell, Frank Furstenberg, and Theodore Hershberg, "Social Change and Transitions to Adulthood in Historical Perspective," *Journal of Family History* 1 (Autumn, 1976): 7–33; and Rotundo, *American Manhood*, pp. 53–54.

12. Kevin White, *The First Sexual Revolution: The Emergence of Male Heterosexuality in Modern America* (New York: New York University Press, 1993), p. 147.

13. Cantor, *My Life Is in Your Hands*, p. 49.

14. Ibid., p. 39.

15. Rotundo, *American Manhood*, pp. 60–61.

16. White, *The First Sexual Revolution*, pp. 9–10.

17. Rotundo, *American Manhood*, p. 245–46; Joseph Kett, *Rites of Passage: Adolescence in America, 1790 to the Present* (New York: Basic Books, 1977), p. 173; Elliott Gorn, *The Manly Art: Bare-Knuckle Prize Fighting in America* (Ithaca, N.Y.: Cornell University Press, 1986), p. 193; Griffen, "Reconstructing Masculinity," p. 203; Peter G. Filene, *Him, Her, Self: Sex Roles in Modern America* (New York: Harcourt Brace Jovanovich, 1975), pp. 169–75; Bederman, *Manliness and Civilization*, pp. 10–15.

18. Leonard Ellis, "Men among Men: An Exploration of All-Male Relationships in Victorian America" (Ph.D. diss., Columbia University, 1982), pp. 11–14. See Michelle Zimbalist Rosaldo, "Women, Culture, and Society: A Theoretical Overview," in Michelle Zimbalist Rosaldo and Louise Lamphere, eds., *Women, Culture and Society* (Stanford, Calif.: Stanford University Press, 1974), p. 24.

19. White, *The First Sexual Revolution*, pp. 4–9.

20. Melvin Adelman, *A Sporting Time: New York City and the Rise of Modern Athletics, 1820–1870* (Urbana: University of Illinois Press, 1986), p. 286.

21. Rotundo, *American Manhood*, pp. 245–46; Gorn, *The Manly Art*, pp. 193–94; Adelman, *A Sporting Time*, p.286; Elizabeth H. Pleck and Joseph H. Pleck, "Introduction" to Pleck and Pleck, eds., *The American Man* (Englewood Cliffs, N.J.: Prentice-Hall, 1980), p. 24; Ellis, "Men among Men," pp. 339–40.

22. Griffen, "Reconstituting Masculinity," p. 203; Adelman, *A Sporting Time*, p. 286; Rotundo, *American Manhood*, p. 8; Donald J. Mrozek, *Sport and the American Mentality, 1880–1910* (Knoxville: University of Tennessee Press, 1983), chap. 2.

23. Gorn, *The Manly Art*, pp. 142–43. See also, Peter N. Stearns, *Be a Man! Males in Modern Society* (New York: Holmes & Meier, 1979), pp. 52–53; Benjamin G. Rader, *American Sports: From the Age of Folk Games to the Age of Spectators* (Englewood Cliffs, N.J.: Prentice-Hall, 1983), p. 34; Jon M. Kingsdale, "The 'Poor Man's Club': Social Functions of the Urban Working-Class Saloon," *American Quarterly* 25 (October 1973): 480; White, *The First Sexual Revolution*, p. 9.

24. White, *The First Sexual Revolution*, pp. 17–20.

25. Gorn, *The Manly Art*, p. 193; Ellis, "Men among Men," p. xv.

Rotundo, *American Manhood*, pp. 192–93, notes that some middle-class men found a similar kind of retreat in neurasthenia, the condition of mental stress usually identified with middle-class women in the late nineteenth century. Rotundo claims that neurasthenia gave men a path to escape the ordeal of work in order to indulge themselves in the cure of relaxation. The disease, however, differed from other masculine forms of escape because it provided a retreat into the feminine realm of vulnerability, dependence, passivity, and invalidism.

26. See, for example, Rotundo, *American Manhood*, pp. 144, 201.

27. John Burnham, *Bad Habits: Drinking, Smoking, Taking Drugs, Gambling, Sexual Misbehavior, and Swearing in American History* (New York: New York University Press, 1993), pp. 88–101.

28. Ibid., p. 59; Rotundo, *American Manhood*, pp. 123–26, 203, 250–57.

29. Harry Kemp, *Tramping on Life, An Autobiographical Narrative* (New York: Boni and Liveright, 1922), p. 27.

30. Jack Black, *You Can't Win* (New York: Macmillan, 1927), p. 19.

31. Lillian Rubin, *Intimate Strangers: Men and Women Together* (New York: Harper and Row, 1983), p. 135.

32. Rotundo, *American Manhood*, p. 156.

33. See Rotundo, *American Manhood*, pp. 75–77; Charles E. Rosenberg, "Sexuality, Class, and Role in Nineteenth-Century America," in Elizabeth H. and Joseph H. Pleck, eds., *The American Man* (Englewood Cliff, N.J.: Prentice-Hall, 1980), pp. 221–41. On the romantic relationships between women, see Carroll Smith-Rosenberg, "The Female World of Love and Ritual."

34. Homer Croy, *Country Cured* (New York: Harper and Brothers, 1943), p. 139.

35. Ferris Greenslet, *Under the Bridge: An Autobiography* (Boston: Houghton Mifflin Company, 1943), pp. 157–58.

36. Frederick Shelley Ryman Papers, "Notes and Notations," vol. 6, 1882–83, Cortland, N.Y., Massachusetts Historical Society, p. 160. Hereafter cited as FSR. Emphases are Ryman's.

37. FSR, vol. 6, November 17, 1883, p. 533.

38. FSR, vol. 6, April 9, 1883, p. 532.

39. FSR, vol. 10, September 30, 1886, p. 310.

40. Material on Ryman's experiences with prostitutes is taken from John D'Emilio and Estelle B. Freedman, *Intimate Matters: A*

History of Sexuality in America (New York: Harper & Row Publishers, 1988), pp. 109–11.

41. FSR, vol. 6, February 15, 1882, p. 313.

42. FSR, vol. 6, April 25, 1883, p. 535.

43. FSR, vol. 6, April 27, 1883, p. 535.

44. FRR, vol. 6, April 28, 1883, p.536.

45. FSR, vol. 7, October 11, 1883, p. 160.

46. FSR, vol. 10, September 6, 1886, p. 217. Ryman expressed his desire to keep this part of his journal secret by marking across its contents, "Private! Do Not Open This for Any Purpose Whatsoever."

47. FSR, vol. 18, November 5, 1903. Ryman seems to have regretted this outburst, because the next day he wrote over this passage with a different pen, "Cut it no matter what you feel."

48. Scott Swain, "Covert Intimacy: Closeness in Men's Friendships," in B. J. Risman and P. Schwartz, eds., *Gender and Intimate Relationships: A Micro-Structural Approach* (Belmont, Calif.: Wadsworth Publishing Company, 1989), pp. 71, 85, as cited in Messner, *Power at Play*, p. 92.

49. See Rotundo, *American Manhood*, pp. 280–82; Alan G. Davis and Philip M. Strong, "Working without a Net: The Bachelor as a Social Problem," *Sociological Review*, n.s., 25 (February 1977), 109–29.

50. Rotundo, *American Manhood*, pp. 250–57; Burnham, *Bad Habits*, pp. 278–79; Ellis, "Men among Men," pp. 11–14.

51. See, for example, Mrozek, *Sport and the American Mentality*, pp. 46–51, 63–65; Bederman, *Manliness and Civilization*, pp. 172–77; Kimmel, *Manhood in America*, pp. 181–87.

52. These essays can be found in *The Works of Theodore Roosevelt* 16 vols. (New York: Collier, 1905).

53. Theodore Roosevelt to G. Stanley Hall, November 29, 1899, quoted in Kimmel, *Manhood in America*, p. 66.

54. Gorn, *The Manly Art*, p. 247.

55. This oft-quoted boast originally appeared in Sullivan's ghost-written autobiography, *Life and Reminiscences of a Nineteenth-Century Gladiator: By John L. Sullivan* (1892). See R. F. Dibble, *John L. Sullivan: An Intimate Narrative* (Boston: Little, Brown, and Company, 1925), p. 8.

56. Dibble, *John L. Sullivan*, pp. 10–20; Gorn, *The Manly Art*,

pp. 207–10; Michael T. Isenberg, *John L. Sullivan and His America* (Urbana: University of Illinois Press, 1988), pp. 17–38.

57. Dibble, *John L. Sullivan*, pp. 179–82; Isenberg, *John L. Sullivan and His America*, pp. 131–32.

58. Isenberg, *John L. Sullivan and His America*, pp. 129–32. See also Hasia Diner, *Erin's Daughters: Irish Immigrant Women in the Nineteenth Century* (Baltimore, Md.: The Johns Hopkins University Press, 1983), p. 55.

59. Gorn, *The Manly Art*, p. 222; Isenberg, *John L. Sullivan and His America*, pp. 111, 118.

60. Dibble, *John L. Sullivan*, pp. 44–45; Isenberg, *John L. Sullivan and His America*, pp. 48–59.

61. Isenberg, *John L. Sullivan and His America*, p. 140.

62. Sullivan was not actually a bare-knuckle fighter; all but three of his official forty-seven matches were fought with gloves, according to Marquis of Queensbury rules.

63. Gorn, *The Manly Art*, pp. 230–45.

64. Theodore Dreiser, *A Book about Myself* (New York: Boni and Liveright, Inc., 1922), p. 151.

65. Isenberg, *John L. Sullivan and His America*, pp. 377–84.

66. U.S. Bureau of the Census, *Fifteenth Census of the United States, 1930: Volume 2: General Report, Statistics by Subjects* (Washington, D.C.: Government Printing Office, 1933), p. 842.

67. Paul Harold Jacobson, *American Marriage and Divorce* (New York: Rinehart, 1959), p. 21; Kingsley Davis, "The American Family in Relation to Demographic Change," in Charles F. Westoff and Robert Parke, Jr., eds., *Commission of Population Growth and the American Future: Volume 1, Demographic and Social Aspects of Population Growth* (Washington, D.C.: Government Printing Office, 1972), table 2, p. 243.

68. This notion of rebellion against eighteenth- and early-nineteenth-century norms of civilization has been ably articulated and developed in Rotundo, *American Manhood*, pp. 251–57.

69. Michael Oates Palmer, "Bachelor Ads: How the Attributes of the Unmarried Population Were Depicted in Magazine Advertising, 1880–1930" (unpublished paper, Brown University, 1994).

70. *Harper's*, September 3, 1910, p. 21.

71. *Outing*, August 19, 1920, p. 231.

72. Burnham, in *Bad Habits*, makes the point that the repeal of Prohibition in 1933 signaled the culmination of a trend in which Americans had transformed previously defined "bad habits" into acceptable, even desired behavior. I believe that Burnham could have expanded his interpretation by adding that this transformation, which took place in the closing decades of the nineteenth century and first third of the twentieth century, was in large part, though not exclusively, brought about by the proportionately high numbers of bachelors in the general population, among whom such "bad habits" were already common.

73. *Life*, January 1920, p. 903 and *New Yorker*, October 8, 1927, p. 20, quoted in White, *The First Sexual Revolution*, p. 171.

74. William Johnson, "Why Men Won't Marry the New Woman," *Colliers*, March 14, 1925, quoted in White, *The First Sexual Revolution*, p. 171.

CHAPTER EIGHT

THE DECLINE AND RESURGENCE OF BACHELORHOOD, 1930–1995

1. "Games Singles Play," *Newsweek* 82 (July 16, 1973), 52.

2. Bonnie Miller Rubin, "Singles Looking before Leaping into Marriage," *Chicago Tribune*, March 28, 1996, pp. 1, 23.

3. Bernard Glueck, "Are You Emotionally Mature?" in Hilda Holland, ed., *Why Are You Single?* (New York: Farrar, Straus, 1949), pp. 199–220.

4. "Games Singles Play," 53.

5. "The Way 'Singles' Are Changing the U.S.," *U.S. News and World Report* (January 31, 1977), 59–60.

6. U.S. Bureau of the Census, *Current Population Reports: Marital Status and Living Arrangements, March 1994* (Washington, D.C.: Government Printing Office, 1996), table A–2, p. A–3; U.S. Bureau of the Census, *Historical Statistics of the United States, Colonial Times to 1970*, Part 1 (Washington, D.C.: Government Printing Office, 1975), derived from table, p. 20.

7. Landon Jones, *Great Expectations: America and the Baby Boom Generation* (New York: Coward, McCann, & Geoghegan, 1980), pp. 11, 23–24.

8. "Introduction," in Holland, *Why Are You Single?*, pp. viii–ix. The noted handbook on marriage authored by Ernest R. Groves in-

cluded similar passages on the "problem" of the unmarried. See Groves, *Marriage*, rev. ed. (New York: Henry Holt and Company, 1941), pp. 606–7.

9. Theodore Reik, "The Marriage-Shyness of the Male," in Holland, *Why Are You Single?*, pp. 23–37.

10. Cliffod R. Adams, "Why Are You Single?" in Holland, *Why Are You Single?*, pp. 251–72.

11. Richard A. Easterlin, *Birth and Fortune: The Impact of Numbers on Personal Welfare* (New York: Basic Books, 1980), cited in Andrew J. Cherlin, *Marriage, Divorce, Remarriage*, rev. and enl. ed. (Cambridge: Harvard University Press, 1992), pp. 41–42.

12. U.S. Bureau of the Census, *Current Population Reports: Population Characteristics, Marital Status and Living Arrangements: March 1977* (Washington, D.C.: Government Printing Office, 1978), pp. 1–2. The proportions of women remaining single also rose, as did the median age of first marriage. In 1960, 19.0 percent of women were single, compared to 23.4 percent in 1977. More remarkably, among women aged 20 to 24, the proportion who had never married increased by more than half between 1960 and 1977, from 28 percent to 45 percent.

13. Ibid., pp. 2–3; Mary Jo Bane, *Here to Stay: American Families in the Twentieth Century* (New York: Basic Books, 1976), appendix, table A–7; Robert T. Michael, Victor R. Fuchs, and Sharon R. Scott, "Changes in the Propensity to Live Alone, 1950–1976," *Demography* 17 (February 1980): 41.

14. Michael, Fuchs, and Scott, "Changes in the Propensity to Live Alone," p. 39. The authors found that nonwhites had a somewhat lower propensity to live alone than did whites, but they did not elaborate on this finding. See also Fred C. Pampel, "Changes in the Propensity to Live Alone: Evidence from Consecutive Cross-Sectional Surveys, 1960–1976," *Demography* 20 (November 1983): 433–46.

15. Genevieve Knupfer, Walter Clark, and Robin Room, "The Mental Health of the Unmarried," *American Journal of Psychiatry* 122 (1966): 850–51.

16. Michael Kimmel, *Manhood in America: A Cultural History* (New York: The Free Press, 1996), p. 255. Hefner quote is reproduced in Kimmel, p. 255.

17. *Jane and Michael Stern's Encyclopedia of Pop Culture* (New York: Harper Perennial, 1987), pp. 388–94.

18. Ibid.

19. Barbara Ehrenreich, "Playboy Joins the Battle of the Sexes," in Ehrenreich, *The Hearts of Men: American Dreams and the Flight from Commitment* (Garden City, N.Y.: Anchor Press/Doubleday, 1983), p. 42.

20. "Meet the Playboy Reader," *Playboy*, April 1958, p. 63.

21. Ibid., p. 51.

22. Kimmel, *Manhood in America*, p. 255.

23. Andrew J. Cherlin, *Marriage, Divorce, Remarriage*, p. 10.

24. "Games Singles Play," p. 57.

25. See Cherlin, *Marriage, Divorce, Remarriage*, p. 38.

26. "Games Singles Play," p. 58.

27. John D'Emilio and Estelle Freedman, *Intimate Matters: A History of Sexuality in America* (New York: Harper & Row, 1988), pp. 303–5. See also Steven Mintz and Susan Kellogg, *Domestic Revolutions: A Social History of American Family Life* (New York: The Free Press, 1988), p. 209.

28. *Current Population Reports: Marital Status and Living Arrangements: March 1977* pp. 1–2; *Current Population Reports: Marital and Living Arrangements: March 1994*, pp. vi–viii.

29. The term "unmarried partner" was defined as "a person who is not related to the householder, who shares living quarters, and who has a close personal relationship with the householder." This category was intended to differ from the "roomer/boarder" and "housemate/roommate" categories, where the person's main function was to reduce housing expenses rather than providing emotional functions. *Current Population Reports: Marital Status and Living Arrangements: March 1994*, pp. xiii and table A–9, p. A–10. See also, Paul C. Glick, "Marriage, Divorce, and Living Arrangements: Prospective Changes," in Arlene S. Skolnick and Jerome H. Skolnick, *The Family in Transition* 5th ed. (Boston: Little, Brown and Company, 1986), pp. 89–103.

30. Ibid., pp. 12 and table A–7, p. A–8 and table A–8, p. A–9.

31. Cherlin, *Marriage, Divorce, Remarriage*, p. 61; Frank Levy, *Dollars and Dreams: The Changing American Income Distribution* (New York: Russell Sage Foundation, 1987).

32. Kent Black, "The New Lonely Guys," *Mademoiselle*, August 1990, p. 199.

33. Peter Nelson, "An Unmarried Man," *Mademoiselle*, October 1985, pp. 166, 259.

34. Linda Schwartzbaum, "Is He a Bachelor for Now . . . or Forever?" *Mademoiselle*, April 1992, p. 106.

35. Cherlin, *Marriage, Divorce, Remarriage*, pp. 20–25; James Weed, "Duration of U.S. Marriage Tables: A 1985 Update," cited in Cherlin, p. 24.

36. Ibid., p. 28 and D'Emilio and Freedman, *Intimate Matters*, pp. 331–32.

37. Roderick Thorp, "A Wary Bachelor," *New York Times Magazine* (March 31, 1985), p. 88.

38. D'Emilio and Freedman, *Intimate Matters*, pp. 288–92. See also John D'Emilio, *Sexual Politics, Sexual Communities: The Making of a Homosexual Minority in the United States, 1940–1970* (Chicago: University of Chicago Press, 1983) and D'Emilio, "Gay Politics and Community in San Francisco Since World War II," in Martin Bauml Duberman, Martha Vicinus, and George Chauncey, Jr., eds., *Hidden from History: Reclaiming the Gay and Lesbian Past* (New York: New American Library, 1989), pp. 456–73.

39. D'Emilio and Freedman, *Intimate Matters*, pp. 318–24, 340–41, 358–59. See also Toby Marotta, *The Politics of Homosexuality* (Boston: Houghton Mifflin, 1981).

40. See, for example, D'Emilio and Freedman, *Intimate Matters*, p. 323.

41. "The American Male," *U.S. News and World Report*, June 6, 1985, pp. 44–45.

42. The most cogent analysis and expression of "men's liberation" was made by psychologist Joseph Pleck in *The Myth of Masculinity* (Cambridge: The M.I.T. Press, 1981) and "The Theory of Male Sex Role Identity: Its Rise and Fall, 1936 to the Present," in M. Lewin, ed., *In the Shadow of the Past: Psychology Views the Sexes* (New York: Columbia University Press, 1984).

43. The major spokesman of men's liberation was author Herb Goldberg, whose multiple books, such as *The Hazards of Being Male* (New York: Nash, 1976), *The New Male* (New York: New American Library, 1979), *The New Male-Female Relationship* (New York: William Morrow, 1983), *The Inner Male* (New York: New American

Library, 1987), and *What Men Really Want* (New York: Signet, 1991), were best-sellers.

44. See Kimmel, *Manhood in America*, pp. 300–303.

45. Robert Bly, *Iron John: A Book about Men* (Reading, Mass.: Addision-Wesley, 1990). See also, Kimmel, *Manhood in America*, pp. 316–17; Rotundo, *American Manhood*, pp. 288–89; Diane Johnson, "Something for the Boys," *New York Review of Books* 39 (January 16, 1992): 13–17; Charles Gaines, "Robert Bly, Wild Thing," *Esquire* 116 (October 1991), pp. 125–28; Tom Lowry, "What Men Can't Get from Women," *Ladies Home Journal* 109 (January 1992), pp. 77–78; and Barbara Grizuti Harrison, "Campfire Boys: Why the Men's Movement is Hot," *Mademoiselle* 97 (October 1991), pp. 94–96. Several critics speculated that a considerable number of those who purchased Bly's book consisted of women who were soothing their man's ego by giving him a literary reinforcement for his masculine ego.

46. Sam Keen, *Fire in the Belly: On Being a Man* (New York: Bantam Books, 1991).

47. *Esquire* 116 (October 1991), p. 138. To a considerable extent, as well, the sentiments of male bonding flowed through the Million Man March of African Americans who gathered in Washington, D.C. in 1996.

48. Leonard Ellis, "Men among Men: An Exploration of All-Male Relationships in Victorian America" (Ph.D. diss., Columbia University, 1982), p. 629.

Index *

335